Writing after Retirement

Writing after Retirement

Tips from Successful Retired Writers

Edited by Carol Smallwood and
Christine Redman-Waldeyer

ROWMAN & LITTLEFIELD
Lanham • Boulder • New York • London

Published by Rowman & Littlefield
A wholly owned subsidiary of The Rowman & Littlefield Publishing Group, Inc.
4501 Forbes Boulevard, Suite 200, Lanham, Maryland 20706
www.rowman.com

16 Carlisle Street, London W1D 3BT, United Kingdom

British Library Cataloguing in Publication Information Available

Library of Congress Cataloging-in-Publication Data

Writing after retirement : tips from successful retired writers / edited by Carol Smallwood, Christine
Redman-Waldeyer.
pages cm
Includes bibliographical references and index.
I ISBN 978-1-4422-3829-9 (cloth : alk. paper) -- ISBN 978-1-4422-3830-5 (pbk. : alk. paper) --
ISBN 978-1-4422-3831-2 (ebook) 1. Authorship--Vocational guidance. I. Smallwood, Carol, 1939-
editor. II. Redman-Waldeyer, Christine, editor.
PN151.W77 2014
808.02'023--dc23
2014016396

∞™ The paper used in this publication meets the minimum requirements of American
National Standard for Information Sciences Permanence of Paper for Printed Library
Materials, ANSI/NISO Z39.48-1992.

Printed in the United States of America

To
The Contributors. (CS)

To floods and fortunes
and the courage to write about it.
And those who inspire imagination—
To Jonathan Austin and his love of animal talk. (CRW)

"Live first, write afterwards."
John Galsworthy, *Glimpses & Reflections*

"Live first, write afterwards." "If I Only Knew. . . ." *Glimpses & Reflections*, John Galsworthy, 1937, London, Toronto: William Heineman.

Contents

Acknowledgments

Sheila Bender, founder, Writing It Real.com

Laura Boss, founder and editor, *Lips*, *Flashlight* (2010)

Vandella Brown, *What Is a Zawadi to We?* (2007)

Maria Mazziotti Gillan, *Writing Poetry to Save Your Life: How to Find the Courage to Tell Your Stories* (2013)

Mark Hillringhouse, *Between Frames* (2012)

Richard Marranca, *Dragon Sutra* (2012)

Ellen Ryan, Ph.D., McMaster University, host of the website *Writing, Aging, and Spirit*

Lura Sanborn, research and instruction librarian, St. Paul's School

Foreword

The topics of the anthologies Carol Smallwood has edited in the recent past are very close to my heart, and I am delighted once again that this anthology comes at a very opportune time for me, personally, as I have started thinking of retirement and the more regular writing I will be doing then. After years of taking writing workshops and classes in creative writing, and reading all the articles and interviews that I have edited for the *Writer's Chronicle*, I am convinced that writing as such cannot be taught. It can be nurtured, yes, but it has to be an inherent trait that you enjoy and want to pursue. When it comes to writing after retirement, it has to be an activity that has been dormant in our lives or something most of us have done only sporadically up until then as we raised our families and worked for a living. The desire to want to write and the natural instinct to do so has to be present. This desire can, then, in retirement, take the form of regular writing or attending workshops and classes to hone those inherent skills.

Reading what these very qualified writers have to say in the various sections of this anthology strengthens my belief. I also tend to identify with titles like "Following Dreams Put on Hold" by Stanley Klemetson and "Using and Tuning Life Experiences" by Jinny Batterson. What these and other writers in this enlightening anthology have to say in their essays is what I have believed all along, and now I find credibility in what I have come to believe: life experiences lend depth and dimension and, most importantly, authority to what I write. As a writer, I can now confidently introspect and ponder and apply philosophy to what I think.

What especially draws me to this collection is that Carol Smallwood and Christine Redman-Waldeyer do not just concentrate on poetry and prose alone. They have wisely included *all* aspects of writing. One thinks of estate planning only in the material sense, but Robert Runté talks about royalties, artistic control, unfinished manuscripts at the time of the author's demise, and whether the author had an online presence. Had you thought about including all this in your will? Likely not.

This anthology strives to tell us that writing poetry or stories or essays is not everything. We have entered a digital age, and there are other aspects of writing we can think of. Grant writing has become very lucrative. Nancy Kalikow Maxwell tells us how we can use our flexible schedules to freelance, and her wonderful essay has all the nuts and bolts of grant writing. Similarly, Sarah Bartlett tells us about blogging. The beauty of blogging is that you can write about *anything*. Reading this essay has made me want to start blogging right away!

In my teenage years, I would devour romance novels, and I loved being spirited to faraway destinations in my imagination. I would be transported to nineteenth-century Victorian England after reading a Barbara Cartland novel or move forward a century to be in twentieth-century Barbados after reading stories from the Mills & Boon series! I am now tempted to follow Lori Leger's advice and write romance in retirement. In one of my undergrad writing classes, we were asked to expand on a writing prompt, and I managed successfully to recreate the language from the romance novels I had read. Maybe I can find success as a romance writer.

But then I read further in the anthology, and now I have decided to write children's stories after reading what Angela Narth has to say. I am confused indeed! There is such a wealth of knowledge here about the diverse writing one can do. How about a how-to book? How about joining a writers' group? Do you know everything about self-publishing? And lastly, but most importantly, do you know how to market your writing? We do write for ourselves, but nothing gives us greater pleasure than to see our words in print, whether they are on paper or online. Marketing one's writing is a tedious and time-consuming process. Ann McCauley talks about book reviews, press kits, advertising, marketing plans, and all other aspects of selling our work.

Of course just knowing what you want to write about is not enough. Writing is a disciplined endeavor that requires dedication and hard work. Granted that it does become easier to find time after retirement, the fact remains that the will has to be there. Easier said than done, but after I retire I am determined to set aside a set time everyday to write. For someone who is ready to do this now, this anthology is a perfect guide to have on the desk—to refer to again and again or to read through for inspiration and knowledge. Personally I am now looking forward to the day I can write every day without the constraint of time. Though, whether I write essays or try the romance genre or write for children is yet to be seen!

Supriya Bhatnagar, Director of Publications/Editor
The Association of Writers & Writing Programs (AWP)
George Mason University
Fairfax, Virginia

Preface

When people begin writing after retirement, they have the advantage of experience to draw on, whether it is poetry, fiction, nonfiction, or creative nonfiction—yet this very variety and the vast opportunities that the Internet provides make it daunting to know how to begin much less how to continue. Retired writers have time to dip their toes in or opt for lengthy work, which again raises questions. Or they can go for the genre that seems easiest only to discover that the one taking the most effort ends up being the most rewarding. The retired writer will soon find that when more than one genre of writing is explored it spurs others and expands overall craftsmanship.

Retired people, whether just retired or long retired, are in advantageous position to write after seeing many things in their lifetime: brooding, the time needed to think over events, is elemental to writing. In retirement we can take advantage of the time now available to hatch what we always wanted to bring into being, give birth to what we have long desired to see in print.

Edward Hirsch, in *How to Read a Poem and Fall in Love with Poetry*, asked readers in his opening chapter to "imagine you have gone down to the shore and there, amidst the other debris—the seaweed and rotten wood, the crushed cans and dead fish—you find an unlikely looking bottle from the past."[1] Hirsch is referring to the great Russian poet Osip Mandelstam, who wrote, "I read the message, note the date, the last will and testament of one who has passed on."[2] In retirement you also find the opportunities to discover the past, of family matters and experiences that have been floating for sometime on the open sea. This process affords every yearning writer the time to find the whole shell or precious stone we always have searched for along the shoreline.

The contributors of *Writing after Retirement: Tips from Successful Retired Writers* come from a variety of backgrounds from the United States and Canada. The twenty-seven chapters are divided into Starting In, Practical Aspects, Finding Your Niche, and Publication and Marketing. We wish to thank the contributors and foreword writer for sharing their experiences to help others.

The Editors

NOTES

1. Edward Hirsch, *How to Read a Poem and Fall in Love with Poetry* (San Diego, New York, London: A Harvest Book, 1999), 1.
2. Osip Mandelstam, (San Diego, New York, London: A Harvest Book, 1999), 2.

Part I

Starting In

ONE

After Retirement

Building a New Writing Life
by Connecting to the Community

Arlene L. Mandell

In 1999, after saying goodbye to my university colleagues, I packed a lifetime's worth of possessions, along with a husband who was also retiring, and our cat and dog, and headed for California, the Golden State, where I would, at last, *write*.

Retiring and moving when I was fifty-nine wasn't really my decision, though I had hoped someday to relocate to California. My husband had reached a turning point and needed to depart the nerve-wracking business of mortgage banking. I would be leaving everyone I had ever known in the New York metropolitan area, including my daughter, Tracey, and beloved five-year-old grandson, Derek.

Santa Rosa, two weeks later, Larry was settled across the hall in his own office, our computers were up and running, and I had reams of paper at the ready. I happily revised my "great American novel" and mailed it to a few friends. Their response was tepid. So I started a second novel. Then I stopped, looked around, and realized I didn't have any friends, tribe of congenial writers, or even a book group where I might discuss literary matters.

I tried joining local organizations but couldn't find a good fit. I tried another tactic: I volunteered. First I volunteered to interview people who want to be matched up with community-service jobs. Then I tutored Latino immigrants studying for their citizenship exams. I also mentored a

fifth-grade girl with learning disabilities. These were all worthwhile activities, but at the end of the day I was still alone with my writing.

Receding from memory were my multiple careers:

- award-winning newspaper reporter in New Jersey
- staff writer/editor at *Good Housekeeping* magazine
- vice president of an international public-relations firm in New York
  City
- and, last, a decade as an adjunct professor teaching composition,
  literature, and women's studies at William Paterson University in
  Wayne, New Jersey.

It was time to step up and use all those skills for whatever needed
writing in Sonoma County. But first I needed to find a new writing
group. Back in New Jersey I had been a member of a small circle of
writers who'd met regularly. I missed them terribly.

FORMING A NEW WRITING GROUP

I put an ad in *Poets & Writers Magazine* and received one response. A
month later I attended a Writers Connection event at the Sebastopol Center for the Arts for everyone who wanted to be in a writing group. Some
were novelists, some mystery writers. I proposed forming a group of
folks who were interested in shorter projects — poetry, essays, chapters of
memoirs.

Presto! The Scribe Tribe came into being, seven women ranging in age
from thirty-two to seventy-three. Tonya was a teacher trainer. Jan was a
retired PanAm stewardess who had spent many years abroad. Maryann
was a retired social worker. Jodi and Stephanie were high school English
teachers. And Kathleen was an attorney who wanted to be a poet.

Group Goals

- Provide a creative, supportive environment for writing and revising. Believe in the possibilities of the piece. Be both honest and
  tactful. Suggest outlets for publication. Cheer successes.

Nuts and Bolts

- The group needs a minimum of four and maximum of eight members, preferably writers who live within a half hour's drive of each
  other.
- Each person brings a maximum of fifteen hundred words. Novel-
  writing groups need a different format — for example, sending a
  chapter in advance with a summary of the previous chapters.

- Pick a schedule that works for the group—for example, the second and fourth Thursdays of the month. Adjust as needed for holidays and summer vacations.
- Take turns meeting at each other's homes or at a convenient coffeehouse at a set time.
- The hostess offers coffee, tea, and cookies.
- Once a year, plan a celebration.

Format

- The group gathers by 6:30 or 7:00 p.m. The first twenty minutes are devoted to announcements and calls for submissions. Then the hostess reads a short meditation: a quotation or brief paragraph for inspiration. (Optional, but a nice touch.)
- The author provides copies, reads with no detailed explanation as to how/why the piece was written, except to say, for example, "This is the first part of a short story" or "one of a series of poems about birds." The author may request that the group focus on a possible problem area—for example, the first paragraph or last stanza.
- Clockwise to reader's left, the group provides brief, specific responses, starting with positive comments:
  - What is interesting?
  - What is strong?
  - What is unclear or might need expansion?
  - Don't try to rewrite the piece.
  - If you don't like or understand a piece, it's all right to say, "This doesn't resonate with me" or "I don't like to read about incontinence."
- While the group is responding, the author remains silent and can take notes on the feedback. The author may ask a question or two afterward. This is necessary to avoiding debates and long-winded discussions.
- Editing—Suggestions about word usage and punctuation can be made on the page, but it's not necessary to take up the group's time. Members should sign the copies with their comments before returning them to the writer.
- Although something may have happened in real life, that isn't a defense of an incident that reads as unbelievable.
- Equal time is allotted to group members, based on the number of people present. The timekeeper for each meeting helps avoid short-changing the last reader. If someone is tired or needs to leave early, she may go first. The hostess goes last.

Housekeeping

- Take turns hosting.
- Call or e-mail the hostess if you cannot attend.
- Bring enough copies for everyone.
- Double space or use 1.5 spaces for prose.[1]

I also joined an organization that offered book clubs and foreign-policy discussions, the American Association of University Women. The Santa Rosa Rose Branch was filled with lively, well-informed women, many in my age group. Quite a few were retired teachers, and a few had doctorates, but it seemed as if they'd all known each other forever. When they learned I had been at *Good Housekeeping*, however, they wanted to turn over the editorship of the newsletter. No, no, no. Layouts, deadlines—no.

I did agree to write the new-member profiles each month, which involved brief phone interviews with newcomers. I joined one of their four book groups. Each group meets in May to plan the year's reading schedule. We've read everything from books about the tragic Donner Party to a celebration of women's shoes. We also support some local authors by selecting their work and inviting them to the discussion.

TAKING ADVANTAGE OF THINGS LITERARY AND QUIRKY

Since arriving in Sonoma County, I've been going to writers' workshops, attending and participating in poetry readings, and dropping in at Copperfields, the local bookstore, to hear authors read from their latest works. The number of these events has kept expanding, so Terry Ehret, a poet laureate, started the Sonoma County Literary Update. I was one of many who supported its development. The Update is e-mailed monthly at no cost to any and all who want it.[2]

The *Press Democrat*, our local newspaper, also lists events, some unique to Sonoma County, such as a Wiccan solstice celebration and a swim party for dogs. This fall the Blessing of the Animals at the St. Francis Winery welcomed 125 dogs, a turtle, and a llama, all of whom were blessed by not one, but two Catholic priests. Our dogs, Maxwell and Ringo, behaved admirably.

I continue to absorb some of the local culture and color by going to farmers' markets and craft fairs. Visits to winery events, olive pressings, and tomato festivals provide material for many poems and essays. My writing has been enhanced by the fragrance of lavender at the Lavender Festival and the flavor of Mexican oregano in an olive-oil dip.

Coming from the New York metropolitan area, I was initially underwhelmed by the local celebrities and landmarks but gradually realized there are historical societies and world-famous writers whose homesteads have become museums and preserves. The tiny town of Glen Ellen, just down the road, boasts Wolf House, the residence of Jack London, and the Bouverie Preserve, the home and estate of M. F. K Fisher, the renowned food writer. Right here in Santa Rosa is a museum devoted to the world's most famous cartoonist, Charles Schultz. And over the Mayacamas Mountains in Napa County is a small museum dedicated to the life and works of Robert Louis Stevenson.

While visiting these places, I gather information that may find its way into my poems and stories. I wrote a prose poem, "Another Murder of Crows," inspired by the fireplace at the Saddle Club down the hill. The fireplace was used by Alfred Hitchcock in a famous scene from *The Birds*.

MAKING TIME FOR SOLITUDE

One danger with immersing myself in all things cultural and literary is that I sometimes relegate writing time to the margins between other activities. To heed make the best use of my time, I carry a tiny composition book in my purse. At an art exhibit, for example, I might take detailed notes on a painting I admire. At a museum I take copies of all the free handouts.

Then on hot summer days or during deluges in the rainy season (roughly mid-December to late March) I sometimes go through my notes and assorted materials. I visited the Sonoma County Museum in Santa Rosa to view an exhibit on the birth of American landscape painting featuring Thomas Cole's 1827 painting, *The Close, Catskills*. The exhibit included some of the materials he used: tiny canvas bags of ground colors, plus linseed oil and turpentine, and the information that oil paint in tubes first appeared in 1849. This made it possible for artists to paint en plein air.

I'm not sure how or when this material will find its way into my writing but am pretty sure it will.

BUILDING RELATIONSHIPS

It took about eight years until I was truly a part of the extensive Sonoma County literary community, but I'm happy to share these experiences so you can become one of the literary gang in your town much sooner. You can begin by exploring the historical and cultural resources of your new community. You might consider becoming a docent at a small museum or an usher at the local theater. Or you could help out at the house and garden tour that the women's club organizes each spring. While making yourself useful, you're also gathering material and making connections.

GETTING INVOLVED IN BOOK-RELATED ACTIVITIES

It's not enough to embrace history—you can also take part in creating it. When I had been here a year, I volunteered to help with the Sonoma County Book Festival, which had begun in 1999. It remains the largest festival north of the Golden Gate Bridge. My first assignment was writing three-line bios for each of the sixty-plus authors who would be reading. Taking those long author bios and condensing each into three sentences was a challenge, and a mundane task, but one that needed doing.

A few years later I graduated to chair of the Adult Authors Committee, which involved searching for the most diverse and prestigious writers on the West Coast to fill the Forum Room of the central library. Working with writers, editors, and publishers helped me learn about some of the behind-the-scenes machinations of the book world. Not unlike the New York literary scene, it's more than a network—it's a labyrinth of relationships that build over time. They all compete yet also support each other.

A bonus of my volunteer efforts with the festival is that I realized novel writing was not a talent I possessed. Each year I noticed which books were best sellers and which, often self-published, were bypassed by the thousands who attended the festival. I also saw how much self-promotion was necessary to put a book in a reader's hands.

I realized where I fit into the vast literary world: Writing short, pithy essays. Capturing the movement of a dragonfly over a pond in a six-line poem. Supporting the efforts of Sonoma County and California authors by buying and reading their books. Novels #1 (_Slow Kissing_) and #2 (_Machiavelli's Daughter_) were laid to rest.

Since libraries had been a source of delight to me since I was five years old, I also became a member of the Santa Rosa Library Advisory Board. Looking for ways to call attention to the thirteen libraries in Sonoma County, I helped create a "What the Library Means to Me" art and essay contest open to all forty thousand kindergarten through sixth-grade students in the county.

I was inspired by an article I read about an eight-year-old Chinese-American girl who had written an essay for a Santa Rosa contest fifty years earlier. She won a savings bond and a transistor radio. Her name was Amy Tan. I reasoned that if this world-famous author of Chinese-American stories, including _The Joy Luck Club_, was recognized for her talent and encouraged at a young age, perhaps we could do the same for a new generation of children.

For this huge project, I wrote proposals, pitch letters, and press releases, employing PR skills I hadn't used in two decades. Winners received cash and acclaim at a celebration in the central library. One of the most amazing entries was by a six-year-old boy, written in Japanese, describing his visits to the Petaluma library as being like swimming in an aquarium with books that were like multicolored fish. He arrived for the ceremony with parents, grandparents, his teacher, and his school principal.

Amy Tan sent autographed copies of one of her books for the libraries in each child's school. My reward was seeing the pride and enthusiasm of the children, their parents, and teachers as the superintendent of schools handed each one a certificate and a check.

SUPPORTING OTHER COMMUNITY ORGANIZATIONS

Here's another example of making connections: In Santa Rosa, renown for botanist Luther Burbank, the Garden Club is a revered seventy-five-year-old institution. Their monthly meetings feature specialists in everything from bats to xeriscape gardening. Their members maintain a butterfly garden at Sonoma State University and win awards at flower-arranging competitions. Enter yours truly, who can identify marigolds and zinnias but failed at Sunflowers 101.

Their president overheard that I'd written for *Good Housekeeping* and invited me to write a monthly column. I explained my limited gardening abilities and assured her I shouldn't be giving advice. Maeve persevered. And so I began by writing about their oldest member, who is 101 and comes to every meeting. I wrote about the perennials group and how they propagate plants for the April plant sale. I wrote about the herbs in Shakespeare's garden. People know me now, and I've even learned how to keep a Meyer lemon tree alive.

Being part of a community can also mean sharing your opinions. I write the occasional letter to the editor of our local newspaper. When the paper put out a call for stories about best gifts ever received, I wrote about Ricky, the parakeet I had when I was seven. I've also sent photos of Gatsby the cat and Maxwell the golden retriever to the Weather Page, which features a photo each day. Friends and neighbors call to congratulate me.

Admittedly these are not high literary pursuits, but I've learned to find niches and get work published. In fact, after taking a number of writing workshops at the nearby Sebastopol Center for the Arts, I was asked to teach a seminar on getting published. Then I was invited to join the Poet Laureate Selection Committee, which every two years selects a poet from Sonoma County who not only writes powerful verse but also engages the community in various poetic activities. Being with other, more accomplished, poets is inspiring. It is also rewarding to be part of their inner circle.

In 2010 I became involved in another project, Bibliophoria, which was a series of events and exhibits to draw more people to the small town of Sebastopol to support their artistic and literary offerings. That's where I met Luci Edwards and Eric Johnson of Iota Press, who joined me in launching the Poetry Chapbook Contest. Seventy-one poets submitted chapbooks. Our committee met to read entries, judge them, and organize a celebration of the winning works. Eric and the first place winner printed the chapbook on his hand letterpress.

My bonus: I got to read some wonderful poetry and got a crash course in what makes a chapbook successful. If and when I decide which of my seven hundred–plus poems to publish together, I now have a connection with a unique printing operation and an opportunity to create a beautiful chapbook.

SIX STEPS TOWARD BUILDING YOUR POSTRETIREMENT WRITING CAREER

How might my experiences help you in your particular situation? Regardless of where you relocate, if you're a competent, quick, and flexible writer, you are *useful* and you are *needed*. Whether you live in a retirement community with its own newspaper or join an organization that communicates by e-newsletter, you have a skill they are seeking. At the same time, you'll be immersing yourself in the local culture so you'll come to know what they're all talking about and won't remain an outsider.

I can sum up my advice by urging new writer/retirees to

- get involved in local activities
- use your writing skills for worthwhile community purposes
- visit unusual shops, galleries, and museums
- attend readings, plays, concerts, and festivals
- join a few organizations that reflect your interests
- and write every day when possible. Too busy? Take notes of fascinating events.

NOTES

1. The Scribe Tribe of Santa Rosa, California, has developed and used these guidelines successfully for ten years. Our seven members range in age from thirty-five to eighty-three. Not all members have been interested in publication. However, we have had a vast number of poems and essays published, along with three poetry chapbooks, a book providing support to caregivers, and several teacher-training manuals.

2. You can access it at http://literaryfolk.wordpress.com.

TWO

Following Dreams Put on Hold

Stanley L. Klemetson

As a teenager I used to gather family records, histories, and pictures. I would write to distant relatives asking for more information about our family. I suppose my interest in writing started with my mother's example. She was an unpublished writer who wrote poems and short stories, mainly about all of the trouble I caused her. She gave her collection a title, *Wildlife in the Home.*

Before I was twenty-three years old both my mother and father died, I married, and my wife Peggy and I had our first child. My life's focus became one of working and getting an education to support my family. As a young college professor I had an obligation—no, I should say, an opportunity—to write again, but the focus was more on professional research papers, books, and other publications. When I was forty-six years old I left my job at Brigham Young University and joined an environmental-engineering consulting firm in Walnut Creek, California. The move away from the university setting turned my focus to technical reports. Finally, at sixty-eight years old, I decided it was time to go back to what had I wanted to be in the beginning: a writer.

A NEW BEGINNING

Retirement presented an opportunity for me to work in an environment that encouraged writing while I was sharing my professional experience with young adults. I became a university professor again and began teaching engineering students. While some might not consider this to be retirement, I had found that preparing lectures, reading for pleasure, and writing go hand in hand.

Colleges and universities provide an added benefit. As a professor I can take college classes for free and work with young students in a workshop setting. I have been given assignments to read about various writing methods, and then I practice those methods in my creative-writing classes, where they can be critiqued by the students and the professor. After many years writing technical materials, these classes have opened up a whole new world in my mind about creative thought. In the following sections I will list some of the opportunities I have found and explain some things I have learned about writing.

WRITERS' GROUPS

In most geographical areas there will be groups of writers that want to support the development of new writers. Since I was living in Lake Charles, Louisiana, when I started to write again I used a simple Internet search to find such a group. Many writers' groups have monthly meetings with workshops, before the general meeting and a speaker, where writers can share a manuscript with others and have it critiqued. The larger groups also have annual conferences where speakers from a variety of genres provide opportunities to ask questions. Many of the participants have published books to sell. Often there are publishers or agent representatives available that will meet with writers on a one-to-one basis. If the monthly meetings are too far from the writer's home, there are also chapters that meet by e-mail, Skype, and other electronic means.

The meetings of the writers groups allow the novice writer to just sit and listen, ask questions, or have their writing reviewed. It is also a good way to determine personal writing interests. Although I have written some poetry, I have found that my interests are more in the creative-nonfiction genre used to write family histories and memoirs in a format that is both publishable and readable to my children and grandchildren. That experience has led to my essay, "Living Alone Together," which was published in 2012 as part of *My Love to You Always*, an anthology.[1]

Some of the writers' groups also host writing contests for several genres—like flash, first page, first chapter, prose, picture books, early readers, young adult, novels, and scripts. There is often a reading fee that is used for prize money, and in return feedback or critique on the manuscript is often provided.

The Benefits of Joining a Writing Group

- *Networking*—A writers' group provides an association with experienced writers who are willing to help a beginning writer. Representatives from the publishing industry and other specialists often attend these meetings. Useful information and writing opportunities are available through the personal contacts and group newsletters.

- *Discipline*—The desire to have something written for the next meeting or contest becomes a time-management tool that promotes writing. At the meetings, writing prompts may be given to provide a focused writing exercise. Fellow writers share the methods they use to complete their writing projects.
- *Reading Aloud*—The opportunity to read aloud in front of a friendly group of writers improves presentation skills. The author's voice becomes more evident in the written materials during an oral presentation, and the author gets a better feel for the flow of his or her writing.
- *Critiques*—A writers' group can be a friendly audience that makes suggestions for improvement to the individual writer. The author can then decide what suggestions to utilize during his or her revision process.
- *Community*—The members of a writing group function as a supportive group that can help the growth of a writer.
- *Education*—Writers' groups are also educational. Invited speakers and members share knowledge on publishing and marketing manuscripts. Experts are often available to help improve the quality of the writing. New techniques may also be learned and applied.
- *Motivation*—When friends are interested in writing it is easier to be interested in writing and to be more productive. Writers may also be motivated by the friendly competition between writers.
- *Promotion*—Writing friends are more likely to read what you have published, write reviews, and promote your work on their websites and blogs. Some groups also publish the works of their contest winners.
- *Special Events*—Writers' groups often sponsor special events that add more benefits than their monthly meetings. These may be workshops, conferences, or special training opportunities.

WORKSHOPS

While writers' groups often host workshops, I also like to attend those that feature a single author for one day or longer. These workshops may be announced in the writers' group's newsletters or through the local university. I attended a two-day workshop held by Orson Scott Card to learn the elements of good writing. In his workshop we were given assignments to fulfill, and I had the opportunity to read what I had written to the workshop and receive a critique from Mr. Card. I found that the insights offered by published authors have been very helpful.

Internet searches and writers' publications, such as Poets & Writers, contain notices of longer workshops held with authors or groups of authors.[2] The longer workshops often require preapproval for submitted manuscripts in progress. The requirements are clearly spelled-out in the announcements.

The Benefits of Attending Workshops

- *Networking*—This can be an opportunity to meet editors, agents, publishers, and other writers. It serves to widen the writer's circle of connections within the writing community.
- *Writing and Critiquing*—Workshops are set up to give writing prompts to sharpen writing skills. There will be opportunities to critique the work of others and have your writing critiqued as well. During longer workshops there is additional time to work on the revision of your manuscript submitted for acceptance to the workshop.
- *Publishing Trends*—The speakers and panels at the workshops will often address the latest trends in the writing and publishing process. The question-and-answer opportunities can provide significant information on writing and publishing.
- *Expanding Writing Experiences*—At workshops, writers may be given writing prompts or challenges that they have avoided in the past. Gaining experience with a new genre or writing method opens up new ways to look at your writing.
- *National Workshops*—These meetings can transport a writer to new and exciting places, cultures, and people that can broaden writing experiences. While writing in new surroundings the author may find that the separation from a familiar home will actually help them focus on more details of what was left behind than if they'd actually stayed at home. Meeting writers from other parts of the country may also enrich the experience.

CONTINUING-EDUCATION WRITING CLASSES

Adult education and university continuing-education programs often provide short-term classes on writing. The formats are generally lectures but may include writing practices, presentations, and critiques. The continuing-education writing classes are noncredit classes that provide a low-risk exposure to writing. A wide variety of genres is often provided at a very reasonable cost. Some of the types of classes may focus on travel, children, teens, personal essays, memoirs, novels, or screenplays.

UNIVERSITY CLASSES

University writing classes take a longer time commitment because of the academic formatting, but I have found that the teachers provide so much useful writing information in a short time that they are well worth the effort. Classes can be audited or taken for credit. Check with the university before enrolling to determine whether they have an easy path for entry for older students. Transcripts may not be required when classes are taken for pleasure, and tuition costs are generally much lower. However, taking a class for credit can be beneficial when pursuing a degree.

The typical classes offered are poetry, fiction, and creative nonfiction, but don't forget that English departments also offer a wide variety of reading and critiquing classes that will broaden the writer's background in literature. Every writer needs to be a good reader to be a good writer.

Older adults often wonder how they will fit in to the class. In my recent classes I have found that students about one-third my age have considered me to be just one of the students and often looked forward to my writing and comments because I have a different perspective achieved by a lifetime of experiences. In a creative nonfiction class the younger students seemed to focus on the hard and painful experiences of life, whereas my writing was reflective of the good experiences.

The Benefits of Auditing College Writing Classes

- *Audit vs. Credit*—Auditing a college writing class provides a full-semester course without any required assignments, but the maximum benefit of the course can be achieved by doing all of the required work without the risk of the grade that would have been achieved. However, the writer should consider taking the course for credit because interest in one class may lead to taking several more.
- *Systematic Learning*—College writing classes are designed to achieve student-learning outcomes. The courses are designed for the learning of writing concepts and methods as the writer progresses through the course. The teachers have organized the lectures, assignments, and reading materials to give students the knowledge and experience necessary to succeeding in writing. The expected workload includes writing assignments, critical review of writing methods, preparation of draft manuscripts, presentations by the students, and critiquing of the manuscripts by the class members and the teacher in a workshop session. Finally students are expected to revise their manuscripts and resubmit them to the teacher for a second review. Often the students are encouraged to submit their manuscripts to on-campus or off-campus publications for review and publication.

While college courses require attendance several times each week for the entire semester or term, the classes are structured to provide a balanced system of teaching. The college or university classes each focus on one genre, such as fiction writing, whereas workshops and conferences generally cover a wide range of genres. Both education methods have their place in a writer's training.

BLOGS

A blog is an easy way to practice writing skills. Posting on Facebook or Twitter or uploading a video is considered blogging. Blogging can start with comments on someone else's post or by submitting a new post on an established blog hosted by a writing group or a special-interest group. New blogs can be created by using WordPress.org or Blogger.com. There are numerous webpages and posts about the benefits of blogging for both personal and business use. The following is a condensed list of the benefits of blogging for beginning writers.

The Benefits of Blogging

- *Pursuing Your Passion*—Blogging gives an opportunity to share with others the things that are important to you. A prospective poet can share poems and let others give feedback. A fiction writer can post initial drafts or final manuscripts and receive suggestions and critiques. Families can write memoirs and family histories and ask family and friends to comment. The author can share information with the public or a very limited group.
- *Writing Practice*—Blogging provides an opportunity to become a better writer because of the discipline required to write things that people want to read. Frequent writing for blogs will improve writing skills.
- *Increased Knowledge*—Creating a blog that has a high readership requires that the site owner read a lot to stay on top of topics. The questions raised by others will make it necessary for the writer to learn more about the topic. Perhaps the responses to posts will lead the writer along paths never before considered.
- *Visibility*—People will hear about the blog, and that will improve the readership. For an author or leader of an organization who wants to influence others, this platform provides an excellent method for showing expertise and passion.
- *Expert Status*—Writers who post frequently are often perceived to be experts on the posted topic in question. The more blog posts that are written by an author, the more likely the author will come to be regarded as having knowledge on the post topic.

- *Research*—Hunting down information and resources for the blog from a need to stay informed about the topic will improve research skills.
- *Networking*—You can become a power networker people will seek out for their events. Relationships will develop with others who share common interests. If you desire to publish a book, the networking benefits of blogging can create a following and a support structure for the book. The blog becomes a personal branding tool.
- *Memory Improvement*—Blogging can improve memory because of the stimulation and stretching of thinking.
- *Creativity*—Blog author creativity will increase because of the author's need to think outside the box. Blogging allows the testing of creativity while working from the beginning of a thought or product to the completion or application.
- *Synergy*—The feedback on posts and responses will help to focus your mind. Blogging will also make a person a better listener because of the need to analyze responses before posting a reply.

I have found blogging to be a good way to become known to other writers. The short posting of responses on any blog topic can give some of the benefits listed above, but I generally post longer articles to give others a chance to comment. Blogs are fast and interactive, but a writer has to be careful not to become so involved that there is no time to write outside of blog postings.

BECOMING A TEACHER

Those finishing their professional careers and preparing to embark on new adventures that include stimulating environments for writing might consider teaching at a college or university. No Ph.D.? No problem. Many universities hire adjunct professors based on their work experiences, not their degrees. A professional can teach one or more classes on campus or online. The pay is not great, but the advantage of this type of work to the writer is to be thrown together with young students who will help stimulate thinking. As a writer, you may want to write about the subject that you are teaching, a seminar that occurred on campus, campus life, or teaching methods. While working on campus you might want to take some fun classes that will open up new topics to write about.

Preparing lectures, or even working as a university administrator, have brought me into contact with a community of writers and students. You are always reading and writing for the job. The habit of reading and writing has carried over into writing for the literary genre as well.

APPLYING WHAT HAS BEEN LEARNED

When I was a teenager my father and I would watch people walking by and discuss their possible life stories. I find that I like stories about people living normal lives with the conflicts and resolutions that we all face. Most of my short stories are fictionalized accounts of real people and situations, falling into either a fiction or creative-nonfiction genre. Prompts have been the start of much of my writing. They may be assigned prompts, such as contests, or they may be situational prompts. Often my stories have been composite characters and what-if situations. I have also enjoyed writing poetry, but most of that has come from emotional situations.

For the last several years I have gathered books I used in my classes and others that I purchased on the recommendation of writer-friends. Some contain writing exercises, or prompts, to practice writing techniques. Others expound on the nuts and bolts of writing, while others still critique published stories to practice on.

As a technical writer I was taught to write without emotion. I am learning to overcome that trait as I write fiction and nonfiction stories. I have to learn to add detailed scenes that will do more showing and less telling. I have to think in the context of story arcs, conflicts, resolutions, characters, and many more writing elements, and as I do this my critique comments have gotten better.

I posted to a blog an essay titled "The Blank Page."[3] I explained in that post that as a relatively new writer I am filling in that blank page now by the choices I make to become a better writer. While the past is no longer a blank page in my mind, it will remain blank to others if I don't make the effort to get it down on paper. Now that I have retired from my past professional life and embarked onto a new phase within a university setting, I have the opportunity to fill those blank pages, both the past and the future. My interest in family history and writing about fictional lives has come alive again. I have the opportunity to see the fulfillment of a dream I had put on hold so many years ago.

RECOMMENDED READING

Judith Barrington, *Writing the Memoir, 2nd ed.* (Portland, OR: The Eight Mountain Press, 2002).

Larry Brooks, *Story Engineering: Mastering the Six Core Competencies of Successful Writing* (Cincinnati: Writer's Digest Books, 2011).

Carolyn Forche and Philip Gerard, *Writing Creative Nonfiction* (Cincinnati: Story Press, 2001).

Robin Hemley, *Turning Life into Fiction* (Cincinnati: Story Press, 1994).

X. J. Kennedy and Dana Gioia, *An Introduction to Poetry, 13th ed.* (New York: Longman, 2010).

Stephen King, *On Writing: A Memoir of the Craft* (New York: Scribner, 2000).

Alice LaPlante, *Methods and Madness: The Making of a Story* (New York: W. W. Norton & Company, 2009).

Walter Mosley, *This Year You Write Your Novel* (New York: Little Brown and Company, 2007).

Bill Roorbach and Kristen Keckler, *Writing Life Stories* (Cincinnati: Writer's Digest Books, 2008).

NOTES

1. Ramona Tucker and Jennifer Wessner, *My Love to You Always* (Waterford, VA: OakTara Publishers, 2012).

2. Visit them at http://www.pw.org.

3. Stanley Klemetson, "The Blank Page," June 27, 2011, http://bayouwritersgroup.blogspot.com/2011_0_01_archive, 2011.

THREE

A Muse of One's Own

Finding Inspiration for Your Writing Life

Alice Lowe

O for a muse of fire, that would ascend / the brightest heaven of invention
—William Shakespeare, *Henry V*

Writers need good teaching and models, encouragement, and motivation. This is especially important for those writers who are getting a late start and approaching their craft through less-traditional means. In Greek mythology, the Muses were the goddesses of inspiration, and Mentor was Odysseus's trusted counselor. We still seek muses and mentors, those who will serve as guiding spirits, those who teach us, often by example, and serve as successful models. Students majoring in literature or creative writing have teachers they look up to, assigned readings from masters of the craft, and a built-in affinity group of peers to provide motivation. Mature writers starting out have to be more deliberate about finding guides to help them along the way.

When I accompanied a friend to England for six months in 1990, one of my goals was to "find myself" as a writer. I had the luxury of unencumbered time to read and write and ponder—to determine whether my dormant talent was still alive and if the long-ignored tug toward writing was worth pursuing. Browsing through the bookshelves of my temporary home in a Devon village, I came across *A Writer's Diary* by Virginia Woolf. It was a fragile first edition, the lettering on the worn binding barely legible, but still it seemed to leap off the shelf and into my hands.

In this slim volume, compiled by her husband shortly after her death and years before the publication of her complete diaries, Woolf reflects on her writing and reading, the influences and inspirations that served as her own muses. I was awed by her eloquence and stirred by the skill with which she could capture a person, place, or mood in a few well-chosen words. In one of the earliest entries, written when she was in her thirties, she makes the first of several addresses to her older self, to "Virginia Woolf at the age of fifty, when she sits down to build her memoirs out of these books . . ."[1]

It was as if she was speaking to me, in my late forties at the time.

I'd read *To the Lighthouse* years earlier, but it hadn't made much of an impression. A bit too obscure for my tastes at the time. So why Woolf? Why now? Between jobs, between worlds, I was at a critical juncture in my life, and her words resounded like seismic activity at my core. I turned next to her novels, reading them sequentially.[2] Curled up with endless cups of tea and the uniquely British dark chocolate digestive biscuits that remain my weakness, I marveled at her forays into ever-new territory. I kept *A Writer's Diary* at hand and would refer to her entries while she was generating and revising each novel, when she would express her goals and strivings, her euphoria, her admissions of fear and doubt.

I read and pondered but didn't do any creative writing or make any decisions about it during that interlude. Back home a challenging new job absorbed my time and mental energy. Writing would have to wait. But I didn't give up Virginia Woolf—quite the contrary. During the years that followed I devoured her work: five volumes of diaries and six of letters, hundreds of essays and stories, then the profusion of biographies and analyses by the vast army of Woolf scholars. I didn't realize it at the time, but this would be the framework for my own research and writing, something that might not have come to pass without Virginia Woolf leading the way.

I WASN'T SEARCHING FOR A MUSE, BUT THERE SHE WAS

Aspiring writers at any age must read to learn their craft. Read good writers, and study what they do. Reread them. Read bad writing (but not too much), and learn what not to do. Read about writing. In addition to what can be gained from absorbing the written word, writers-to-be may discover the authors, past and present, whose work resonates with them. These authors may have written the kinds of books or stories we aspire to write; maybe they trod a similar path to our own, overcame obstacles that we also faced. It was during that time in England that I also discovered Mary Wesley, whose first novel, *Jumping the Queue*, was published when she was seventy.[3] Wesley became a role model, assuaging my concerns that it already might be too late for me. She wrote nine more novels, one of them made into a British TV series, during her seventies and eighties. Today, having just turned seventy myself, I'm even more wowed by her achievements.

But my primary inspiration was and continues to be Virginia Woolf. After gorging myself on her work, I joined the Virginia Woolf Society, comprised mostly of academics who teach literature and women's studies in universities. The high level of scholarship in their publications was both impressive and intimidating, and it was years before I cooked up the courage to attend an annual conference, and then with trepidation, an outsider looking in, mouth agape, overwhelmed to meet and hear these Woolfian authorities.

As my long-awaited retirement grew near, I made a plan, what's now known as a "bucket list." Dominating it were four ambitious but achievable goals. I would participate in the Susan B. Komen Three-Day Walk to raise money and awareness for the fight against breast cancer (sixty miles over three days—I did it twice), be a supernumerary (nonsinging extra) for the San Diego Opera, become a certified master gardener, and, present a paper at a Woolf conference. Three out of four became reality— I made the first but not the final cut for master gardener and then lost interest.

The theme for the next Woolf conference, the year after my retirement, was editing: Virginia Woolf as editor or the editing of her work. This was a perfect opportunity to explore Leonard Woolf's controversial selections and omissions as editor of what remains my personal bible, *A Writer's Diary*. My proposal was accepted, and in June of 2008 at the University of Denver I presented my paper to a roomful of Woolf scholars. It was later selected for publication in a volume of conference essays. The most exciting part for me was the awareness of how much I had enjoyed the whole process—research, writing, editing, and—oh, my, yes—the feedback and recognition. It made me certain that I wanted to write and confident that I could, especially now that I had the time and energy to commit to it.

I wasn't searching for a muse, but there she was, a perpetual source of inspiration. It wasn't that I would or could aspire to her unique style or her distinctive voice, so what was it? Her beautiful prose, evocative descriptions, keen observations. Her masterful command of the language: sentence structure and balance, even her use of punctuation. One of my favorite examples is on the first page of *To the Lighthouse* . She uses eleven commas to create a lilting hundred-word sentence; she follows it with one consisting of five words before a full stop: "It was fringed with joy." [4]

And then another: 105 words, paced and spaced by fourteen commas and one dash. What symmetry, what authority; my heart flutters at the very thought of it.

MUSES, MENTORS, AND MODELS EVOLVE
FROM READING AND REFLECTING

Muses aren't sprites that float through the window and alight on your pen or keyboard every morning after you sit down at your desk with your second cup of coffee. "Okay, muse, I'm ready—pour it on!" They're not servants—they don't buy groceries or wash the car, don't perch at our elbows awaiting our commands. Muses were once thought to be male artists' birthrights, near-ethereal beings—wives or more often lovers, who served as subjects and models, sometimes unattainable visions. Think Dante and Beatrice. At some point it was acknowledged that women could have muses too—rarely their husbands and sometimes, as in the case of Charlotte and Emily Brontë, imaginary. Creative couples often were said to be each other's muses: Henry Miller and Anaïs Nin, Jean-Paul Sartre and Simone de Beauvoir, Virginia and Leonard Woolf. A supportive spouse or other who acts as proofreader and cheerleader is a marvelous asset but not what I would consider a muse (unless you're married to Alice Munro).

Well, then, where are they? No, you can't look on Craigslist under *M*. Muses, mentors, and models, whether mortal or make-believe, evolve from reading and reflecting—also called *musing!*—in the course of which your own preferences and passions emerge from the poems, novels, stories, or essays that accelerate your heartbeat and spur you into action. They might be two-hundred-year-old classics (Jane Austen's followers are legion), current literary pop stars, or unknown contemporaries you stumble across in a magazine or anthology. Muses living and dead can play a significant role in stimulating a latent yearning to write among those who want to stretch and grow but need reassurance that it's possible. Consider the disparate examples of two of my friends.

Zohreh Ghahremani has published two novels set in her native Iran. She tells me, "I'm a writer because of Charles Dickens." It was her admiration for Dickens's prose that prompted her to pen stories as a child, although she didn't become a writer until after she had raised her children and given up her profession as a pediatric dentist. Then, she says, "I discovered the art in his simplicity and realized there's more to writing than an effortless outpour of emotions. I left my job, enrolled in a creative writing class, and became a writer."[5]

Zohreh continues to find sustenance and inspiration for her own unique storytelling by rereading Dickens.

I met Jim Brega in a memoir-writing class where he introduced himself by saying that he wanted to write like David Sedaris. Recently retired from the world of finance, Jim had just started writing about some compelling experiences in his life, and he demonstrated both a way with words and a wry wit, like his model. He says that he admires authors like David Sedaris and Augusten Burroughs for their ability to write comically about family interactions that often border on the horrifying. He describes their effect on him as "deeply affecting and deeply funny at the same time," adding that "this is a deliciously compelling combination, one that strikes the exact tone I strive to achieve in my own writing. And as these writers develop and share their experiments with subject, voice, and language, they inspire in me a similar adventurousness."[6]

Jim recently started drafting a humorous essay about corporate slogans, and then he found that Sedaris, in his latest collection, had upstaged him. Now Jim's essay is homage to Sedaris as muse and mentor, target of envy.

Even muses have muses. In *A Room of One's Own* and in her essays Virginia Woolf speaks admiringly, almost worshipfully, of the women she calls the forerunners. She holds up literature's "fab four"—Jane Austen, Charlotte Brontë, Emily Brontë, and George Eliot—as models for women who want to write, herself included. In the midst of writing one of her novels, she makes a note to herself: "I think the next lap ought to be objective, realistic, in the manner of Jane Austen: carrying the story on all the time."[7]

Her most glowing words, however, were bestowed on two writers who epitomized the art for her, William Shakespeare and Michel de Montaigne. Woolf first read Shakespeare and Montaigne in her teens, when she was turned loose in her father's library, and both are cited frequently in her diaries, letters, and essays. In 1930, at the pinnacle of her achievement, she waxes effusively after reading Shakespeare: "I never yet knew how amazing his stretch and speed and word-coining power is . . . I see him do things I could not in my wildest tumult and utmost press of mind imagine. Evidently the pliancy of his mind was so complete that he could furbish out any train of thought; and, relaxing, let fall a shower of such unregarded flowers. Why then should anyone else attempt to write?"[8]

Her own writing was spurred by the brilliance of Shakespeare's work, and she returned to the well again and again. While Shakespeare was her model of excellence for fiction, she sought the person known as the father of the essay for sustenance in that form: "After all, in the whole of literature, how many people have succeeded in drawing themselves with a pen? But this talking of oneself, following one's own vagaries, giving the whole map, weight, colour, and circumference of the soul in its confusion, its variety, its imperfections—this art belonged to one man only: to Montaigne."[9]

In 1931 she paid her first visit to Montaigne's tower in France, and letters home reveal her reverence. To her friend Ethel Smith she wrote, "My word, Ethel, the very door he opened is there; the steps, worn into deep waves, up to the tower: the three windows: writing table, chair, view, vine, dogs, everything precisely as it was."[10]

A 1934 road trip with Leonard included a stop at Stratford on Avon, which she reported in her diary: ". . . when the clock struck, that was the sound Shakespeare heard . . . to think of writing *The Tempest* looking out on that garden: what a rage and storm of thought to have gone over any mind . . . his genius flowed out of him and is still there, in Stratford."[11]

I bubbled over with similar feelings the first time (and each time thereafter) I visited Monks House, Virginia Woolf's country home in Sussex, now a National Trust property. "Janeites" express the same awe when they make the pilgrimage to Austen's Chawton.

A MUSE, MENTOR, OR MODEL OF YOUR OWN

As a recluse of sorts, I used to say that "writing isn't a team sport." But I've found that it isn't true; we need others as we take on new challenges. We need examples of success so that we know we can do it too. Older writers who seek out a writing community may be rewarded when muses and mentors disclose themselves in that milieu. In book clubs, read-and-critique groups, classes, and workshops, you expose yourself to writers and writing at all levels, and the potential for growth and incentive is unlimited. As is the likelihood that you will find, among the people you meet or the ones you read or hear about, muses, mentors, or models of your own. Someone might take you under her or his wing, providing guidance, support, and encouragement. Or someone might say, "Have you read so-and-so? Your style is a lot like hers," leading you to an important new discovery.

As you're exposed to the writing world, you will have writing manuals recommended to you. Their merit is another discussion, but suffice it to say, they're like the bowls of porridge that Goldilocks found at the three bears' cottage: some too cold, some too hot, and some just right. You have to find what works for you. Personally I love to read about writing by authors who already have my respect as successful and accomplished writers themselves, potential mentors. E. M. Forster, George Orwell, Eudora Welty, and Stephen King have written books about writing—their own writing, their advice to writers. I'm willing to bet that they become muses to burgeoning writers who turn to these volumes after they've been exposed to and impressed by the authors' creative works.

I'm wary of how-to guides that want to impose steps and rules. It makes sense with a new piece of machinery, but I'm old enough to figure some things out for myself. When I read books like Anne Lamott's *Bird by Bird*, it's for the authors' own story and style more than for their tutoring.[12] A while back I came across Carolyn See's *Making a Literary Life*. I was familiar with her novels, and her subtitle, *Advice for Writers and Other Dreamers*, made me think this was a volume for people like me who didn't get degrees in creative writing at the age of twenty-two. I ignored her strict admonition to write "A thousand words a day. Five days a week. For the rest of your life" but I was struck by her suggestion that we send "charming notes" to writers whose work we admire.[13] See regretted that she never told E. M. Forster while he was still alive that he'd changed her life, and she vowed she would never again forgo the opportunity to thank writers for their work. She describes the stationery and the structure for these love notes, but forget all that—we have e-mail, and writers are accessible through their websites and social media. My attempts have resulted in gracious responses more often than not, some ongoing communications, and additions to my roster of mentors. I've corresponded with Helen Humphreys, whose breathtaking novel *The Lost Garden* is one of my all-time favorites.[14] It pays homage to Virginia Woolf, who is her muse too. I had a fascinating exchange with Amor Towles after I was blown away by *Rules of Civility*, his first novel after a career as an investment counselor.[15] I wrote to Sonya Huber after reading her powerful essay "Breastfeeding Dick Cheney" (really, can you believe the title?) in *Creative Nonfiction*.[16] Sonya in turn read some of my published work and responded with praise and encouragement. She told me that she too was a Virginia Woolf devotee, saying, "She is such a guiding force for me, and well ahead of her time in her beautiful tracking of consciousness."[17]

Since our communiqué, she has published *The Backwards Research Guide for Writers: Using Your Life for Reflection, Connection and Inspiration,* which sounds like another rich resource for those of us with long lives on which to reflect and connect.[18] See, it all comes around.

LEARN CRAFT FROM MODELS OF VIRTUOSO WRITING

What can we learn from our muses? As older writers, not so reliant on didactic instruction, I think we're more receptive to models of excellence, better able to extract nuggets from these rich resources.

Priscilla Long, a friend and literary model, wrote *The Writer's Portable Mentor: A Guide to Art, Craft and the Writing Life* not as a repository of dos and don'ts but rather to guide writers through process and practice. She emphasizes that "our core strategy, our quintessential tool, is to learn craft from models of virtuoso writing. Our best teachers are the masterworks we scrutinize."[19]

As we develop our own voices, we learn strategy, structure, and technique by the examples of these models. In response to my query, Priscilla reiterates the importance of finding and learning from models, muses, and mentors, whatever our age or level of skill.

Tracy Kidder and Richard Todd emphasize in *Good Prose* that a writer's voice can't be contrived but will emerge as we listen to the voices that precede and learn to define ourselves. They note that Hunter Thompson claimed to have taught himself to write by typing out *The Great Gatsby*—not to try to write like Fitzgerald but to learn from him. "Listen to yourself," they say, "and listen to those writers who are so great that they cannot be imitated."[20]

I think about what Virginia Woolf has given me as a writer. She didn't tell me what to do or not to do, but she made her day-to-day experience relevant to me. She assured me that writing isn't a smooth and predictable path; there are highs that can deceive us into thinking we've arrived, once and for all, and there are lows that might make us want to hang up our pens. How reassuring for me to find that Virginia Woolf, brilliant consummate artist that she was, had the same doubts and flailings that I have.

In my personal essays, I have on a few occasions tackled the subject of aging—I confess it's much on my mind. Virginia Woolf didn't live to the age when many of us are just starting out on this new path. She considered herself "elderly" if not old at fifty and took her own life in 1941 at the age of fifty-nine. My mind boggles at what she might have done in her sixties and seventies and beyond. The maxim (ever-changing for the benefit of the Baby Boomers) that "Seventy is the new fifty" might sound trite, but it says that not only are we living longer today, we're healthier and more productive at a time when our ancestors took to their rocking chairs. Woolf considered aging and death as worthy topics to explore. At fifty-seven she wrote, "How interesting it would be to describe the approach of age, and the gradual coming of death. As people describe love. To note every symptom of failure: but why failure? To treat age as an experience that is different from the others."[21]

And in one of her last diary entries she was still planning future research and writing projects.

Yoko Ono is going strong into her eighties, still productive as a musician, performer, writer, visual artist, and activist, and she's a creative muse for many of her followers. In an interview she was asked about retirement from her artistry. Her words were a tonic to me, reading them within a couple of weeks of my seventieth birthday: "It's like my second life is opening up. When I became seventy, I thought, *Wow. It's great!* I'd like people to know, especially women. They're always thinking, *I'm going to be forty! What am I going to do?* Well, seventy was great. Eighty's even better."[22]

Another addition to my pantheon of muses—you can claim her too.

NOTES

1. Virginia Woolf, *A Writer's Diary*, ed. Leonard Woolf (New York: Harvest Book, 1982), 7.

2. In addition to the other of Woolf's novels I reference in this chapter, I read both *Orlando*, 1928 (New York: Harvest/HBJ, 1973), and *A Room of One's Own*, 1929 (New York: Harvest/HBJ, 1957).

3. Mary Wesley, *Jumping the Queue* (London: Macmillen London, 1983).

4. Virginia Woolf, *To the Lighthouse* (New York: Harvest Book, 2005), 7.

5. Zohreh Ghahremani, e-mail message to author, November 10, 2013.

6. Jim Brega, e-mail message to author, November 2, 2013.

7. Woolf, *A Writer's Diary*, 202.

8. Ibid., 154.

9. Virginia Woolf, "Montaigne," in *The Common Reader* (New York: Harvest Book, 1953), 59.

10. Virginia Woolf, *The Letters of Virginia Woolf, Volume Four*, ed. Nigel Nicolson and Joanne Trautman (New York: HBJ, 1978), 321.

11. Woolf, *A Writer's Diary*, 209–10.

12. Anne Lamott, *Bird by Bird: Some Instructions on Writing and Life* (New York: Anchor Books, 1995).

13. Carolyn See, *Making a Literary Life* (New York: Random House, 2002), 35.

14. Helen Humphreys, *The Lost Garden* (New York: Norton, 2002).

15. Amor Towles, *Rules of Civility* (New York: Viking, 2011).

16. Sonya Huber, "Breastfeeding Dick Cheney," *Creative Nonfiction* 34 (Fall/Winter 2011).

17. Sonya Huber, e-mail message to author, February 8, 2012.

18. Sonya Huber, *The Backwards Research Guide for Writers: Using Your Life for Reflection, Connection and Inspiration* (Oakville: Equinox Pub., 2011).

19. Priscilla Long, *The Writer's Portable Mentor: A Guide to Art, Craft and the Writing Life* (Seattle: Wallingford Press, 2010), 8.

20. Tracy Kidder and Richard Todd, *Good Prose: The Art of Nonfiction* (New York: Random House, 2013), 125.

21. Woolf, *A Writer's Diary*, 14.

22. Lily Rothman, "10 Questions for Yoko Ono," *Time Magazine*, September 16, 2013, 62, available online at http://content.time.com/time/magazine/article/0,9171,2151142,00.html.

FOUR

Starting Fresh into Poetry

A Plan for a Late Career

Elizabeth Bodien

Like many, I was drawn to poetry as a child. Then poetry slipped under the louder parts of my life until I was close to retirement. Then I took a poetry workshop, and poems started spilling out, calling me to pay attention. But how does anyone start a second career, or a third or fourth, so late in life?

If the urge is there to write, write! Put paper in front of you, grab a pencil, and start writing. Whether trickle or flood, let it show up on the page. It may surprise you, if you don't stop to change anything.

I began by writing every day with pencil on yellow legal pads, filling one pad after another. That part was easy—you can dribble all sorts of words onto the page. But was any of it poetry? I had a lot to learn. And being in my sixties, I had to make up for lost time with not many years left to go.

What next? If you want to learn about poetry, improve your writing, build a career, what do you do next? For those who discover poetry late in life, here are some practical ideas for launching a writing life that might differ substantially from any previous career.

ADDRESS THE CONFIDENCE ISSUE

Alongside that urge to write, there can be another voice, maybe not a very friendly one, that undermines the writing urge. It says, *What could you write that anyone would want to read? How could you add anything worth-*

while to the wealth of poetry? This voice, maybe a real one from a friend or a family member, seems determined to sabotage all your efforts. If you are coming from a successful career in another field, you may not have experienced such a lack of confidence for a long time.

Confront that other voice whenever it appears. Speaking to that voice may work to dissipate its power. For example, say to it, *I hear you. You may be right, but I'm going to write anyway and see if I can work to get better at it,* or something similar. Acknowledge that troublesome voice, deal with it, and get back to work.

FIND SUPPORT

As you build confidence, it is helpful to have support, both financial and emotional. Retirement may have come with sufficient resources to allow the writing. If not, part-time work may be necessary, because it is unlikely you will make a living solely by writing poetry, especially if you are new to the work. Instead the expenses involved will far outweigh any income.

What about emotional support? Writers differ in terms of the support they need. It can also vary depending on how the writing is going, how loud that devilish, undermining voice gets, and how many rejection letters show up in the mailbox when you begin to send work out for publication.

At first I was lucky. Soon after I retired, I attended a day-long poetry festival in a park near my home. I stood up to read a poem at the open mike, and two wonderful things happened: An independent publisher asked if I had a manuscript because he might be interested in publishing it (which became my first chapbook). And a woman approached me and asked if I would like to join a women's critique group. I said yes to both, and I was on my way.

You can find similar poetry events at bookstores, libraries, and cafés. Let people know that you are looking. There are also online groups and LISTSERVs. I joined WOMPO, a women's poetry LISTSERV, managed by Amy King, who also manages the POETICS LISTSERV.

Immersing yourself in the world of poetry is like spinning a web that keeps getting larger and larger. You catch news of opportunities and resources. I was stunned recently at a doctor's appointment to hear my doctor say, "But you never hear or see much about poetry. Isn't it dying out?" (I made a mental note to myself to send her some poetry so her life would not be devoid of it.)

MAKE TIME TO WRITE

After retirement there are still the expectations of families, friends, and others that will be placed on you. Everyone may be happy with your avowed intent to write until it interferes with their expectations for you. Women especially may find this so. And if you are living with a spouse or partner who is still working, you may need to sort out who is contributing what to the shared household.

Let any drive or deadlines from your preretirement work help you to establish a good writing schedule before you discover procrastination. You must zealously guard your writing time. Make time also for reading poetry, going to poetry events, and keeping your poetry life organized.

Support yourself with the usual healthy habits of good diet, adequate sleep, and especially regular exercise, as writing is such a sedentary activity. While writing, getting up periodically to stir old muscles will help combat stiffness and will stir up your thinking too. But be careful when you take a break, making sure it is not just to avoid some difficult stretch you've come to in the writing. Sometimes it's better to push on through this resistance to what may be important material.

FIND WHICH WRITING TIME, PLACE, AND MATERIALS WORK BEST FOR YOU

Time of day may not be significant for everyone's writing, but it would be worth paying attention to see if one or another time of day is more fruitful for you. I've discovered that I need two kinds of writing time—one for the first writing and another for later revision. My mindset is not the same for these different activities. The first writing comes most easily in a sort of liminal, trance-like state of mind, so the best times for me to write are at the borders of my waking and going to sleep, or during intentionally induced trance states. My state of mind when first writing is uncritical and receptive to whatever strange things appear on the page. This writing seems to come from more right-hemispheric brain activity[1] and differs from the kind of prose or report writing you might have written, preretirement, in a business report, an academic paper, a medical report, or the like.

Revising is different. That involves a more critical faculty. If the first writing is the inspiration, the revising is the perspiration. Revising requires work and concentration but in a more normal state of consciousness. If I am interrupted, I can usually regain my focus of concentration after the interruption.

Many writers have personal rituals to begin their work, such as going for a walk, playing certain music, and so forth. Many write consistently in the same place and using the same tools. I start with yellow legal pads and pencils. I like the thick children's pencils, because my hand doesn't get as tired as when clutching thinner pencils. I revise either with pencil or computer. Some people write first drafts on a computer. See what works best for you.

RECOGNIZE HOW OFTEN TO WRITE

I strongly urge you to write every day. A big risk in waiting for inspiration is that you may put off writing while you acquiesce to other demands in your life. Of course, if you write every day you will have more stuff to weed through to find the quality in the quantity.

If the urge to write has been strong and until retirement you have not had time for creative writing, the time you now have to write will be a treasure. But you may be surprised at how much time writing takes, not just to put the first things on paper but the subsequent, much more difficult, revising.

DISCOVER YOUR SOURCES OF INSPIRATION

Although you have the urge to write, that doesn't always mean that you have a clear sense of what you want to say. This may sound surprising. It was to me. William Stafford, often quoted, once wrote, "A writer is not so much someone who has something to say as he is someone who has found a process that will bring about new things he would not have thought of if he had not started to say them."[2]

Other than free-writing regularly, what sources serve to prompt one's writing?

Memoir

By retirement, you'll have a lifetime of experience to draw on. Poetry could take the form of memoir on its own, or you may write with the intention of creating memoir pieces. This may seem a daunting task.

Michael Czarnecki, publisher-poet at FootHills Publishing, offers an entrance into memoir writing. He suggests "palm of the hand" stories, a term he borrowed from author Yasunari Kawabata. In his workshop Czarnecki suggests that writers list the decades of their lives. Then they take the first memory that comes, identify its decade, and write down just enough of a phrase to remember that event later. When a decent-sized list of memories has been compiled, pick any one, and write just one page about it—a bit of memoir that could fit in the palm of your hand.

Current Events

What issues do you care about? What community programs have you been involved in—education, politics, religion, international issues? Start with what you care about, and go from there.

Other Poetry

Read as much poetry, old and new, as you can. As you immerse yourself in the literature, respond to poems with poems of your own. The margins of many of my poetry books are filled with notes, the fragments of new poems. For me the more surrealist poets often encourage that state of mind for first writing.

You may also use fragments of your own poems that you have jettisoned when revising. Words that don't fit one poem may work splendidly in another. Remembering this makes it less painful when you must make those difficult but necessary cuts.

Other Art Forms

Poetry has a long tradition of responding to other art forms—often the visual arts, such as painting and photography. This "ekphrasic" poetry runs the gamut from poems that offer a written description of the art to poems that take a work of art as merely a jumping-off point toward subject matter ranging far from the original source of inspiration. Other forms of art, such as dance and architecture, may also give rise to poems.

Daily Life

Simply going about your day reveals dialogue, rhythms, colors, sounds, textures, signs, and ideas that can set a poem going. This is good to remember if you get frustrated by not having time to write. Writers who insist on isolating themselves too much may miss some of the richest observations life has to offer. Keeping a notebook handy to jot down those occasional gems helps later when you sit down to write.

Another matter is audience—both the addressee of the poem and its likely reader. Poems vary in terms of the person or group addressed, if anyone is addressed at all. As for likely readers, some poets write for other poets, often including references that only other poets would understand. I prefer to imagine a broader reading audience and connections between poetry and almost everything else.

LEARN ABOUT POETRY

Master of Fine Arts Degrees

You may think now of pursuing a master of fine arts degree. If you have settled down in place, with family and so forth, it's not so easy to go live on a campus as a student again. If you can and wish to do so, you have a huge number of colleges and universities to choose from for creative-writing degree programs.

Luckily an increasing number of low-residency MFA programs require only brief periods of on-campus residency. The rest of the two to three years students work with faculty members from home, by mail, e-mail, and telephone. When I considered this option, it seemed the programs—at least the ones I investigated—were not looking for the over-sixty student with long-out-of-date transcripts. That may change as the Baby Boomer generation retires and more people want to pursue education in their later years.[3]

Poetry Courses

Other than MFA programs, poetry courses can be found at colleges, universities, and writing centers. Community colleges are a good bet for finding nondegree courses, either in a traditional classroom setting or online.

Workshops, Conferences, Festivals

I decided I would try to design my own program of workshops. There are plenty to choose from and at less expense than full-degree programs. For example, the Fine Arts Work Center in Provincetown (Cape Cod), Massachusetts, offers week-long workshops in their summer program. The center recently added an online set of workshops called 24 Pearl Street, which is also the name of an even newer online publication from the center.

Another offering is the West Chester Poetry Conference for formalist and neoformalist poetry, held in June at West Chester University in Pennsylvania. The Palm Beach Poetry Festival in Delray Beach, Florida, also offers weeklong workshops each January. These are just a few of many such centers for learning about poetry and working on one's own writing. They can be found in *Poets &Writers Magazine*, *Poet's Market*, online, and by word of mouth from others.[4] Poetry festivals—such as the huge Dodge Poetry Festival in New Jersey (with recordings online)—are excellent places to hear poetry.

FAMILIARIZE YOURSELF WITH RESOURCES FOR LEARNING

Read. Try writing in the style of the poets you are reading. It is a good way to study the moves they make in their poems. Don't worry about losing your own voice. That will emerge on its own.

Bookstores and Libraries

Bookstores are a resource for books, of course, and also for poetry readings and critique groups. Where no such groups exist, consider starting one. Be sure to seek out the smaller, independent bookstores as well as the big chain ones. Public libraries and college libraries are another good resource. If you live far from libraries, many have online resources, including e-books. During National Poetry Month in April, there are numerous poetry events.

Internet

The most humongous source is of course the Internet where you can find poems, glossaries of poetry terms, poetry journals, poets' websites and blogs, poetry organizations, information about conferences, workshops, and special events.

There are also online classes. A new development is the MOOC—the massive open online courses that the company Coursera began in January of 2012. One example is the free semester-long course in Modern and Contemporary American Poetry taught by Al Filreis and teaching assistants from the University of Pennsylvania with more than 30,000 (that's not a typo!) students from around the world in one class.

SUPPORT THOSE WHO SUPPORT POETRY

In addition to buying and borrowing books and journals, become familiar with the organizations that support poetry. It is even better to become a member (as your budget allows), contributing toward their costs and benefitting yourself in the process.

The Academy of American Poets, the Poetry Society of America, Poets House, and the Poetry Foundation offer extensive websites. They also offer print publications, such as *Poetry* magazine from the Poetry Foundation, and events, such as the Poets Forum sponsored by the Academy of American Poets in October in New York City.

The Association of Writers and Writing Programs is geared more to academic programs but accepts memberships from individuals unaffiliated with any institution. Their annual conference is huge and includes an enormous book fair as well. The AWP publishes *The Writers Chronicle*.

The National Writers Union functions on behalf of writers, including help negotiating publishing contracts.

There are also specialized poetry organizations, such as the Haiku Society of America, the Tanka Society of America—with their own meetings, publications, and websites—Cave Canem for African American poetry, and the International Women's Writing Guild, which sponsors one big annual conference and smaller ones in and near New York City.

States have their own poetry organizations—such as the Pennsylvania Poetry Society—that sponsor meetings, small groups, conferences, and poetry contests. The National Federation of State Poetry Societies has its own annual conference. There are also local groups. Look for the ones near you.

SHARE YOUR WRITING WITH OTHERS

Publishing

Most of us want others to read what we have written. In fact you may be so eager to get something published that you send work out before it has been polished to its best possible form.

One thing I've realized is that one of the best editors is time itself. Put a poem, seemingly finished, in a drawer and wait months before pulling it out again. The changes that would improve the poem become obvious, especially if you are not attached to the idea that the first wording must be the best.

After revising to the final best version, look for the most appropriate journal for the poem. If you read a variety of publications, online and in print, you will begin to get an idea of where your poem seems to fit best. Of course what any editor thinks fits may differ from your own wishful thinking on the subject. Duotrope is an online compendium of publications, both print and online journals, and includes useful information, such as which publications are the slowest and fastest to respond, which are "most challenging," and which are "most approachable." You can also track your own submissions on their website. Whatever system you use, keeping track of submissions is important. I keep an Excel file with column headings indicating the following:

- name of poem
- where submitted
- whether the publication permits submissions to other journals at the same time (simultaneous submissions)
- name of the editor, judge, contact person
- physical address
- website address
- date sent

- expected date of response (Some publications/contests tell their turn-around times, while many don't.)
- date returned or rejected
- date accepted
- comments

Often poets publish poems singly at first. Submitting to journals should cost nothing more than postage (for snail mail) unless you submit to a contest. Contest fees may be as much as $25 and may or may not include a subscription to the journal. Some journals, such as *Passager*, want poems from older writers.

Submissions of individual poems, chapbooks, or books may be made in print or online, using a site such as Submittable. Publications have their preferences on submission details. You must pay attention to their guidelines, which you should think of as requirements.

Prepare yourself to get rejections. As discouraging as rejection letters are, try to remember several things: You may have rushed to publish before the poem was ready. Or you may have sent a good poem but to an inappropriate journal. Or you may have misread guidelines.

Eventually when you have a collection of poems, especially if they follow a theme, you can arrange them into a chapbook of between eight and forty poems or pages. Some poets skip the chapbook step and wait until they have a full-length collection that would make a book, usually between fifty and one hundred pages. Much poetry publishing today involves submitting to contests. These involve entry fees between $10 and $25 for chapbooks and $25 and up for full-length books. The fee may or may not include a copy of the winning book. These fees can add up quickly, so it is worth paying attention to the most likely places to submit your work.

Steer clear of self-publishing and vanity or subsidy publishers. Books so published usually are disqualified from most contests and library collections. You will benefit, as you start out, from the imprimatur of a press that thinks your work is worth publishing.

I'd advise keeping a poetry rèsumè. Mine includes headings with the following information:

- publications (collections and individual poems)
- articles and blog pieces (not poems) published
- workshops and talks given
- invited featured and group poetry readings I've given
- mass media (radio and TV) appearances
- poetry education (the poets I have studied with, where and when)
- poetry memberships
- nonpoetry education
- very brief summary of preretirement work

Social Media

I have not yet immersed myself in Facebook, Twitter, and other social media as I am not convinced that the time and attention they take away from writing time is worth the benefits. But I do find it useful to maintain a website with a couple of photos and pages similar to my rèsumè headings:

- welcome page
- sample poems
- publications
- elsewhere on the Web (links to my presence online)
- awards
- events (both past readings, workshops, etc. and upcoming ones)
- mass-media appearances
- contact information

You might also include videos of readings, links to other good sites, and the URL for your blog.

Readings

Reading your poems aloud is another way to share them. Seek out open mikes to begin with. Resist the temptation to read more than one or two poems. Some venues have rules. Abide by them. Practice what you intend to read.

If and when you are invited to be a featured reader, plan what you will read, practice it, and time it. You can also observe what works and what doesn't by attending readings. One tip: Don't read too fast. You are very familiar with your poem, but your listeners are probably hearing it for the first time. Help them with an appropriate speed and clear diction.

A final note: These ideas come from some years into writing after retirement. I suspect with more years of experience I might want to amend these ideas substantially. Meanwhile, reading, writing, listening, speaking—poetry offers riches. Partake and enjoy!

POETRY ONLINE

- The Wise Guide (http://www.loc.gov/wiseguide/dec04/poet.html)
- Poets.org's Browse Poems & Poets page (http://www.poets.org/poetsorg/browse-poems-poets)
- Poetry Foundation's Essential American Poets (http://www.poetryfoundation.org/features/audio?show=Essential American Poets)
- From the Fishouse (http://www.fishousepoems.org/)

- National Public Radio's Poetry page (http://www.npr.org/books/genres/10125/poetry/)
- PennSound (http://writing.upenn.edu/pennsound/)
- The Writer's Almanac with Garrison Keillor (http://writersalmanac.publicradio.org/)

POEMS AND POETRY NEWSLETTERS

These poems and newsletters can be e-mailed to you upon request.

- Poetry Daily (http://poems.com/)
- Poets.org's Poem-a-Day (http://www.poets.org/poetsorg/poem-day)
- American Life in Poetry (http://www.americanlifeinpoetry.org/)
- Poetry International's weblog (http://pionline.wordpress.com/)
- Gwarlingo (http://www.gwarlingo.com/)
- Diane Lockward's monthly poetry newsletter
- Knopf/Borzoi reader's Poem-a-Day (in April)

LISTS OF PUBLISHING OPPORTUNITIES

The following are places to submit your work.

- Creative Writers Opportunities List (CRWROPPS-B) (https://groups.yahoo.com/neo/groups/CRWROPPS-B/info)
- *Poets & Writers Magazine* (print and online at http://www.pw.org)
- New Pages (http://www.newpages.com/)
- MadPoetry.org's lists of contests by month (http://www.madpoetry.org/). Click on link for poetry contests.

ELECTRONIC TOOLS AND RESOURCES I HAVE FOUND HELPFUL

- *ReadPlease*—A software program that allows you to copy poems and paste them into the reader. In the free version, you can choose a reading voice from two male or two female voices. You can adjust the speed. Whether or not you use ReadPlease, reading your poems aloud while revising them helps to get grammar and line breaks right and allows you to hear the music of your poems (and where the beat might be off).
- *Visual Thesaurus*—Articles about words e-mailed to you upon request
- *A Word a Day*—e-mailed to you upon request

- *Smart Phone Apps*—such as Dictionary, Notes, Dragon Dictation, Rhyme Now, WGBH Poetry, Poetry (Poetry Foundation), Poetry Daily, Story Tracker, and Secure Safe

NOTES

1. Julie Kane, "Poetry as Right-Hemispheric Language," *Journal of Consciousness Studies* 11 (2004): 21–59.

2. William Stafford, "A Way of Writing," in *Writing the Australian Crawl: Views on the Writer's Vocation* (Ann Arbor: University of Michigan Press, 1978), 17.

3. I have not encountered overt ageism, but I don't look for it either. I don't know if my age works as an advantage or disadvantage in terms of people's receptiveness to my work, but, of course, if the poems have no heart in their message or language, my white hair won't help.

4. *Poets & Writers Magazine* can be found online at http://www.pw.org/magazine. *Poet's Market* can be found online at http://www.writersdigestshop.com/2014-poets-market-group.

FIVE

Transition from Teacher to Author

Rosemary McKinley

I suppose it had been a good life lesson to have had to work hard for everything I'd ever wanted. My first teenage hurdle was to earn a scholarship so I could attend college; it wasn't easy, but I did earn it. I am from a large family, so I knew I needed scholarship money, because my parents could not have afforded the whole cost. I visited my guidance counselor every day senior year to look at the scholarship board. After a lengthy and grueling interview, I was miraculously granted the college scholarship. While in college I realized that I had to study hard to attain those high grades to keep my award each year. I did just that and was happy that I did. The more prepared I'd been in my study of historical eras, the better prepared I was to teach it later on.

After graduation from college the next hurdle was landing a job as a high school history teacher. At first every interviewer said that I looked too young and could not coach football because I was female. I was not able to secure a full-time job in the early 1970s. When I did find a part-time teaching position, I appreciated it, and it fit into my lifestyle. My husband and I started a family, so teaching part time and being home the rest of the week worked for us.

Since I taught history, I grew used to researching facts and writing nonfiction. Of course I learned to present the history in an entertaining way that drew my students in. My thought processes were always working because my presentations had to be entertaining as well as factual. Again this style of writing would help me later as an author. I could not be boring, and yet the facts had to be true.

My part-time career eventually worked into a full-time job teaching history at the high school level and later morphed into teaching English

43

language arts on a middle-school level. I realized that I needed to improve on my teaching of writing skills, so I attended two summer Writing Institutes at Columbia's Teachers' College in 1991 and 1992. It was an intense and rewarding experience because I was expected to approach writing workshop just as if I were a student. Apparently the professors there had studied how professional writers worked, developing their writing workshop from it. When I returned to the front of my own classroom, I asked my students to do as I had been taught at the institutes:

- Keep a notebook, and write down everything that is important, everyday. Any kind of writing is acceptable in the notebook, including lists, fragments, poetry, and pictures with captions.
- Read through the notebook after twenty days or so, and look for a pattern or thread to write a story about.
- Write your first draft of the story that means something to you.
- After some peer editing with a writing buddy or writing group, write a second draft.
- Write a third and final draft, and share the work with the class.

I had no trouble doing this once I saw the reason for it. I wrote a very powerful story about being stalked by a student. The process I had just learned allowed the words to flow. Little did I know that by working to become a better writing teacher I would eventually be bitten by the writing bug. I still did not think of myself as anything but a teacher. In that class I was reluctant to share my story because this was all new to me and I was unsure of my writing. While I was taking the courses, though, I did realize that many of my colleagues wanted to become writers. I did not share their desire at the time. However, I compiled several notebooks over the years and I pushed myself to write poetry and stories along with my students. Part of the thinking in this approach is to model the writing for and with your students. It did help my classes to see what good writing looked like. It also aided me by encouraging me to write in genres I had never dreamed of. I wrote poetry and some fiction for the fun of it. I shared everything I wrote with my students, and they liked reading my work along with theirs. The added bonus was that I became accustomed to doing this. Before I had attended the workshops at Columbia, I never would have written poetry, and now I was writing it often and reading it aloud.

THE CHALLENGE OF A NEW CAREER

After retiring in 2003, I began to write, in earnest, and continued my quest to become published. The challenge in accomplishing this goal was surprisingly what I needed when I retired. It was staring me right in the face, but I only thought of the end result—being published. I did not realize until *after* I was somewhat successful that the writing was only a part of why I wanted to become a writer. The process of writing, submitting, promoting, and selling my work was just as important to me. This was my new career, and it was daunting for me personally. Before, as a teacher, I'd written lesson plans and delivered what I'd wanted to say in front of my students. I not only had developed a style, but I'd enjoyed standing up in front of a class stating information and offering encouragement. I was comfortable doing this. My writing always centered on helping children learn and on providing facts.

As many would-be authors come to know, it is very difficult to get published. I was not a celebrity, nor did I know anyone in the publishing industry. I sent my work anywhere and everywhere I could find a call for submissions. My inexperience did not help me one bit. In fact I made a big mistake in not realizing that the writing sent has to fit what the submission calls for. I was so anxious to send my work that I did not pay close attention to that part. I would feel dejected about my writing and then elated when I did receive an acceptance. In fact I would do a dance in my writing room just for my own sake. It would help lift my spirits and give me the will to keep on writing.

SUBMITTING WORK

After a while I realized that I needed to change my approach to submitting work. Here are a few suggestions that might seem basic, but they are sound for a new writer:

- Read all of the submission guidelines carefully, and follow them as closely as you can. Guidelines differ from place to place. Some editors will not even read your work if you do not do this.
- If an editor is kind enough to send back a critique, read it carefully, and adapt your work accordingly.
- Welcome constructive criticism, because it can only help make you become a better writer. Sometimes the advice does not work for that particular piece. For example, I had written a story in the first person, and one editor suggested I write it in the third person. It just would not have been as forceful, I believed. And, lo and behold, the original piece went on to be published by another editor at a later date, in the first person. I learned a good lesson that day: writing is very subjective, and it depends on what the audience and editor want.
- Subscribe to *Poets & Writers* online, and you will find calls for submissions and contests.
- Subscribe to free writing newsletters. *Writing World* is a good resource for suggestions on how to become a better writer and how to solve problems related to this profession.

- One article I read on a site mentioned websites that were good sources of suggestions and advice from other authors. The best website by far is *Funds for Writers,* written by C. Hope Clark. Her advice goes straight to the core of what new writers need to do. In addition, her newsletter is free, and she sets a theme for calls for submissions and contests. Most of my contacts have come from her newsletter, and her advice has helped me immensely. Her mantra comes through loud and clear: writing is hard work, and authors need to practice and improve every day.

When I began this career I slowly realized that, like everything else in my life, it was hard work. I had left a career that I had improved upon for thirty years, and now I was embarking on a completely new venture. As a teacher, I did not have to sell myself; I had proven that I could do my job well. Now I had to write well and keep editing to improve my style, but I also had to sell my writing. It was all new and overwhelming at times. One year I took a six-month break after a teary few days. I thought to myself, maybe I wasn't cut out for this. Then I proceeded to write again. I learned to keep my own mantra going inside my head: *I will be published someday. I can do this as long as I grow as an author.*

PROS AND CONS OF WRITERS' GROUPS

In becoming an author, I had to continue to edit and re-edit my work and focus on details. That was one part of the job. Yet it was almost impossible to edit my own work, so I joined a writers' group. I found that it can be helpful for others to critique your work, and it can also be damaging. Not everyone is looking at your work objectively. One man tore one of my essays apart and said it sounded "like a high school student wrote it." I was really upset by his comment, but soon thereafter that essay was accepted for publication. So you never know for sure if your piece is what an editor is looking for.

In order to have someone else edit your work, consider starting a writing group among a few writers you know for the sole purpose of critiquing and giving support.

- Take their advice into consideration only if you see the point.
- If most have similar suggestions and you can see the flaws, you should consider revamping your story.
- Another suggestion that might work for you is to find one writing friend through one of these groups. I trust my writing buddy's judgment. We both know that the critiques are based on best writing practices, not biases. We are also kind in our approach to giving advice. It works.

PROMOTING YOUR WORK

Promoting and selling my work are the hardest for me. I did not know how to start the process. I did not like selling my books, but I sure had to learn. My mouth would get dry, and my hands would shake. but I forced myself to do this. Here are a few tips to starting your promotions:

- Start local. Since my books are set in the local area and highlight history, I began with libraries and historical societies.
- Next visit the school librarians with a book in hand and a smile on your face. Donate a book or offer an e-book.
- E-mail schools and historical societies in the neighboring areas. Offer to do free book talks as long as you can sell your books.
- Offer to do book talks in specialty stores that do sell books along with local items.
- Ask if you can leave small posters of your books on community message boards, along with upcoming events.
- Exposure helps. I read a poem at the library in honor of Poetry Month. People in the audience asked about my recent memoir article and books I'd written.
- Use free online services offered through local newspapers to advertise book presentations on their events pages.

Another truth I have learned in this profession is that sometimes people you think would love to sell your books are just not inclined while others you would not expect to have interest do. It happens all the time. You have to keep presenting your books and yourself and not give up. You have to become a good salesperson if you want your books to sell. Persistence does pay off.

I have used my teaching skills as a presenter. I dressed in costume and showed pictures of how people lived during the era of my story. I asked the children a lot of questions about the culture of the era. They were enthusiastic about answering and adding to the discussion. I showed shells, wampum, settlers' homes, wigwams, and a mortar and pestle. It kept the children involved in the presentation.

It took several years and piles of rejections, but I now can say that I have attained my goal of becoming a published author. Working toward this goal has not been easy, but, as in my youth, I have learned that it was worth the time and effort. Success is sweeter when it does not come easily, all part of that life lesson I learned long ago.

THE SPARK THAT SENT MY WRITING IN MOTION

When my mother died in 2001, I reevaluated my life. After reflecting on my career, I thought that it was time for me to move on to becoming a writer. Many people hold down full-time jobs and write on the side. I wanted to become a writer full time. That was ten years after my stint at Columbia. And so I began to write vignettes of my childhood and attend writing classes to improve my skills. I retired from teaching two years later and wrote every morning. I was still grieving and I found that putting pen to paper helped me keep my happy childhood memories alive. Sometimes I laughed, and sometimes I cried, but either way it was cathartic. My memoir glimpses kept flowing and emerging when I was not even thinking about them. I would have to grab my notebook and quickly write down what I was thinking so I would not forget.

The first piece published that was not an essay was about the night my mother died — "A Mother's Roses," published in *Fate Magazine*. It was so important to me that that story was about my mother; it became the spark that precipitated my retirement.

FIRST BOOK DEAL

I submitted a short story of historical fiction set in 1905 to a book publisher calling for submissions. I received the nicest rejection I had ever gotten to the effect that my piece was too short. The next day the same editor asked me to write a book for them about the area in which I live. I was flabbergasted and thrilled all at the same time. I accepted, of course, and still was not sure what was expected of me. Because it was to be of a nonfiction genre, I knew I could do it. Again, all of this helped me to continue writing and to continue to improve upon my skills.

My first book deal included sizing and formatting pictures for the local history book. I did not know a thing about performing this task. I hesitated to accept the book contract and then realized that not knowing how to do something is part of venturing into a new career. I accepted the contract with the idea of asking for help from experts in this area. It all came together. I was fortunate enough to reach out to the right people, and they made it happen. Again, if I had not taken the plunge, I would never have had a book contract. I have to admit to a lot of sleepless nights, but I did accomplish my goal of being published. I also had the satisfaction of completing a task I found challenging and exciting. Another learning experience.

RESEARCH

While I was researching my first book, *101 Glimpses of the North Fork and Islands*, ideas for a new story were emerging. I kept referring back to my notes when the main plot for *The Wampum Exchange* was brewing in my mind. I ran with it and kept writing and researching. I spent hours reading and taking pencil notes fitted with white gloves and seated in special library collections. Information from the 1600s here on Long Island was difficult to find. I read and read and read about Colonial times but had to filter out what was factual about this area. It was not easy, but my teaching skills pulled me through. When I asked an archivist about what the inside of a typical house looked like in 1640, I was pleasantly surprised when she told me they had a miniature in the local museum. I needed to see the inside so I could describe it in my book. She offered to take me to see it.

Doing the research of the everyday details of life back then was fun for me. It brought me back to my own childhood even though times were so different; the closeness of the family was similar. I relived some of my early memories and thought of my mother often. As I was writing my book and telling the story of Daniel as it unfolded in 1650, I would take time to write more vignettes of growing up in a large family household in the 1950s.

I dedicated my second book to my mother. All while I was writing it, I was thanking her for all of the encouragement I'd received in my growing-up years. She would have loved the fact that I reached my goal, and because of that my life has changed dramatically in a good way.

SIX

What Shall I Write Today?

Lynne Davis

In retirement, I am lucky to be able to do what I always dreamed of—to write.

It starts every morning, when I make the coffee and then sit down with my spiral notebook to write my morning pages.

This ritual comes from Julia Cameron's *The Artist's Way*, a book of exercises, activities, and inspiration. I did the exercises with a group of seven other women when I was fifty.[1] Week by week, chapter by chapter, we explored our creativity, beginning with childhood pursuits, wishes, and dreams.

Our group included two painters, an art quilter, a woodworker, two writers, and a singer. For some of them, this was a chore, a difficult discipline. For me, it was a discipline, but one that I welcomed. Morning pages take me half an hour, usually. Through this discipline of three pages a day, I write.

I took to it right away, and every morning since then, with very rare exceptions, I've done my three pages. It's my best tool. It's my refuge; I pour out everything into these three pages—what happened yesterday, who I'm angry at, what problem I need to solve. Also I get ideas for other things I want to write. I start something brand new. I'm already here on the page, so why not write it now?

In retirement, I write what I want to write. I've done four basic types of writing.

ESL RELATED

As an ESL teacher at a university I submitted articles to professional journals. After retiring I had more time to put my language-teaching and -learning ideas into articles. No longer constrained by the requirements of academia, I had fun writing for a beautiful, glossy magazine called *Global Study*, which included plenty of photographs and great design. They took articles that never would have played in the academic journals. I wrote an article called "Your Teacher Will Love You" about what to expect in a teacher-student relationship as a student of English as a second language in the United States; "Travel Is Broadening," about how I always gain weight when I go to another country and experience the culture through food; in "Don't Forget the Popcorn!" I advised ESL students to watch movies in English in order to learn the language.[2] These articles were all based on my experiences as a language teacher and a language learner.

"Fifty Tips for Language Learners" was the first article I wrote for *Global Study*.[3] They are not able to pay contributors, but they are grateful and gracious, and with their superb design they make your articles look really good!

ART-QUILTING ARTICLES

I also had the opportunity, through my fiber-artist friend Karen Linduska, to write several articles for *SAQA Journal*, a magazine devoted to art quilting. I'm not a quilter myself, although I've tried my hand at it. I found a pattern for The Weekend Quilt in a women's magazine and finished it in about two years! I love quilts though, so when my friend asked me to do a feature on her latest series of art quilts, I was delighted. It was inspiring to interview her, to look through her collage-like journals, and to see her workspace. After my article on Karen's series, "Rebuilding the Wall on My Own Terms," was published on the magazine's website, I was able to get more assignments from this magazine, writing about collecting art quilts, setting up a museum exhibit, advertising and marketing one's work, getting inspiration, and teaching.[4] I got paid a decent amount of money for each article, and I also loved the process of writing these articles. The editor sent me portions of various artists' or curators' or collectors' comments on a topic, and I put them together—much like quilt pieces, it seemed—into one article. It was colorful, fun writing.

THE *SUN* PIECES

I hadn't heard of the *Sun* magazine until a friend recommended it and let me borrow a copy. (Since then I've seen it at the library and in coffee shops, have heard from friends who read it and have seen my pieces.) It is a black and white glossy magazine with just a touch of color on the front and back covers.

The *Sun* is different from other magazines in that it has no ads. Also no recipes, no articles about celebrities or how to lose abdominal fat. It has, in each issue, an interview with a thoughtful, principled person: a nun challenging patriarchy in the Catholic Church, a poet with a fierce attachment to his personal spirituality, an animal shelter–reform activist.

The magazine always features poetry, fiction and nonfiction, and beautiful photographs, but what attracted me right away was the Readers Write section, with its invitation to readers to submit short, heartfelt pieces of writing on one topic.[5]

I like working small. I like creativity with parameters. These *Sun* assignments were perfect for me.

The first two topics I tried were True Love and Coffee. The first was easy for me. I wrote about having a child as my first experience of pure, selfless love. Coffee, too, came easily. I had returned, inspired, from a weeklong homestay in Mexico, where I studied Spanish. My gracious hostess was dismayed when I left the house before breakfast, to sit in a restaurant and have coffee and write in my journal. The next day she brought coffee to me in my room, early. *Café por amanecer*, she called it, "coffee for daybreak." I was touched. I thought others would be, too.

However, this story was not published. Nor was my True Love.

But I persisted, enjoying the process of writing on these topics—the brainstorming, drafting, editing, and polishing of each small piece. They were short, averaging 250 to 500 words each.

Feeling a need for a community of writers, I started a group based on Readers Write. Everyone in the group (which varied, monthly, from three to eight participants) wrote on the theme that the magazine's editors specified for that month.

These themes were always broad and general, allowing for many takes on the same topic. We wrote our own personal stories on, for example, Coming Home, Truth, Rivals, Keepsakes, Airports, and In the Middle of the Night.

You can see how many stories could fit into these categories. I discovered that stories I had been wanting to tell for many years often fit comfortably into one of these themes. I would choose and write one, sometimes two of these stories.

We met once a month in a coffee shop to share our writing on that month's topic. It was interesting to see how the others had interpreted the theme and instructive for us to get feedback—both oral and written—on our writing. There was a nice camaraderie to our group, and an efficiency, too, due to the narrow focus.

We read our stories to the group, then listened as they shared their reactions, suggestions, and criticism. This was a big step for most of us. It was so useful, though, to have readers who would tell you what didn't make sense to them, what was repetitive (I hadn't noticed I used *really* so much), and, most important, what was good.

We submitted many stories to Readers Write. If the story was too personal, we asked to have our name withheld if they chose to publish it. And they did sometimes publish our stories.

The *Sun* sends a page proof in the mail via Fed Ex when they think they are going to publish your story, space permitting. That's how you find out. My heart leapt every time I saw that envelope on my porch. The magazine pays for publication in Readers Write with a free one-year subscription—a generous gift from a business with no advertising revenue.

Though it's been a couple of years since our group disbanded, I still submit to Readers Write.

YAHOO VOICES ONLINE

When you are a writer, people like to tell you what to write—usually their life story! Today the suggestion is, Why don't you write a blog? When I got that question, my answer was, Because I don't know the first thing about it.

But the seed had been planted. I saw a course, Writing for the Web, in the summer continuing-education catalog from the local junior college. I thought, This could be interesting. Plus, it was free for seniors. I had nothing to lose, so I signed up.

I loved the class. It was taught by a woman who wrote and published articles online and elsewhere when she wasn't helping her husband run their storage-rental business. She introduced the class to "content sites" where we could submit writing. This was a whole new world to me, a big and roomy one. There must have been twenty websites on the list she handed out to us. Here are some that I remember:

- About.com
- Associatedcontent.com
- Brighthub.com
- Constant-Content.com
- Dailyarticle.com
- Demandstudios.com
- Experts123.com
- Seed.com

Our teacher proceeded to explain in general how to submit to the various sites, how much they paid, and how to write articles that people would search for on the Web.

Equally important, she told us how to make an article easy to find among the millions published. That was called search-engine optimization (SEO). It meant: choose keywords for your article, then make sure that those words, and their synonyms, are in the title and the first paragraph, sprinkled through your article and repeated at the end.

I chose to focus on one website, Associated Content, which has since become Yahoo Voices.[6] In the three years I've been writing articles for that site, I've been learning more about SEO. It involves thinking about the words and phrases people will use to find an article like yours, perhaps trying these out in a search and discovering other phrases people are searching for, and then placing these words and phrases prominently in your title, the first paragraph, and again at the end. It is similar to the who, what, when, where, and why at the front of a newspaper article, and maybe even more important.

If I write an article with a lesson plan for ESL teachers on prepositions, for example, I want to have the key words *lesson plan, ESL teachers*, and *prepositions* in my title, and in the first paragraph as well. I can also use phrases like *ESL class, ESL classroom, English as a second language, teaching international students*, and *English prepositions*. Yahoo always asks me to list two to five key words and phrases. I try to include both broad (*ESL teachers*) and narrow (*lesson plan for English prepositions*) ones, repeating them frequently in my article, yet without "stuffing" them obviously into every sentence—which is considered a violation.

So rather than using a title like "Little Words, Big Problems," which might be cute and catchy, I stick with key words: "ESL Teachers: Use This Lesson Plan to Teach Prepositions." Readers will search for these words, and they will find my article.

Our teacher also recommended writing often on "evergreen" topics: articles about things that are perennially popular—like Halloween or parenting or sex—will pay you over and over, for years to come, because articles on the Web stay on the Web.

I wrote my first article, since it was summertime, about Campus Lake at Southern Illinois University. I wrote about their free boat rentals, times open, and directions to the place. I took a couple of pictures of the lake and the boat dock, which I included in my article.

As of today, this article has received 737 hits. Not huge, but it's evergreen: it will be read year after year. It could be compared, I suppose, to a stock that performs consistently if not extremely well.

But I have had instant successes as well. A short, simple article I wrote about dealing with culture shock in South Korea has received 4,550 hits.[7] This happened suddenly, and it surprised me. With a little research, I discovered that the article had been referenced in a military publication and read by a lot of service people in South Korea. Some of them commented on my article, pro and con, adding their own ideas to mine.

I've been able to publish articles about issues important to me. One of these issues is gun violence. When I received an onslaught of negative, disparaging comments on one article on that topic, I was hurt and embarrassed. But then two very supportive and understanding comments appeared.

I got an avalanche of hits on "I Can't Wait for the Movie Version of *Snow Flower and the Secret Fan.*" To this day, I still haven't figured why this article garnered 4,500 hits, most of them in the same time frame.

Writing for the Web is not a get-rich-quick scheme, at least in my case. But it earns me more than the interest on my savings account—and when those little payments start trickling in, it's gratifying. When I submit an article on Yahoo Voices, I can opt for an upfront payment, performance payments based on the number of hits the article gets each month, or both. Performance payments are a little above a dollar per thousand hits right now. Upfront payments vary. An average upfront payment for me has been between three and four dollars. There are also specific assignments on Yahoo, targeted to certain groups of writers—based on age, for example. Accepting one of these assignments usually means writing for a deadline, but it also usually means upfront payment.

Our teacher invited three guest speakers to the class. The first one was a blogger whose subject is low-carb diets. She's very successful, with product reviews and even a TV appearance or two.

More power to her! But she only cemented my conviction that blogging was not for me. She has to write regularly, and always on the same topic, and keep up with all the news on that topic.

The second speaker was more to my taste. She wrote for several content sites, choosing her own topics at times, accepting assignments at other times. This woman told us that she went from $5 a month to $300 a month between January and June. I still can't figure out how she did that. But I know that she writes a lot more articles than I write, or want to write. She approaches this writing as a full-time, forty-hours-a-week job.

The third writer was just right for me. She said that she writes whatever she feels like writing, that she wakes up every morning thinking, What shall I write about today?

She really expressed the freedom and fun that I wanted and have found in writing for the Web. I write about whatever I want to write about, when I want to—a wide range of topics that includes, for example,

- travel experiences and advice
- ESL teaching tips and lesson plans
- how to solve the Word Jumble
- descriptions of concerts and local theater performances
- sinus problems common in Southern Illinois

- reviews of local places and events—a festival, a Christmas ginger-bread display
- assistive devices that were helpful after hip replacement
- and (in the same time period) how to extend the life of flower arrangements.

I enjoy learning through the research most articles require. I might submit an article one day on the *Metropolitan Opera Live in HD* in movie theaters and the next day a review of the *Bachelorette* show. If I have an idea, and then details on that subject come quickly to mind, I know that's a good topic for me to write about.

If the first question is, What do I want to write about? the second is, What do others want to read about? In terms of hits, my most-read topics have usually been celebrities, TV shows, and movies:

- "Nicole Kidman to Star in and Produce *Little Bee*," 5,940 hits
- "I Can't Wait for the Movie Version of *Snow Flower and the Secret Fan*," 4,496
- "Kudos to Natalie Portman for Her Lovely Dancing in *Black Swan*," 1,987
- "'Final Rose Ceremony Is Our Superbowl,' *Bachelorette* Staffer Says," 1,771
- "Who Is Chloe Malle?" 1,750
- "Emily Stone, Viola Davis, Cicely Tyson, Octavia Spencer and Sissy Spacek to Star in *The Help*," 1,477
- "Jennifer Aniston's Beau Justin Theroux More than Just a 'Bad Boy,'" 1,341
- "Frank Turns the Tables on Bachelorette Ali," 1,239
- "Outsourced Starts Season with Bollywood-Type Show," 1,216

I like being retired and having a lot of free time. But I also like having something to do. I feel lucky that the something I've discovered is fun and interesting, gives me an opportunity to learn and grow, and is there when I need it.

With my online writing I have access to tutorials, well-organized lessons on everything from choosing key words to writing clearly and succinctly to choosing key words. It's so much easier than the old days when I pored over *Literary Market Place* trying to find a magazine that might publish something I had written, even though their description of what they wanted was never an exact fit for what I had. I collected rejection letters, and the thrill then was to get one that said they almost published my work.

I'm happy waking up in the morning and asking myself, What shall I write today? I have the life I've wanted, the writing life.

NOTES

1. Julia Cameron, *The Artist's Way: A Spiritual Path to Higher Creativity* (New York: Jeremy P. Tarcher/Perigee Books, 1992).

2. Lynne Davis, "Your Teachers Will Love You," 5, no. 2 (2009): 16–17, http://www.globalspl.com/site/articles/445/; Lynn Davis, "Travel Is Broadening," 6, no. 1 (2010): 70–73, http://www.globalspl.com/site/articles/505/; and Lynne Davis, "Don't Forget the Popcorn! How Watching Movies Can Assist Your Language Learning," 5, no. 1 (2009): 35, 37, http://www.globalspl.com/site/articles/384/.

3. Lynne Davis, "50 Tips for Language Learners," 4, no. 1 (2008): 6–9, http://www.globalspl.com/site/articles/274/.

4. Lynne Davis, "Rebuilding the Wall on My Own Terms," *SAQA Journal*, Spring 2006 Addendum, pp. 1–2; Lynne Davis, "The First Quilt," *SAQA Journal* (Summer 2007): 26–27, http://www.saqa.com/media/file/journal/SAQAJournalSummer07.pdf; Lynn Davis, "Making a Group Show Cohesive," *SAQA Journal* (Fall 2009): 26–27, http://www.saqa.com/media/file/journal/IssueV19N4_Fall09.pdf; Lynne Davis, "Advertising Art Quilts," *SAQA Journal* (Winter 2007): 12–13, http://www.saqa.com/media/file/journal/%20SAQA%20Journal%20Winter07.pdf; Lynne Davis, "Dry Spells," *SAQA Journal* (Summer 2010): 32, 39, http://www.saqa.com/media/file/journal/IssueV20N3_Summer10.pdf; Lynne Davis, "International Teaching," *SAQA Journal* (Fall 2010): 22–23, 35, http://www.saqa.com/media/file/journal/IssueV20N4_Fall10.pdf.

5. "Readers Write," *Sun*, http://thesunmagazine.org/about/submission_guidelines/readers_write.

6. Yahoo Voices online, "Lynne Davis," http://contributor.yahoo.com/user/837798/lynne_davis.html.

7. Lynne Davis, "Enjoying the Ride in Korea," *Global Study Magazine* 3, no. 3 (2007): 96–97, http://www.globalspl.com/site/articles/267/.

SEVEN

Using and Tuning Life Experiences

Jinny V. Batterson

Few of us have earned our primary incomes as full-time professional writers of any kind for all of our careers. We've needed to get and pay for our educations, raise families, care for elders, participate in community and civic life. Those of us now reaching retirement age, with pensions, Social Security, or investments providing for at least some of our monetary needs, with family and civic responsibilities lessening, may at last be contemplating more regular, more "serious" writing. This chapter explores several themes for embarking on later-life writing:

- crossfertilizing the different aspects of our lives
- seeking mentors and mentoring
- aiming for an audience
- being playful

CROSSFERTILIZING THE DIFFERENT ASPECTS OF OUR LIVES

I may have a fresh perspective in my writings precisely because I have not been primarily a paid writer all of my life. My experiences of many years in the information-technology world, first as an employee and later as a consultant and small-business owner, help inform my writing. My family experiences, likewise, become part of who I am as a writer.

Half a century ago, British author and scientist C. P. Snow's *The Two Cultures and the Scientific Revolution* observed that in post–World War II Britain practitioners of the "hard sciences," such as chemistry and physics, rarely conversed with fiction writers or artists.[1] Both science and the arts were diminished, he postulated, by being kept separate or touted as the only relevant features of an overall education. We can lose a great deal by overcompartmentalizing our lives and clustering only in groups with similar backgrounds and interests. Computer nerds and performance artists, unless they are members of the same biological family, rarely sit at the same table.

I have yet to figure out how best to "translate" the constrained and highly systematized writing of software specifications and computer code into essays and stories with more human characteristics, but I'm working on it. Along with a fair number of other computer professionals I've known, I've written jingles and musical parodies, partly as a tension reliever after a day job of dealing with an "editor" (a computer) who does exactly what, and only what, it is told to do. One of my early mentors in systems thinking, Gerald M. Weinberg, has branched into crafting mystery and science-fiction plots built around computer nerds.[2]

During the 1970s and 1980s, when I was first learning my IT craft, rapid advances in computer hardware and software made it possible to move from "flat files" to "hierarchical databases" and then to "relational databases" in short order. Each successive change made accessing and analyzing data easier, allowing for more thorough and more accurate predictions of real-life phenomena. How might our social and political evolutions parallel these continuing changes in our computer-assisted capacity to handle information? How might we solve problems of blight, environmental degradation, and polarity of wealth by meshing increasing technological sophistication in information gathering with a core of humanistic teachings? What are the best examples, the worst counterexamples, of this sort of crossfertilization?

SEEKING MENTORS AND MENTORING

The older I get, the more I cherish examples of elders who've made notable written and cultural contributions much later in life. My literary favorite is Helen Hoover Santmyer, whose best-known novel, *And Ladies of the Club*, became a best-seller after its second publication in 1984, when she was eighty-eight years old.[3] It turns out that Santmyer, who lived most of her life in and around Xenia, Ohio, was not an "instant bestselling author." After university, graduate study, and early publication as a poet and novelist, she forestalled a full-time writing career due to family and economic constraints.

I also take inspiration from Doris Haddock, "Granny D," in her youth an aspiring actress before marriage, family, factory work, and then extended caregiving for an infirm husband intervened. As an activist widow, she campaigned successfully for national campaign-finance reform by walking across the United States from west to east, starting on New Year's Day in 1999, just shy of her eighty-ninth birthday. Along her 3,200-

mile way, she wrote portions of a memoir later published with coauthor Dennis Burke as *Granny D: Walking across America in My 90th Year.*[4] A frequently quoted slogan, "You're never too old to raise a little hell," became the title of a second volume of memoirs.[5] Her low-budget, non-winning 2004 campaign for a New Hampshire U.S. Senate seat was turned into a film documentary, *Run Granny Run.* Part of her platform in that race was a promise to serve just a single term if elected (she was, after all, 94 at the time). A posthumous collection of Granny D's writings was completed and published by coauthor Dennis Burke in 2012. In it, Doris explained her basic philosophy: "You have to keep the young adventurer inside your heart alive long enough for it to someday re-emerge."[6]

Mentors remind us that our expectations, in writing as in life, need to focus on small incremental steps—not one mammoth memoir or novel or play or poetry collection spun from whole cloth, but a few more words or paragraphs or lines of poetry or revisions with each writing session. Being mentors can be just as important as having them; in my various experiences of both technical and nontechnical teaching assignments, I've certainly learned volumes from my students.

Legendary basketball coach John Wooden's memoir, *A Game Plan for Life: The Power of Mentoring*, lays out the importance of both mentoring and being mentored.[7] His first mentor was his struggling farmer father, who accepted reverses with good grace and avoided bitterness despite some questionable dealings by colleagues. His final mentor was someone he'd never met: Mother Teresa of Calcutta. Her late-life questioning of her faith helped him come to terms with the painful death of his wife and lifelong helpmate. Wooden's book, published with coauthor Don Yaeger when Wooden was nearly one hundred, also contains testimonials from players he coached to become better humans as well as better basketball players.

AIMING FOR AN AUDIENCE

One of the most difficult tasks for an aspiring writer is defining and finding an audience. Family and close friends are a logical first step. For many of us this may be enough. In addition to being a goad to my writing efforts, Mom also provided me with an important part of my audience so far. The longest piece of finished writing I've done up to now is a self-published family memoir composed of narrative, poetry, and pictures that I created in 1999. During the 1990s my father finally expired physically after suffering years of declining memory and function due to Alzheimer's disease. It seemed an appropriate time to record as many remaining family stories as I could before any more memories were lost. Mom, whose memory was still intact, helped me fill in the parts of my parents' and her parents' lives that came before I was around to know them. The stories she told me, along with stories of my paternal grandparents and their forebears from my dad's one surviving sister, became *Images in Transition*, developed with help from a semester's course at a local community college. At Christmas that year I used the community-college computer lab to burn CDs. I engaged a local print shop to produce a limited number of hard copies of the memoir. I distributed them, with CDs on the inside front cover, to surviving family members.

Researching and crafting the memoir taught me a lot, including how to frame the not-so-good episodes in ways that preserved the essence of the experiences, while also maintaining the dignity of the participants. Emily Dickinson's caution to "Tell all the truth but tell it slant" applies here. For example, I chose not to dwell on the long-term estrangement that developed between my maternal grandfather and his only son when my uncle refused to attend college. As it turned out, Uncle Stu would have been a serious drain on family finances as a collegian during the Great Depression. Instead, starting in 1929, he initially earned an income as a grocery clerk, progressing rapidly into management. After about a decade, he had the skills, savings, and business-networking resources to purchase and manage the general store and service station in the small town where he and his parents still lived. After my grandfather lost his last full-time job in 1930, he eventually wound up working for Uncle Stu. The sketch I wrote of Grandpa and his struggles, titled "A Good Failure," was one of my mother's favorite vignettes of the entire memoir. I cherish the memory of her reading and rereading this sketch and telling me how well she thought it captured the essence of her father.

If we're ready to go beyond family and close friends, it can take a while to find and develop our niche. How do we get the word(s) out? As the publishing industry changes, and as the Internet becomes evermore ubiquitous, finding audiences for our work can be easier but also considerably more complex. There are some generally useful practices:

- Read widely; especially read in genres where we aspire to write.
- Get feedback from friends who are tactful enough so we'll listen and honest enough not to gloss over our shortcomings.
- Join formal or informal writers' groups, especially those geographically close to us and/or focused on the genre of writing we aim to write.
- Attend writing workshops and conferences; take community-college courses on various genres of writing.
- Get peer reviews of our work.
- Find and cultivate good editors for our efforts.
- Enter contests (and read the winning entries when we don't win).
- Set aside regular intervals for writing and revising our work.
- Write, write, and write some more.

I've probably submitted at least three entries for every one that has been published by anyone besides me. I am still something of a neophyte at the craft of marketing my work—a craft that is separate, and just as important, as doing the actual writing. My longest string of publishing "successes" so far was a set of seven opinion pieces that I wrote over the course of a decade during the 1990s and early 2000s. An understanding editor at the alternative weekly in Richmond, Virginia, where I then lived, gave me useful feedback about tuning my original drafts and had enough clout at the magazine to sometimes bend the rules that opinion pieces on the "Back Page" needed to focus on strictly local controversies. This editor left Richmond for the hereafter at about the same time I left for a year-long overseas teaching assignment and then relocated to another state.

As I continue to write and to submit work for possible publication, I'm learning increasingly to value the feedback of editors and possible distributors of my work who take the time to say, in essence, "Not yet, but . . ." rather than a pat, formulaic "No." One of the most wonderful rejection notices I ever received was a handwritten note from a member of the Capitol Steps musical satire troupe. I'd sent off to their office in Washington, D.C., a few of the numbers of a winter-holiday political-parody show that I'd composed for a local Richmond audience. The response has since been lost in a move. As I remember it, it said something like, "Sorry, Jinny, we write all of our own material, but what you've sent shows promise. Get yourself an accompanist, a talented group of singers, and keep at it!"

The bar for entry into the category of "established writers" can be high and somewhat fickle. If I'm even somewhat honest with myself, I realize that I may not have either the stamina or the talent of a Helen Hoover Santmyer or a Granny D. When I've been successful at finding a wider hearing, it's more often been for a particular niche audience with whom I share an interest or a life experience—I once had a poem published about surviving an episode of breast cancer; another that made it into a local magazine described a winter snow storm in a part of the country where such storms are rare.

The Internet can provide nearly instant access to a wealth of information that increases almost exponentially. Its very richness can be daunting. This is why personal contact is an important adjunct to surfing for appropriate publications and calls for submissions, even those already prescreened by a local or regional writers' network. I am just starting to learn the relevant styles for publications in the area where I now live. It's not quite the same as my previous stomping ground—the differences between Virginia and North Carolina can be subtle, but they exist. I'm not yet a native in the market where I currently reside and not yet widely enough known for that not to make a difference. The local newspaper sometimes publishes my letters to the editor; the editor of the alternative weekly here already has a stable of regular and gifted writers to hash over current events and controversies, writers whose experience of central North Carolina is both deeper and broader than my own.

The niches in which I aspire to write are developing, though—*sustainability* and *resilience* are buzzwords whose time seems to be coming. "Writing after Retirement" will likely occupy a fair number of us boomers as golf and rocking chairs lose any interest they might initially have held. Urban agriculture is taking off—our area for the past several years has hosted an annual Tour de Coop. International and crosscultural exposure are more and more important. A possible memoir I've begun several times about a decade of travel and teaching in early twenty-first-century China will need a lot more revisions and a lot more contacts, though, before it is ready to find a published niche beyond an occasional blog entry. The friends who read my initial draft were kind enough to point this out.

Friends, writing groups, and editors will continue to be the main sources of feedback for those of us who want to write more. All of us crave feedback. Few of us are totally capable of disentangling feedback about our work from our sense of worth as human beings. I've not yet learned to look forward to having my work dissected by peers. In the 1980s and '90s, feedback for computer designs and computer code was sometimes done via peer reviews called *walk-throughs*. I was grateful when reviewers found and pointed out errors before they could become more costly later on. I also learned that the intended purpose or audience for a particular set of software was often unclear at the outset. Resolving ambiguities about who would sponsor and control the project could be crucial to a project's success (or, if too difficult to discern, a good reason for scuttling a project before it progressed further). I continue to learn that many of my writing drafts will not see further distribution. However, these "failed" efforts will often contain the germs of future pieces of better-crafted, better-aimed work.

BEING PLAYFUL

Those of you who've read this far probably have noticed that I'm partly a reformer, sometimes too insistent on my capacity, paraphrasing Robert Kennedy, "to see things that never were, and to ask, Why not?" So why insist on the importance of being playful as a writer? Isn't the work of a reformist writer serious? Perhaps the work is, but the writer who takes him- or herself too seriously has lost touch with an important aspect of self. The writers I most aspire to emulate, the ones I deem to be most effective, manage to wear their reformist tendencies lightly.

You cannot, no matter how gifted your writing style, bludgeon someone into agreeing with you. If you are powerful and well-respected, you may be able for a time to override dissenting opinions, but they will assuredly pop up again. (Their existence is much more vital to advancing your understanding than is fawning praise.) In our overly media-saturated era, too much of what passes for considered written opinion consists of increasingly hostile factions of the powerful lobbing rhetoric and insults at each other. Finding or being an amused, quiet voice of sanity can be difficult. We still have a few gifted but understated satirists among us. We would, I believe, greatly benefit from having more.

FINALLY, A CAVEAT

Most later-life writers have been writing in some form since childhood. If you are just starting out as a retirement-phase writer, and you have a memoir, nonfiction essay, or piece of fiction that cries out to be written, you may want to engage a coauthor. Many talented ones exist, and writers' networks typically include some. Part of who I am has always been a writer, even before that winning fifth-grade essay. As a teen I journaled and wrote sappy poems about my many crushes and disappointing love affairs. I later resumed journaling when as mother of a kindergartner and a preschooler I tried to cope with my children's growth and to foster my own. From time to time I penned more public efforts: letters to the editor, parodies, opinion pieces, poems, essays. As I continue to write, rejection slips for my efforts will continue to come in. I remember, after some initial defensiveness, that they are not rejecting me. I go back to nurturing the piece of me that writes, that needs this particular form of expression. Though I may not ever complete the great American novel, or craft the poem that defuses the next war before it starts, I will continue to search for a wider audience. On some days, my "audience" will turn out to be just nudging forward my best self, and that will be enough.

NOTES

1. C. P. Snow, *The Two Cultures and the Scientific Revolution* (Cambridge: Cambridge University Press, 1959).
2. Gerald M. Weinberg's official site is at http://www.geraldmweinberg.com. The latest "Nerd novels" are the *Aremac Project* series.
3. Helen Hoover Santmyer, *And Ladies of the Club* (New York: G. P. Putnam's Sons, 1984).
4. Doris Haddock with Dennis Burke, *Granny D: Walking across America in My Ninetieth Year* (New York: Villard Books, 2001).
5. Doris Haddock and Dennis Michael Burke, *Granny D: You're Never Too Old to Raise a Little Hell* (New York: Villard Books, 2003).
6. Doris Haddock and Dennis Michael Burke, *Granny D's American Century* (Durham, NH: University of New Hampshire Press, 2012).
7. John Wooden and Don Yaeger, *A Game Plan for Life: The Power of Mentoring* (New York: Bloomsbury USA, 2009).

Part II

Practical Aspects

EIGHT

Estate Planning for Authors

Robert Runté

When my brother passed unexpectedly, it took over five years to settle his estate. It was depressing, tedious, time-consuming labor that took me away from my own family far too many weekends and was potentially divisive as various relatives argued with my decisions as executor. So my wife and I went home and made out our wills, told the relevant people where our wills could be found, simplified and updated our banking and asset records, and did what we could to ensure that our executor and heirs would not have to go through all that.

Retirement is a good time to pause and take stock, and estate planning should be a key part of that. Few writers think through the implications of their literary careers for their wills, but your estate planning is incomplete if it does not include clauses outlining who gets control of your literary properties and what they should do with it.

There are four issues to be addressed here:

1. who gets the royalties (if any) from one's work
2. who has *artistic* control over one's published work
3. what is to be done with any unfinished manuscripts left after one is gone
4. and what is to be done with one's online presence.

THE NEED FOR A SEPARATE LITERARY EXECUTOR

The easiest approach, of course, is simply to leave the estate in the hands of a single executor, but the individual charged as executor for dealing with the regular sort of assets may not be the best person to look after one's literary legacy. Unless one's spouse, close relative, or trusted friend also happens to be one's collaborator or a writer in their own right—and so qualified to make appropriate judgments about one's literary legacy— they may not be the best choice as literary executor.

For example, it is not uncommon for an executor unfamiliar with publishing to quickly glance at the current revenues for a particular title and, if sales are low, conclude that it is valueless. This may be a mistake.

First, such an evaluation fails to recognize that—commercial or not— keeping their work in print may have mattered to the deceased. I took years to write my novel, and I am inordinately pleased with it, so I would like to think it will have some staying power, even after I am gone. Psychologists tell us that many writers are driven by the desires to achieve a kind of immortality through their works, so shutting that down a few months after their passing may be a bit disrespectful. That is probably less true for magazine writers (who expect their work to have only a limited shelf life) than for book authors, but one wants an executor who is aware of how much significance the author placed on "literary heritage."

Second, assessing the earning potential of literary properties is extremely complex, especially given recent shifts in publishing models. It is true under the old model of fixed print runs that if a book were selling below a certain minimum level it was remaindered. *Remaindered* refers to the practice of publisher's listing a book as out of print and then selling off their remaining stock to distributors at massive discounts. Books were remaindered when the cost of storing the remaining copies was thought to exceed any potential profits from the trickle of sales. Authors do not receive royalties on the sale of remaindered books; once a book was remaindered, that was pretty much the end of its earning potential.

With print-on-demand technologies and e-book publishing, however, there are no storage costs, so no reason not to keep a title in print indefinitely. Even as little as a dozen sales a month can still add up to significant revenues when calculated over a period of years. More significantly, titles are increasingly finding their audience through word-of-mouth recommendations that build momentum over time, so that a current trickle of sales may well become a torrent if given sufficient time to grow. Similarly, self-publishing has opened the doors for writers to reprint their backlist, so that even currently out-of-print titles may have the potential to earn again—if left in the hands of someone who understands both the author's work and the marketplace.

Even many authors find the rapidly shifting marketplace extremely confusing, however, so it is unreasonable to expect one's executor to have the necessary expertise. One may, therefore, wish to designate a specific individual (and a backup, just in case one's first choice becomes unavailable) to manage one's manuscripts and publications. Choose a collaborator, a sympathetic colleague, a trusted editor, or even a dedicated fan, as long as it is someone who understands one's work and one's preferences.

CHOOSING A LITERARY EXECUTOR

The goal is to choose someone who can manage one's life's work as closely as possible to one's own wishes. For example, many fans of C. S. Lewis were deeply disturbed when a publisher announced that they would be editing the many Christian references out of the Narnia stories to enable the series to reach a wider, more religiously diverse, modern audience. The decision might well have increased sales and so been welcomed by heirs interested solely in royalty generation but abhorrent to C. S. Lewis himself, who specifically set out to write Christian literature. Or take the long and bitter dispute over the literary estate of Stieg Larsson (author of *The Girl with the Dragon Tattoo* and its sequels) between the family who—in the absence of a will to the contrary—inherited the rights to his famous trilogy, and Larsson's longtime girlfriend and collaborator, who insists Larsson would not have approved of his family's many accommodations to the North American market. Consequently, if one wishes to avoid such conflicts, or the risk that one's work could be left to languish as an uninterested executor fails to promote them or even keep them in print, then it is crucial to specify in one's will who is responsible for what.

My advice would be to leave all one's literary work to be managed by a single literary executor rather than designating specific titles to specific individuals. One drawback of leaving specific copyrights to specific individuals is that such an approach requires frequent updates to one's will whenever one finishes additional manuscripts—an ongoing nuisance and unnecessary expensive. Another drawback is that there may be opportunities for omnibus editions or reprint series or e-book rereleases, etc., that would require package deals that could be fatally stalled if the holder of one or other copyright demurs. Appointing a single literary manager also facilitates determining which unfinished manuscripts should be finished, by whom, and how and by whom published. Coordination of such decisions is especially important where the deceased is the author of multiple series or brands that could otherwise end up competing with each other. Decisions about unfinished manuscripts cannot really be made in advance, since by definition one cannot know how things are going to evolve after one's death. The exception here may be if one is absolutely certain that one does not want anyone else tampering with one's manuscripts. In that case, one could simply order unfinished manuscripts left as is. (I would strongly advise against ordering unfinished work destroyed, however, as descendants or scholars may well be legitimately interested in one's unfinished work.)

It goes without saying that one needs to check with the person one is thinking of designating as one's literary executor (and a reliable backup as well) to ensure that they are able and willing to take on this responsibility, before assigning them in one's will.

ROYALTIES

I am no lawyer, and even if I were I likely do not live in the same jurisdiction as you, so I am not about to give legal advice here; but I do want to raise some issues you might wish to consider or discuss with a lawyer when drawing up a will.

If one's writing income comes from topical articles, then it is likely that income stream will quickly dry up after one stops writing. In such cases, it may be sufficient to simply have royalties accrue to the estate, on the assumption that a year after one passes, there will be no more checks coming in and the executor will be free to wrap the estate up. If, on the other hand, one anticipates continuing royalties, the executor may need to keep the estate active so that payments may be received and efficiently disbursed.

This can get a bit tricky, because one needs to strike a balance between ensuring sufficient clarity in the will that the money goes where intended and becoming so detailed that the will becomes a burden on those left behind. For example, one of my relatives specified down to each teacup and rusting tool which object went to each of an innumerable list of relatives. Finding, identifying, sorting, and distributing each item was, frankly, maddening. The cost of shipping many items greatly exceeded their value, sentimental or market. Besides having to deal with the fact that many of the items had been disposed of or gone missing years before, the recipients were often mystified as to why a particular tool or teacup came their way, and largely unappreciative. Objects that are of import and sentimental value in one generation may be received as less significant by the next. One needs, therefore, to ensure that one does not saddle one's heirs with a will that generates resentment rather than fond remembrance.

The difficulty with literary properties is that income streams, particularly in a rapidly changing publishing environment, are highly unpredictable. Specifying who should receive royalties from which titles is therefore probably a mistake, since—as with my relative with the teacups—one may have difficulty objectively appraising the actual worth of any particular item. One does not want to bury one's executor in a blizzard of paperwork tracking each small royalty payment, and heirs do not wish to receive checks for eight dollars, especially if the administrative costs of delivering it were ten dollars. Similarly one does not want to specify that the revenues from a title one expects to be wildly successful to one heir, only to have that stream dry up while a less-deserving or needy relative reaps a windfall from a title from which one expected little. Besides leaving the larger sum to the wrong heir, the potential for resentment among family members over which titles get lucky—or, worse, over which titles they perceived to have been more adequately promoted by the executor—could cause considerable friction. My (nonlegal) advice would therefore be to have all royalties accrue to the estate and for revenues to be divided among the heirs according to a predetermined formula, with some leeway to the executor to determine when the amounts are too small to warrant immediate distribution.

I say "predetermined formula" rather than "percentage" because one may wish revenues to be held in trust for some heirs, particularly when underage, with leeway for the executor to disburse funds as needed for their care, education, and so on. Many wills, particularly when the estate is substantial, include provisions for a set percentage of the trust fund to be released on, say, the child's eighteenth, twenty-fifth, and thirty-fifth birthdays so that if they squander the initial amount foolishly, they get a second and third chance to use the remainder sensibly.

Of course royalties may not represent the most significant element of the estate, especially given that I am addressing this chapter to authors who have retired from another, presumably better-paying, career. (Most full-time writers live modest lives from very modest incomes.) On the other hand, the thrust of my argument here has been that one needs a knowledgeable executor to ensure that literary property is not undervalued or carelessly disposed. The greater the income from writing, the greater the need for a separate literary executor and the greater attention to the distribution of royalties. Getting the balance between underestimating and over estimating one's likely posthumous literary success is an interesting test of ego, better entrusted, perhaps, to one's lawyer and executor.

ACCESS TO THE WILL

Having drawn up a will, put a copy somewhere where people can *find it!* Lawyer's offices and bank safety-deposit boxes sound sensible, until one realizes one's survivors may not know the name of one's lawyer or be able to gain access to the safety deposit box without a copy of the will appointing them executor, which is *in* the safety deposit box they are trying to access—an astonishing Catch-22. So leaving a duplicate in an envelope in one's desk drawer makes a lot of sense.

Further, it may be useful to have a list of one's online passwords in the same envelope so that various Web pages, online book-distributor sites (Amazon, Kobo, Smashwords, etc.), and social-networking sites can be immediately updated. This is particularly important if one is self-publishing, as orders, queries, complaints, and so on must be addressed, or at least the explanation posted, so that customers are not left hanging or fans left to speculate.

ONLINE PRESENCE

The literary executor must be explicitly empowered to take down, close off, or maintain one's various online activities. If one's books are selling well, it may be sensible to maintain one's Facebook and Twitter accounts, blog, Web page, and other social media channels as they are so as to better reach one's established audience with ongoing updates. Of course the executor must make it clear that the author is deceased and the reader is now dealing with the literary executor, speaking on the author's behalf. On the other hand, if the executor is closing up the estate, being able to take down all one's sites can be very important—particularly if one's last post happens to be a rant, and not necessarily how one wishes to be remembered.

And while on the topic of online presence, if one is self-publishing, one needs to make provisions for having someone take over and manage one's inventory in the event of illness or mishap. A week's delay while one is abed with the flu will go unremarked, but any extensive illness or absence could create devastatingly ill will if no one is responding to queries, filling orders, or addressing complaints. So I strongly recommend along with a will that all self-publishing authors draw up contingency plans.

DEALING WITH PUBLISHERS

Similarly one should have some sense of whether one's publisher has such contingency plans. If one is published through large enterprises like Penguin or Random House, then one need not worry: if one's editor drops dead, another will be appointed shortly. But with the emergence of many indie publishers, one should be alert to the possibility that even the best-intentioned micropublisher could suffer a sudden mishap or illness that could leave one's book tied up in limbo for years. At a minimum one must ensure that any contract signed includes a revision clause, such that if the book is out of print for more than six months the rights revert automatically to the author.

Indeed it would not hurt to inquire about the publisher's estate planning, especially when dealing with one-person operations. If the publisher passes away, who is going to take over? Anyone? Someone that could be trusted to take the same care with cover art, editing, marketing, and so on? Even if there appears to be a half-dozen individuals involved in the press, if the owner passes without a will, the other members may be powerless to carry on. So ask. (Asking may even spur them to develop a will and contingency plan!)

CONCLUSION

There are two points, then, that I would like you to take away from this chapter.

First, that you need a will. If you do not already have one, you need to write one immediately. Everyone knows that they need a will, but it is just human nature to put off actually drawing one up, because no one likes to dwell on their mortality. So if you were nodding your head and thinking, "I had better get to that soon," you need to know that some indefinite "soon" is not nearly soon enough. Make the appointment with your lawyer right now; or if you are more inclined to the do-it-yourself approach, add "will kit" to today's shopping list. (I do not necessarily recommend a do-it-yourself kit, though, as such kits tend to be very basic and likely will not address issues of intellectual property. But even a basic will may be better than nothing.)

Second, now that you have adopted writing as a second career, you need to recognize that this may have implications for your will. If you already have a will, you may need to update it to acknowledge this shift in careers. One's publishable writing represents intellectual property, which is as much a part of one's estate as one's house or car. Executors are sufficiently familiar with cars and houses to deal with those in a straightforward manner but may require additional direction to address the complexities of intellectual property. Careful consideration needs to be given to the four areas raised in this chapter to ensure that one's wishes are known and followed.

Strive for a balance between providing sufficient direction and not tying the executor's hands. Most authors find it difficult to keep on top of developments within the rapidly evolving publishing industry, let alone predict what challenges and opportunities may present themselves twenty years down the road. One must therefore allow sufficient leeway for one's heirs to respond to the changing environment, but hopefully within the spirit of one's own intentions.

NOTE

Dr. Runté is not a lawyer, and this is not legal advice. You may wish to consult with a lawyer before implementing any of the suggestions in this article.

NINE

In Pursuit of Simultaneous Passions

Writing and Volunteering

Christine Swanberg

Retirement offers the luxury of pursuing long-held passions put on hold. Perhaps you have dreamed of making a difference in the world through a cause you are passionate about. Now, finally, in retirement you can follow your heart, become involved, and, while you're at it, get to that inner writer that has been waiting to come out all these years. Yes, you can have it both ways: writing and volunteering make great partners.

Many communities have literary organizations, scholarship committees, and advocacy of every sort: child, senior, disabled, medical, and foster care to name but a few. Most communities have rescue missions, booster clubs, and veterans' organizations. Libraries have "friends" and support groups, as do school districts and academic organizations.

Philanthropic and fraternal groups still meet regularly for lunches and events all across America. Alumni organizations explode with opportunities for involvement and writing. Park districts, garden clubs, and forest preserves have supporters, as do symphonies and especially local arts councils. (Since organizations vary in their nonprofit status, check with them if you want to know for sure.)

What does this have to do with rekindling your writing in retirement? Let's take a closer look. What do most nonprofits have in common? The ubiquitous newsletter. *Newsletter* with a capital N deserves a great deal of respect, and a good writer can make a newsletter sparkle. Remember those big brown eyes of shelter dogs? Maybe you can't adopt them all, but you could write a description that would persuade someone else to take home the little cutie. Do the homeless tug at your heart? Besides helping with the soup kitchen, you could interview and profile some of the regulars whose stories might surprise you while garnering more support for their cause. By igniting your long-lost inner journalist, you also become a community player, making a difference for the people you are profiling and getting to know them as real folks with real stories.

Be daring. Are you really worried about global warming? You are not alone. Green organizations of every sort could use good writers to explain facts and statistics in a way that isn't just preaching to the choir (pardon the mixed metaphor here). And speaking of choirs, you don't have to qualify for *The Voice* to be in one. Church and community choirs are generally very forgiving.

One of the most unexpected rewards of my recent retirement came about through getting more involved in a church choir. I was a new choir member at a church the same year that a new choir director was appointed. The new director turned out to be a distinguished composer and surprisingly very open to creative collaboration, expressing an interest in my poetry. That lead to several collaborations in which he composed music for the lyrics I wrote. Besides benedictions, we collaborated on Advent songs and Christmas songs, which were well-received not only by the congregation but also by the larger community. Some of the collaborations were also sung by community chorales and for college audiences.

Religious organizations sometimes welcome other forms of writing from lay members. In some religious organizations it is possible to become a lay liturgist, which means that you write part of the service. Perhaps that might take the form of a call to worship, a prayer, or a script for a drama. One very meaningful activity I participated in was helping out with a psalms study class. As the resident poet, it was my job to write a model modern psalm to inspire others in the group to write their own. I used the idea from Psalm 23, "The Lord is my . . ." and had the group fill in their choice of words, then follow that metaphor through the rest of their original psalm. We also wrote lamentations, which were very powerful. Finally we decided to compile a booklet of our psalms to share with others and for use in certain services.

Some people find sacred meaning in nature. It inspires poets to write about trees, birds, canyons, rivers, prairies, and oceans. Nature is fodder for deep memories: the first time you saw a shooting star, a vivid camping trip, cascading down the rapids, hiking a particular trail. Most of us have places that we call our own even though we share that place with the rest of the planet. Many forest preserves, nature centers, and parks might be delighted to have a writer's perspective on their nature trail, a particular landmark, or indigenous animal. Offer them a poem or memoir, and you might be delighted to see it on their website.

Another unexpected reward in retirement came to me via a nature center in my community. After I had contributed a few poems to the website newsletter and offered nature-writing workshops at the center, the program director approached me with a big idea: Could we possibly create a collection of Northern Illinois nature writing that would be an attractive book with visual art? If so, what would we include, and how would we fund it? Nonprofits with certain legal status are eligible for grants and donations, so the writing opportunities inherent in such a project are extensive.

First there were the grant-writing proposals. If you are a clear, concise, yet persuasive writer, this is the job for you. Second, creating the mission statement was an art form: "not too long, not too short, but just right, Goldilocks." Third, writing a call for submissions addressing the mission, scope, and protocol of the editorial process had to be written. Fourth came the editing, the weeding out, the accepting, and the rejecting. That meant composing letters of acceptance and rejection as artfully and graciously as we could. If you have never been on that side of the desk, it's a great experience. Never again will you be offended by a rejection notice once you realize how hard choosing just the right pieces are and just how many good writers are out there. That perspective is simply invaluable. We created an attractive book, well-designed, with a natural feel to the paper and print style. The entire project took over a year but was well worth the effort.

To recap generally about nonprofit organizations:

- Nonprofits offer myriad opportunities for volunteering and writing.
- You can find nonprofits that fit your passions.
- Nonprofits are generally eager for volunteers and writers.
- Some nonprofits are open to your suggestions for writing.

To recap, consider the following types of writing projects for nonprofits:

- profiles of people served by the organization
- descriptions of animals needing homes
- poetry about nature
- memoirs about nature
- lyrics
- grant writing
- proposals
- mission statements
- and calls for submissions.

In addition, pursuing passions simultaneously can lead to

- creative collaborations

- community collaborations
- editing
- compilations
- and surprising rewards.

Let's pursue the notion of surprising rewards further. It's possible to make a real difference in your community by writing for nonprofits. A woman in my writing group who is a retired librarian with a passion for research, education, and history was saddened by the imminent closing of a neighborhood school. She discovered that no history had been written about the school, which had been in the city for a good part of the century. By approaching the school's administration as well as the parent-teacher organization, she convinced them to let her have at the task of writing the school's history. Since she is so adept at desktop publishing, she chose to compile the project herself, creating memorable booklets for those who wanted them. I believe it helped assuage the sting of the school's closing. It had been commemorated in a fitting way.

Larger commemorative projects can also be in the purview of nonprofits. Sometimes this may take the form of fundraising in conjunction with a milestone. When a college celebrates its centennial, it will look to alumni for stories, anecdotes, memoirs, and profiles of students and professors and for coming-of-age stories and the like. When a local college was celebrating a restored classic home that was to be the residence of the president and his family, as well as a meeting place for traveling intellectuals, the president's wife mentioned the phrase *non nobis solum* in reference to the house. It translates to "not for us alone." She asked if I might be interested in a commission to write a commemorative poem on the theme of *non nobis solum*. As an alum and poet, I was thrilled to be asked and answered with an enthusiastic yes. (I took a big gulp afterward and wondered if I was up to the task but decided to be daring.) Fortunately it appeared to be exactly what she had in mind. Her words: "Oh, this is just what I'd hoped for." Much of the work I do for others is volunteer, but in this case the commission came with a nice honorarium. So you see, you never know how your writing talents will be recognized or rewarded.

This commissioned poetry project took on a life of its own, which involved several nonprofits. A local performing-arts center, a woman's-center chorale and visual artists, a local musical composer, and another church collaborated to create an event called Music to My Eyes. It featured the visual artists from the women's center as well as their chorale singing a musical rendition of "*Non Nobis Solum*" in an older downtown church. The event brought together not only various nonprofits but also groups of people who might not have mingled together in this way before. Since all the events were held downtown, it helped bring the community together in a place that had lost its appeal. Grant writing, mission statements, brochures, invitations, and press releases written by various writers paved the path for success. This is an example of the power of pursuing passions through nonprofits.

Have you considered writing for your alma mater? Check out the possibilities. Do you know of someone you think should get a scholarship? Find out how to make that happen, and write a great letter of recommendation. This writing, though not prestigious for the writer, packs a punch for the receiver. If you are an adventurer, you could volunteer not only to help organize an alumni trip but also create the travelogue in the alumni newsletter. Retirement offers the opportunity to stretch, adventure, and even reconnect.

Consider this: writing opportunities for nonprofits hide in plain sight. Local literary organizations themselves are often nonprofits. Do you have a local literary group that meets regularly and produces a journal? Voilà! Is there a nonprofit retirement club or center near you that has a literary component? Literary and retirement groups offer support for writing and publishing and sometimes organize critique groups. Some even offer regular readings and programs. I gave a reading for a retirement group near Seattle. Two cowboy poets also read from their work, a new experience for me. Apparently the group enjoys sharing their writing together and bringing in other writers for inspiration. A bonus was that I was able to combine my passion for traveling (I live in the Midwest and love to get out to the Pacific Northwest) with my passion for poetry.

If you are a woman lucky enough to have a good nonprofit women's organization in your community, you may find many ways to use your writing. Mission statements, advocacy proposals, creative project grant writing, capital grant writing, and creative writing are some possibilities. Did you ever wonder when that old-fashioned rhetoric would come in handy? Writing zesty mission statements, proposals, and grants are really just rhetoric with a special purpose: to help the nonprofit stay afloat. Such organizations usually have newsletters, most likely online, as well as websites. The newsletters often profile members and many include short memoirs and poetry appropriate to theme or season. If you are even luckier, you may find a women's organization that has a strong literary thread running through it, offering women a place to write freely and without stifling them from speaking their truth. Sometimes booklets and anthologies grow out of these workshops and support groups. And never underestimate the power of Facebook and the Internet.

Last year I submitted a few poems to what was going to be a small booklet. That led to an invitation to play a larger role in the project. We placed a little call for submissions on the organization's website, which somehow found its way to various Facebook accounts across the country. In short, it went viral. Suddenly we received hundreds of submissions from women across the United States, England, and Australia. What were we going to do? We hadn't applied for a grant. We'd neither budgeted for a big project nor asked for an entrance fee. Ah, now here's where working with a nonprofit has its advantages. If your organization has legal federal status, tax-deductible donations can be given. A few generous "goddesses" donated boldly to make the project workable. Thanks to them, a beautiful anthology was born. To our further amazement, women from all over the country came to the reading held at the center's pavilion, and within a few weeks the anthology sold out. Never underestimate the power of working with a nonprofit, especially one with a website and Facebook presence.

Perhaps the quirkiest experience I have had with nonprofits was with a food co-op that I dearly love. For many years I had visited a colorful and well-run flagship food co-op during writing residencies at an art center in the Pacific Northwest. One year the produce was so gorgeous and the aroma of fresh coffees so tantalizing that I just had to write a poem. I had the notion that the co-op folks might like it, so I actually took it to the editor of their newsletter personally. Shortly after, it appeared in the co-op newsletter. As a writer who has done due diligence with publishing protocol, waiting sometimes months for acceptances or rejections, wading through the vagaries of poetry etiquette (which is not for the impatient or thin-skinned, though I am diligently both, nonetheless), I find it refreshingly simple and satisfying to do "business" with nonprofits in this way. You make friends, and you get your work out there to people who might actually enjoy or benefit from it.

To recap further possible nonprofits to pursue:

- Consider schools, colleges, and booster clubs.
- Check out literary and retirement organizations in your own community.
- Find nonprofits with websites and Facebook accounts.
- Explore quirky nonprofits.
- Consider bringing various nonprofits together.

To recap, consider the following types of writing assignments for nonprofits:

- Research and write history for organizations.
- Deliver your writing in person.
- Write vibrant press releases, invitations, and brochures.
- Write quirky poetry or prose related to nonprofits.
- Submit prose and poetry to local literary organizations.
- Work on editorial boards.

Besides finding fulfilling nonprofit work within your own community, working with nonprofits can give you the opportunity to cast a wider net. Have you ever felt compelled to respond to a natural disaster? Have you cried or become enraged at the treatment of a veteran? Perhaps the sight of an endangered species moves you deeply. When you have a full-time career, it's pretty hard to respond to these internal calls of compassion and action unless you have an employer willing to give you time off to help a hurricane victim, march with vets in D.C., or save a manatee. But once you have the delicious time that retirement bestows, you can finally dare to follow your heart. All you need is courage, conviction, stamina, and a journal or laptop.

In the wake of natural disasters, many nonprofits send teams to sites to help victims rebuild their lives. Of course you do not go with the intention of "getting a story" out of the experience. The story is the gift. Whether you keep a private journal and never share your reflections with others or you share them with a group, these stories shape your soul. You are making a difference, contributing to a worthy cause, and following a compassionate muse. The choice to write publicly about your experience depends on whether you are compelled to. Sometimes while journaling you discover that a real story or poem is emerging. It has a life of its own. You are tapping into something larger than yourself. That's one of the secrets of good writing.

Some time ago I had the experience of being with a nonprofit work team in Appalachia, helping a particular man restore his house. Over the course of the week, it became clear that there was a real story here, a real character who had lived his entire life in the "hollow" with dogs he'd had for years yet never named, and feuds in the hills that I'd always thought were mythological. The work itself was grueling and involved tarring a roof, rebuilding a snake-infested porch, cleaning, painting, and restoration of every sort. When I pondered over my journal, I realized there was a real narrative here; not only had "our man" had a change of heart, but so had we. When I sat down to write the story, it flowed easily. It ended up being published in a large newspaper, photos included. It had not been my intention to write this story, but I was compelled.

Perhaps you will find stories of courage and compassion in your work with good causes. No doubt you will meet some real characters on your journey. Maybe their stories need to be told and you are the one to tell them. Writing gives you the chance to experience something twice. It affords the opportunity for clarity and meaning. Whether close to home engaging in community or on a longer journey of compassion, involvement with nonprofits can lead to pursuing simultaneous passions. How lucky we are to have that chapter to look forward to in retirement. How fortunate to finally have the time to make a difference while pursuing our passions.

TEN

Joining a Writer's Group for Practical Help, Emotional Support

Louise Nayer

In downtown San Francisco, I pass a sign that reads, "Working alone sucks: Shared office space in this building." This sign speaks to the human need for community. As a retiree author, the reason I get on the BART train, lugging my black rolling case with my computer, my computer cord, some books, some soup in a box, and fruit, is to be around other writers at the San Francisco Writers' Grotto where I rent space and have instant access to a wonderful community of writers. The Grotto is a particular kind of community where writers rent shared writing space to teach classes, share information, and give each other emotional support. For retirees, all kinds of writing groups exist and can take on added significance, as social isolation is one of the potential pitfalls of leaving the workplace behind.

Writing groups can take on many forms:

- *a critique group*—where writers take turns sharing work and get extensive critiques from all the group members either taught by a seasoned writer or led by a group of peers
- *a "free-write group"*—where writers compose pieces in a shared space and then read their work out loud and get feedback
- *the Grotto*—where writers band together, rent shared space, meet for lunch, share information, offer classes, and host speakers
- *conferences*—such as those held in Squaw Valley and Napa, where writers meet peers, agents, and editors in classes
- *online communities*—such as She Writes or Redroom [1]
- *online classes*—such as ones at UCLA or Gotham

Finding or forming a writing group offers writers emotional support and practical tips, all of which aid in the journey to publication.

WHO CARES?

Franz Kafka said, "Writing is utter solitude, the descent into the cold abyss of oneself." Though writers don't all experience the "cold abyss," writing is often a descent into unchartered territory, sometimes uncomfortable territory. Of course, when writers are in the zone, in touch with their imaginations, in touch with the world through their characters, or in settings from a local pub to a Long Island beach crowded with striped beach umbrellas to a subzero weather outpost in Antarctica, words spill on to the page. Hours can go by and, like a child mesmerized by a search for buried treasure in the backyard, you are enchanted by the very act of using your imagination. Anton Chekhov said, "Don't tell me the moon is shining; show me the glint of light on broken glass." Writers love words—the beauty and the power of words. However, as much as writers can be swept up by their own words, eventually a question rears its head: Who cares?

Is it enough to be the only one who cares deeply about your work with no one to validate and encourage you? Most of us crave a cheering section. Many writers go through periods of thinking our writing is terrible, the "shitty first draft," as Anne Lamott talks about in her book *Bird by Bird*.[2] We have all felt moments of *This sucks* about our precious words. Some cold nights, when the fireplace releases brilliant blue and yellow flames into the air, we can think our words are less than brilliant, even worthless, and imagine tossing our manuscripts into the flames. Ashes to ashes. It can get that bad. We need emotional support—someone to say, "Keep on going. You're good. That line is fabulous. You've got something here." We need people who care, a cheering section. We don't always get the support we need for our writing from a partner or trusted friend, as much as friends and loved ones often make Herculean efforts to bolster our spirits. It is often too much to expect that one person, especially someone who is not a writer, will be able to handle everything from "My writing is terrible. I'm done with writing. I hate my last piece" to "My agent must be sick of me. She hasn't called me back" or "My editor wants to take out my favorite scene. What should I do?" Sometimes these thoughts spin like a looped tape in our brains, an obsession. *Lighten up, Go stare at a tree,* and *Put on a meditation tape* often doesn't help, though the suggestions are good ones. Our needs are too great and often can be best taken care of by an outside group—people going through the same feelings about writing wherever they are in the continuum.

EMOTIONAL SUPPORT

Perhaps you have had a story building up inside of you for your whole life: a difficult memory from childhood, the death of a sibling, an alcoholic parent, a move from one town to the next, or, in my case, parents who were severely burned when I was four. You want to finally get the story down on paper. Some of the writers in your writing group have also written about difficult memories, particularly if you're in a memoir class together. The community that develops, even deep friendships at times, creates a sense of safety and, most importantly, others who care about your writing, who care about your story and helping you to make it better. This is a big draw—a reason why many people go to workshops. You no longer ask yourself, *Who cares?* as you are writing. Everyone in the group cares. They want to hear more. Like people gathered around a campfire with you as the storyteller, people ask, "What happens next? Does she pull through? Does the family move? Does the daughter leave her marriage? What about the child? What happens to her?" However, a distinction must be made: Writing groups are not counseling groups. The focus needs to stay on the writing and making it better. That is the ultimate purpose, but these groups often do become a sanctuary, a shared, sacred space. Many times, writers become friends. For retirees who have often lost the community of a workplace, these writing groups are invaluable. *Who cares?* is no longer a constant nagging and at times deeply existential question. All the other writers in the writing group care—offer emotional support as well as critiques—and that is terribly significant.

SETTING UP A SCHEDULE

As well as offering emotional support, groups can help writers set a schedule and stick with it. You are accountable to your group. You need to either write during free-write time or bring in pages for critique. You've signed up for a conference. You're going to meet with an agent and need to get a pitch together. You have deadlines. You have peer pressure to share your writing with others. When I was a new mother, anxious about making sure I still had writing time, I set up Monday nights as my writing night. My husband watched our two small daughters, and eventually, kind man, made the night a special one for them— pizza and a movie. They happily rode their pink and purple bikes to the video store, back when such stores still existed, while I spent the entire night at the desk in our bedroom, sleeping at first, turning the channel from the world of grading papers and the needs of small beings, and then finally typing away at a wooden desk into the night. It helped that I touch-typed, and quickly at that, and I would encourage all writers to learn this skill. I shared my pages with my writing group. They gave me important feedback. They believed in the story. I never gave up. I continue to be in writing groups to this day. My memoir was written that way and finally published. I didn't feel particularly motivated on Monday nights or inspired by the gods, but that was my time to write. The more I wrote, the more I wanted to write. The writer Octavia Butler said, "Forget inspiration. Habit is more dependable . . . Habit is persistence in practice." Schedules are important—in fact, crucial—to your life as a writer. Woody Allen's famous line, "Eighty percent of success is showing up," refers to anyone doing anything—and of course to writers. We need to sit at the desk, café, or wherever we write (waiting in a car for someone), but we need to do it. Having a group that is waiting for the pages helps immeasurably with this discipline. As a writer you create your own deadlines, and the group acts as that external superego catalyst.

TIME CHALLENGES

That said, discipline can be particularly fraught with problems for retirees, who can have issues with time. Time can feel daunting, endless, and stretch on for hours or, the converse, get filled up with projects around the house, from pulling weeds to fixing dry rot to commitments to others—friends, relatives, civic groups, children, grandchildren. You no longer have to squeeze in your writing time at 6 a.m. or in the middle of the night, and the lack of urgency to finally do what you want can affect or alter your ability to be disciplined. Then guilt will set in. *I've got this time, and now I'm not even writing! I must not be a real writer! I'm wasting this gift that was given to me!* Or, as my husband repeats, *There are no voids.* Time will always be filled up, but is this what you imagined? Or you can blame others. *I have too much to do. Everyone is making demands on me. I still can't do what I want.* You cook, take out the garbage, tile the bathroom floor, pay bills, clean closets that haven't been touched for a decade, sort through old photographs, a project that could take hours, weeks, months, even years to finish.

INTERNAL MOTIVATION

Some people find it especially challenging to shift from having an external schedule that they have to follow—the alarm clock, breakfast, the trek to work, accountability to coworkers—to now creating the writing schedule that they have ached for over many years. Of course some days you will not have the time, as life does intervene, but often within seven days and approximately 112 or so weekly hours of waking life we can all find some time to write. Sinclair Lewis said, "It is impossible to discourage the real writers—they don't give a damn what you say, they're going to write." This is, of course, true, but the knowledge that your work will be shared with others can keep you going, especially during difficult times. In one writing group that I taught I paired up students and told them to e-mail or call each other twice during the week to check in on how they were doing with their writing projects. That act of checking in plus knowing that they would share their work with the group transformed their writing. Someone cared, and someone was gently nudging them. Plus they were doing the same for someone else. My students suddenly began to set a schedule for themselves each week and stick with it.

Some authors will not leave the computer or stop writing by hand until they have a certain amount of pages each day or each week. You can say to yourself or mark it on a calendar that you'll write two hundred words a day or a thousand words a day or a thousand words a week, or you can count time by hours. Your writing group, now made up of close friends, is waiting for your work, cheering you on. Even if you stare at the blank page for thirty minutes without any of those magical black squiggles appearing, eventually you will write some words. Similar to a workout schedule, or a calorie count, a definite word count has helped many well-known writers with inner discipline. Along with the word or time count, all relatives and friends need to be notified. "This is my writing time." If your best friend walks into the café where you're writing, you need to politely tell her that you're writing. You are not being rude. You are not a selfish person. When your book is on the shelf at the local bookstore, your friends and family will celebrate your ability to focus. They might even be jealous. You will tell them how you learned to focus, how you joined a group to keep you going. You will help them on their own paths. You are a professional, going to work, even if the work takes place at a desk in your bedroom or at an office or in a corner of a café (switching cafés sometimes helps). Imagining your writing-group friends also dealing with the same challenges helps you find that internal motivation.

Some writers, along with setting a schedule, set up a specific atmosphere. Isabel Allende talks about wearing "writing clothes" and having special photographs that help her write. She talks about her office as "sealed space." Even if you don't have a sealed space, specific rituals can help you turn the channel from ordinary life into the extraordinary world of words. You figure out internal ways to motivate yourself to produce. The external motivation comes from your writing group. Often we think it is a sign of weakness to need others; in fact, reaching out is a sign of strength. Writing groups help with scheduling time to pound the keys:

- Writing groups help authors create tangible deadlines. You have an audience, and you don't want to let them down.
- They also help authors set up uninterrupted time to write, because everyone in the group is writing. They can do it, and so can you.

- You create individual rituals to help you get going. Sharing these ideas with your group can help you find your own best practice.
- Only answer the phone if there is an emergency (meaning you need to glance at the screen if someone is texting you eight times in a row) or if it is someone in your writing group saying, "Keep on writing."

KEEPING THE MOMENTUM GOING

Andrew Chen, a retired surgeon writes, "I have very little discipline to write on my own. I can not keep the momentum going." He spent six months in Europe at one point, with long stretches of time to write, but it was only when he came back to his writing group in the States that he could consistently produce. He has had some pieces published and is working on a beautiful memoir. Sometimes people finally have the time to visit such places as Croatia, the small town where their novel takes place, and perhaps don't feel the same drive to tell their story as they did when they were working. However, when your writing group is waiting—perhaps e-mailing with "How is it? Did you find the town where your protagonist grew up, the special puff pastry that she ate at four year's old or the type of red and yellow flowers that lined that town square?"—the drive returns, and you come back excited about your story, pages in hand. And you get applauded for it. Writing groups help with creating the discipline to get the pages out.

Being in a writer's group can give you the grounding that you need, the motivation to keep going, and the ability to write more and better. Whether the group meets weekly, twice a month, or even once a month, you are suddenly accountable not only to the solitary act of writing but also to producing work to share with others. If it's your week to share with the group, you have to come up with the pages. Janet Thornburg, a retired ESL teacher, has published nine short stories and a short-story collection. She speaks of the importance of writing groups. "Writing for an audience stimulated me to generate livelier work than I was cranking out in isolation." She also talks about how "writing to be heard" kept her going.

NETWORKING

As well as getting emotional support and setting up a schedule, networking, as in any professional community, leads to all kinds of important connections that can guide writers to publication. For those of us over fifty, the new world of social media can be overwhelming. When I joined the Grotto, I met Meghan Ward, whose website, Writerland, is endlessly useful in terms of marketing and connecting writers to each other. In one blog post, "Book Bloggers: The Secret to Book Marketing Success," she says, "self-publishing stars like Amanda Hocking know the secret: book bloggers."[3] Meghan then lists the most prominent book bloggers on the Internet. From "Top Fifty Book Blogs" to Meghan's own Writerland, she helps writers think about which bloggers to approach and how to enter and navigate the world that many writers know so little about. She also blogged on "Multimedia Books: A Comparison of Publishers."[4] Her website is endlessly useful to writers of all ages. However, networking not only catapults writers into online sites and book publishing but can also take on many other forms, such as a kind of serendipity that exists when you are doing what you love. Perhaps you are interested in writing about the local paper that was taken over by the online world. You need to do research and suddenly find that someone who has joined your group used to be the editor, two decades ago. That connection leads to the material you need and perhaps to a friendship. Or your memoir takes place in a remote village in Eastern Canada, and one of the group members, you discover, has a sister who still lives in the same town. She is able to offer invaluable information. When writers open up themselves to others, there is a wealth of information that can be constantly shared. At the Grotto, writers share the names of editors and agents, which gives newer writers an entrée into a world that might take years to crack. The point of a community is to share information. Whatever feelings arise about someone selling an article or book when you are still slogging away, the reality is that in a community where people support each other, each person's success only makes it easier for the next person.

HONING YOUR CRAFT

Writing groups, however, ultimately exist to help you become a better writer. They are there so you can share your writing, listen to others, and give and get critiques. Janet Thornburg warns that it is important to find the right group. "The trick is finding a compatible group and sticking with the purpose of writing rather than wandering off into socializing." Writers can socialize a little bit before the meetings or afterward, but writing groups are about writing and critiques. These critiques—"the more specific the better," as I've told my students for years—help shape a possibly amorphous piece into a work of art. Works of art are what get published. My book, *Burned: A Memoir*, published in 2010, went through multiple revisions. I started it in first person. I added third person. I wanted to fictionalize it. I wanted it as a memoir. Now, with what I know about creating time lines and a better understanding of point-of-view shifts, I can circumvent some of the constant need to revise.

Your peers ask the difficult questions and voice the critical prompts that lead you to revise:

- "We need to care more about the protagonist."
- "You need more sensory detail."
- "Historical context is missing."
- "You need to add more tension."
- "You need foreshadowing."
- "Sentences need to be varied."

Addressing these concerns, whatever you decide to take from the group's suggestions, will inevitably help shape your piece into a work of art. The group is pushing you to create a jewel—or a book with perfect pitch. Michael Alenyikov, a retired writer, runs a free-write group. He says that he wrote one-third of his book, *Ivan and Misha*, in that group. That book went on to win the prestigious Northern California Book Award and recently won the Gina Berriault Award at San Francisco State University. He says, "The idea for the book came from an in-class exercise."

Who knows what will spark the imagination? Our words, our stories live inside us. Writing groups give retiree writers the emotional support and the practical help necessary to going from someone who dabbles in, and perhaps has always had a passion for, writing to someone who can proudly say, "I'm a writer." A community of writers helps us produce our best work, work we can send out into the world, and to form friendships based on a shared love of language.

NOTES

1. Visit She Writes online at http://www.shewrites.com/ and Redroom at http://redroom.com/.

2. Anne Lamott, *Bird by Bird: Some Instructions on Writing and Life* (New York: Anchor Books, 1995).

3. Meghan Ward, "Book Bloggers: The Secret to Book Marketing Success," *Meghan Ward's Writerland*, January 24, 2013, http://meghanward.com/blog/2013/01/24/book-bloggers-the-secret-to-book-marketing-success/.

4. Meghan Ward, "Multimedia Books: A Comparison of Publishers," February 7, 2013, http://meghanward.com/blog/2013/02/07/multimedia-books-a-comparison-of-publishers/.

ELEVEN

The Public Library

A Treasure Trove for Writers

Lisa Fraser

Welcome to the public library! If you haven't been in a library lately—either the bricks-and-mortar or virtual version—you may be in for a surprise. While print books are still a big part of the business, libraries have adapted to the changes in the needs of their patrons by adding a wide variety of services and collections both in the building and online. Writers will find many resources to support their work, from research to refining stories to submitting manuscripts. This chapter focuses on the more commonly available resources, although not all may be offered at every library.

IT'S YOUR LIBRARY

Get a Card

One of the defining features of public libraries is access. Anyone can enter a public library, browse the shelves, and attend events. It has traditionally been the case, however, that to use some of the services it's necessary to first get a library card. With a card you can reserve and check out books and other materials, access services and collections that are provided online, and use the library's public-access computers. The first step, then, is to go to your local library and get a library card.

Mostly Free

The public library is one of the great bargains in our society, providing most of its services for free. In the few cases where libraries do charge for a service, it is typically in an effort to recoup costs associated with that service, such as a per-page charge for printing or copying. Library services are, of course, paid for through a variety of local, district, state, and even some federal funds, as well as grants and gifts from organizations and individuals. Since most funding for most libraries comes from local sources, smaller libraries usually have less money to work with than larger ones. Library administrators work creatively to maximize the impact of the funds they have. This can result in a library providing more services and resources than you might expect.

Get Another Card

Since libraries in the United States get most of their funding from local residents, library services like checking out books are usually limited to people from that local area. However, you may have the ability to get a card from a library other than your local one, gaining access to at least some of the services it provides. There are two common ways to do this: through reciprocal-borrowing agreements and by getting a nonresident library card.

Reciprocal agreements are made between two libraries that serve different localities. Each agrees to issue cards to residents of the other library's service area, providing some level of access to its collections and other offerings. Library cards issued through reciprocal agreements are usually free.

Some libraries allow nonresidents to get a card by paying an annual fee. In Washington state, fees for nonresident cards in 2012 ranged from $10 to $115, with an average cost of about $60.[1] As with reciprocal agreements, nonresident cards may come with some limits to access. Not all libraries offer nonresident cards. If this option is available, information will usually be provided on the library's Web page.

The Librarian Is In

In today's public libraries, librarians are still skilled in finding elusive facts and recommending books, characteristics that many people associate with them. They also provide support with library computers, e-books, and other technology; help patrons develop research strategies; and teach patrons how to use the vast array of resources available. Some librarians have expertise in specific topics, such as local history or business, which can be particularly helpful. Working with a librarian can make better use of your time and introduce you to new resources. To make the most of your interaction with the librarian, keep these things in mind:

- *Develop a research question* — A librarian can certainly locate sources of information on your topic, but if you have a more specific question in mind, it will be easier to weed out those that don't exactly apply.
- *Bring a list of the sources you have already consulted* — This will help the librarian avoid wasting your time by suggesting resources or search strategies that have already been done.
- *You may have to wait* — If your question is complex or the library is busy, the librarian may need time to find the best sources for you. Patience usually pays off, even if you have to come back another day.
- *Ask if you can make an appointment* — Some libraries offer the option of setting up a meeting with a librarian rather than relying on drop-in interactions at the reference desk. This has the added bonus of allowing the librarian time to develop search strategies and look for relevant materials in advance.

The Librarian Is Online

Can't make it to the library? Many offer online help using e-mail or chat technology. An e-mail query usually begins with filling out a form on the library's website. You provide contact information and a description of your research need or question. A librarian receives the message and responds to the e-mail address you provided. This service is usually staffed only when the library is open, and a response can take a couple of hours to a few days.

Contacting a librarian via chat also starts with filling out a form on the library's website. In this case, you will connect to a Web-based messaging program. The librarian will answer the call, usually within a minute or two, and your conversation begins. Chat looks somewhat like text messaging, with the patron's and librarian's messages appearing on the computer screen in real time. Most libraries that provide chat services belong to a nationwide cooperative that allows them to offer the service even when the library is closed. At those times, the service is staffed by librarians from other libraries or freelance librarians. These after-hours librarians may not have access to all of the resources at your library; nonetheless, they can answer most research questions. If they are not able to answer your question fully, they are able to refer it to your home library for follow-up.

RESEARCH

Research is one of the first things most people associate with the library, and for good reason. The library is both a destination and a gateway. The age of the Internet has made this association even more valid; the library offers more to the researcher than ever before. The phrase "at your library" encompasses more every day and is not limited to what is accessible in the physical building. Let's start there and move outward.

Resources

Within your local library you will find a variety of printed materials— books, magazines, and newspapers. The library catalog tells you where they are located in the library, whether they are currently checked in, and other information about the items. Some libraries also keep files of clippings and pamphlets, most commonly on topics of local interest. These files may not be in the catalog and could be in a staff-only area, so be ready to ask the librarian for help in finding them.

Chances are good that your local library also has a website that offers access to valuable online resources, often called *databases* in library jargon. Think of these as virtual libraries, each providing access to a different collection of sources. For example, one might contain articles from newspapers published in the nineteenth century, another might have articles from academic journals, while a third might have the content of a selection of encyclopedias and dictionaries. In most cases, the full text of the articles would be visible, and increasingly that would be in the form of a digital image of the actual page of the newspaper.

The databases can be accessed at computers in the library, and most will also be accessible from anywhere that has an Internet connection. You will typically need your library card, and often a password, to use them. Libraries vary in their offerings and usually start their collections with homework-support sources. Most will have at least one source of newspaper and magazine articles, one with articles about current events and one focusing on business research.

Electronic books, or e-books, can be another source for the researcher. They differ from databases in a couple of ways. First, the entire book can be "checked out" and downloaded to your computer, tablet, or other electronic device. Like a physical book, you can keep it for a predetermined loan period, after which it deactivates. Because the file is saved to your device, you have access to it even when you are not online.

Subject Guides

Subject guides are another type of online resource for researchers. In the time before computers, librarians prepared lists of the best books and other materials on topics that were commonly requested. When a patron asked a question about that topic, the librarian would provide a copy of this subject guide in addition to the other items that were found. Today's subject guides are usually online and include books and other materials from the library's collection, suggested databases, links to relevant websites or blogs, and more. Because much of the information may be from the open Web, subject guides often do not require a library card to view. The Berkeley Public Library has an extensive collection of subject guides.[2]

Interlibrary Loan

Every library is unique, and even the most well-funded public library can't buy everything. Libraries figured this out early on and developed a system for sharing called *interlibrary loan*—often abbreviated to *ILL*. To request an item from another library on ILL, you fill out a paper or online form from your local library, providing the title, author, and as much additional information as you have about the item. Your library looks for a library that will lend that item, arranges the loan, and contacts you when it arrives. It usually takes two to four weeks for an item to be ordered and delivered. If your library is not able to find a library that will lend the item, they will notify you.

There are a few limitations on ILL services, and each library sets its own rules about what it will lend and borrow. In most cases, only books and microfilm are shared in this way; compact discs and DVDs, for example, are not typically available through ILL. Often ILL materials must be used in your library rather than being checked out to you. This is most frequently the case with microfilm and with books that are fragile or hard to replace. Magazine content may be available, usually in the form of a photocopy of the particular pages that are requested. While you will generally have to pay for the photocopies, you will also typically get to keep them.

Interlibrary loan is a relatively expensive service to offer, and some libraries offset that expense by charging a nominal fee. You may have to pay either the lending library, or your local library, or both. Your library will likely provide information about its own fees on the ILL form. You may also be able to tell your library how much you are willing to pay the lending library; if your library can't find a lender within your price range, they will let you know. In most cases, you will be charged a per-page copy fee for magazine articles.

Libraries may also limit the number of ILL requests that one person can make, either in total or at one time. In addition, they usually offer ILL only to their own residents, not to those with cards through reciprocal-borrowing agreements or those holding guest cards. Make ILL requests through your own local library.

WorldCat

Interlibrary loan is a fabulous service, but you may be wondering how to find out about items that your library doesn't have. One convenient way is by searching online in WorldCat.[3] In the same way that your local online catalog tells you what is available at your library, WorldCat shows you what is available at more than ten thousand libraries worldwide.

The basic search is designed to look for all types of materials. Tabs also easily limit searches to books, DVDs, CDs, or articles. After typing your search terms and clicking on the *Search* button, your list of results will appear. If you want to refine your search or limit it by format, year published, topic, or other attributes, select the desired terms on the left-hand side of the page. There is also an advanced search function that lets you begin your search with all of your limit preferences in place.

By clicking on a title in the list of results you will see publishing information about the item. Scroll down to find a list of the libraries that have that item, starting with those that are nearest to the zip code you provide. If you determine that your local library does not have the item, you will have the information needed to place an interlibrary-loan request.

One additional feature of WorldCat can be useful: setting up a free account allows you to create and save lists of items while you are searching. This can be helpful when deciding which items to order or simply for keeping track of possible resources. An account also lets you rate items and write reviews.

TECHNOLOGY

While having a computer and Internet access in your home can be convenient, it's not strictly necessary for someone beginning a writing career. It is likely that a nearby public library has free public-access computers, complete with the programs and Internet access needed for most activities. Like other library services, you will typically use your library card to log in to a system that schedules the computer use. You may be able to reserve a computer in advance. In busy libraries, there may be time limits on computer use in order to ensure that this popular service is shared. Printing is generally available, with most libraries charging a per-page fee to cover the cost of supplies.

The most common arrangement for library computers is to have them grouped together, each one having some work space around it, with a shared printer nearby. However, some libraries now lend laptops for use in the library. The laptops access the Internet through the library's Wi-Fi network, which is also available to patrons who bring their own laptops. Like the desktop computers, the length of time a laptop can be used is often limited. The library may record your use of the laptop using the same system as book checkouts, or there may be a separate process for tracking this equipment. Using a laptop, either the library's or your own, has the advantage of allowing you to work in whatever part of the library you prefer. Remember never to leave a laptop or other valuable equipment unattended; theft happens, even in the library.

The staff at the library are able to assist newcomers unfamiliar with the library's computer systems, which may have different features from the typical home computer. If you think you may need help, try to visit at a less busy time of day to minimize distractions. For those who are new to computing in general, many libraries offer classes in popular programs, like word processing.

For those who prefer to learn at their own pace, many libraries' online collections of databases and e-books include self-study guides and books on specific software programs. Learning Express and Books 24/7 are examples of these resources that can be accessed using the library's computers or from outside via the Internet.

When working on your writing project at the library, you will want to save your work. There are two ways to do this: using some sort of memory media or saving to an online storage service. A flash drive, also known as a *thumb drive* or *memory stick*, is currently the most commonly used memory media. These small devices are about the size of your thumb—hence the name—and connect to the computer using its USB port. They are available in a range of memory capacities and are able to hold hundreds of files. Flash drives can be purchased for less than ten dollars; buy two, and save your files to both so that you always have a backup in case one gets lost or fails.

Saving to an online storage service, also known as *cloud storage*, requires Internet access. Services such as Dropbox and Google Drive provide a limited amount of storage for free.[4] After setting up an account, you are ready to save files to your online folder and retrieve them later. One benefit of cloud storage is the ability to share files with others, like the writer friend who is reading your latest draft.

Opening an account for cloud storage is only one of many tasks that requires an e-mail address. While not technically a service of the library, many people choose to use the library computers to set up an e-mail account on one of the free Web-based e-mail services, such as Gmail or Yahoo!.[5] Some libraries provide classes or other assistance with e-mail.

BECOMING A BETTER WRITER

So far this chapter has discussed library resources that can help with research, and computers that allow you to record what you write. Libraries can also help you to become a better writer by providing resources and support.

Books

Books on the writing process are widely available, covering topics such as mechanics, style, and character development. There are books on writing various genres of fiction, as well as those with tips on writing in specific formats. A search of my local library catalog turned up more than eighty books on writing published in the past two years. Memoirs written by authors can also provide valuable insight.

Writing Workshops and Classes

Writing classes provide both the opportunity to learn from a more experienced writer and support from others in the class. Libraries, especially those in larger cities or college towns, may have access to skilled instructors offering one-time workshops or ongoing classes. Registration may be required. A quick online search of classes at several libraries across the country yielded these examples of class titles:

- Start Writing your Memoir!
- Make your Story Exciting
- Creative Writing Workshop for Older Adults
- Writing Literary Nonfiction

Writing Groups

Writing groups are similar to classes in that members support each other. A group may have one main facilitator, or the structure may be more informal. The groups often read and critique each other's work and can also provide information and advice about other aspects of the business. In some cases, groups are sponsored by the library; others may simply hold their meetings at the library.

Other Writer-Friendly Programs

What if you could ask a best-selling author about his or her writing process or for tips on getting published? It sounds too good to be true, but this is often possible at author events held at the library. While larger cities may get the lion's share of big-name author appearances, smaller libraries sometimes host local authors or those on publisher tours. Many authors talk about their personal experience with writing and publishing as part of the program, and most events include a question-and-answer period. It is tempting to focus on the major authors, but those who are a bit less well-known may have a smaller audience and more time to chat.

A growing number of libraries are supporting participants of National Novel Writing Month, or NaNoWriMo.[6] Participants aim to write a fifty thousand–word novel during the month of November. In 2012, NaNoWriMo reported 341,375 participants, 38,438 of whom won by meeting the word count. Look for increased writing-related programming at your library in November or visit their website for more information.

Libraries that use an online event calendar often provide the option to sign up for e-mail notifications that will alert you to programs that match your interests. This can make it easier to avoid missing that favorite author or new writing class.

THE BUSINESS OF PUBLISHING

If your intention is to be published, it is essential to understand the business end of writing. The annually published *Writer's Market* is one go-to resource, providing chapters on finding, managing, and promoting writing work as well as contact information and descriptions of literary agents, book publishers, consumer magazines, trade journals, and contests. Most libraries will have this book or something similar. Some will also have books on specialty markets, such as *Children's, Writer's, & Illustrator's Market* or *Novel & Short Story Writer's Market*.

Writer's groups, author events, and workshops can also help the new author to learn about navigating the world of publishing. A recent Web search revealed workshops about online marketing for authors and finding an agent offered at public libraries.

Whether you visit the public library in its physical form or its virtual one, you will see an ever-increasing variety of services and resources to support writers. Start by getting a library card now so that you'll be ready when inspiration strikes.

NOTES

1. Washington State Library, "Washington Public Library Statistics 2012 Excel Spreadsheet," http://www.sos.wa.gov/library/libraries/libDev/downloads/statistics/12stats/2012stats.xls.
2. Visit them at http://berkeleypubliclibrary.libguides.com/index.php.
3. Visit them at http://www.worldcat.org.
4. Visit them online at https://www.dropbox.com/ and https://drive.google.com/, respectively.
5. Visit them online at https://mail.google.com/ and https://www.yahoo.com/, respectively.
6. Visit them online at nanowrimo.org.

TWELVE

Some Writing Nuts and Bolts

Stephen P. Sottong

You're thinking about writing after retirement but wondering if it's too late. Let me say from personal experience, not at all. After retirement I took up writing and, after a few years of learning and practice, have had some success, including a recent win in the international Writers of the Future contest.

Writing, like wine, improves with age. Life experience makes memoirs memorable and fiction rich. You have a cast of characters from your life to draw on as well as a wealth of experiences and emotions both good and bad. And now you have the luxury of time in which to practice your new craft. For writing is a craft, as much practiced skill as innate talent. There is much to learn. In this chapter, I'll cover one of the choices you'll need to make for each piece you write, the voice in which it is written, and, after that, some physical considerations related to age so that writing doesn't become a painful experience.

THE VOICE

Point of View

How will you deliver the story to your reader? What will be the point of view, and what person and tense of the verb will you be using to narrate the story?

Point of view refers to which character we experience the story through and who is narrating the story. Some examples:

1. Gerald walked round the corner and saw Gertrude waiting there.

2. Gerald walked round the corner and saw Gertrude, who waited there with the weight of her gun reassuringly below her coat.

The first example is called *close* point of view. The narrator is limited to the point of view of one of the characters in the story, in this case Gerald. When the point of view is limited we can only see, hear, smell, taste, touch, and feel what that specific character does. They are also the only character whose mind we can delve into. Gerald can see Gertrude, but he can't know about the gun concealed under her coat.

The second example is an *omnipotent narrator*. Having an omnipotent narrator broadens the point of view. We can now know what every character is sensing, feeling, and thinking. In this case we not only see Gertrude but know before Gerald does about her concealed weapon and the reassurance she feels in having it. The disadvantage of the omnipotent narrator is that the reader loses identification with the main character. It may even become difficult for the reader to determine who the main character is. Omnipotent narrator was a style broadly used in the past, but it is currently out of favor. You should limit yourself to a close point of view for most stories. Take care while writing to ensure that you do not change the point-of-view character within a section of writing and that you don't go outside the bounds of their senses and thoughts. This is a skill that takes practice. Having a good reader to check your work for point-of-view errors is invaluable.

The actual narrator of the story can either be unnamed or a character within the story. Most stories use an amorphous, unnamed narrator; however, many stories use the main character as the narrator, and some famous books, such as *Wuthering Heights* and *The Great Gatsby*, use a character within the story other than the main character to narrate.[1]

Getting Personal

English has three persons for each verb. Some examples:

1. I walked round the corner and saw Gertrude standing there.
2. You walked round the corner and saw Gertrude standing there.
3. He walked round the corner and saw Gertrude standing there.

Each of the three persons has advantages and disadvantages for the writer. First person draws the reader in. The narrator of the story is the point-of-view character and is generally the main character—although not always, as in *The Great Gatsby*.

The opening line of my award-winning story reads, "I was about to have another beer . . ." In half a line, the reader is already seated on the bar stool next to the narrator as he begins to tell a tale. The effect is personal and intimate. The reader is standing next to the narrator as the story progresses. Reader involvement is heightened. Many modern young-adult novels are written in first person. Another advantage for young readers is the reassurance that, since the main character is the narrator, the character who they identify with will survive (with a few rare exceptions). For the author, of course, this can be a disadvantage.

One disadvantage to first person is the near constant use of the pronoun *I*. Avoiding opening every sentence with *I* adds extra frustration to the writing and editing process, but the primary disadvantage of first person is the narrow point of view. The reader is limited to what one and only one person can see for the entire book. The reader's perspective on other characters in the story and on the world in general is filtered through the perception of the narrator. If an event takes place outside of the view of the narrator, it has to be handled as expository dialogue between the narrator and someone who did see the event or through the narrator reading an account of the event. Either method can be tedious for readers. Some people get around this limitation by writing alternate chapters in the voice of a different character. In one of my novels, I set alternate chapters in the voices of the two brothers who are the main protagonists, since this was the only way to view the major events of the story. In *The Poisonwood Bible*, author Barbara Kingsolver alternates first-person narration between a mother and her four daughters. The problem with this is that the speaking voices of each narrator must be distinct, a difficult skill to master.[2]

Second person is seldom used. The narrator is someone talking to you about you. This gives the story a sense of immediacy while at the same time giving it an oddly disembodied feel, since you're aware the narrator is not really talking about you. Every story requires a certain suspension of disbelief; second-person narration strains that suspension.

Like first person, the point of view is limited to only what the one protagonist can see and a second protagonist is not possible (unless "you" have a split personality). Also, like first person, there is the extra frustration of avoiding opening every sentence with *you*. I have written one and only one story in second person. This was flash fiction (under a thousand words) about a terrorist. In order to get the reader deeper into the mind, emotions, and sensations of the terrorist, I used second person:

> You walk the back streets, narrow, dark—avoiding physical contact with the old men, veiled women, and noisy children—looking straight ahead, businesslike, purposeful, not suspicious. The vest under your loose shirt traps the afternoon heat. You're sweating, light-headed. Fasting this last day has cleared your mind, left you feeling pure and clean. This morning during prayers, the blood rushed to your head; sounds around you melted; the rumble in your ears was like the voice of God. It was glorious—ecstatic. The moment lingers in your mind like a tantalizing promise.
>
> Sweat trickles into your eyes, stings. You wipe your brow on the sleeve of your shirt—slowly, deliberately, not furtively. No one else is

sweating. A second of panic, then you control your breathing, move
eyes forward, try not to steal glances. They ignore you.

Second person is sometimes used in guidebooks and self-help books
but is seldom used in longer works of fiction; however, Jay McInerney
wrote the novel *Bright Lights, Big City* in second person.[3] Here the disembodied feel works well, since the protagonist dislikes the city he's in and
spends much of the novel high on drugs.

Third person is the most common way to write stories. In third person
the narrator is separated from the point-of-view character. The narrator is
an amorphous presence lurking in the background of the story. Third
person can have either close or omnipotent point of view for its narrator
as stated earlier.

The key advantage of third person is that the point-of-view character
can change. Each chapter can have a different point-of-view character.
Even within chapters, the point-of-view character can change if the author indicates a discontinuity by double spacing between paragraphs or
inserting special characters, such as a series of asterisks, or using a transitional word, such as *meanwhile*. This freedom to move between many
points of view allows the reader to see the world you create through
multiple eyes. An event out of sight of one character can be viewed
through the eyes of another. For stories where the events take place simultaneously over a wide area or over extended time, third person is the
best way to write. Weighed against this advantage is some loss of immediacy and personal involvement. The reader may not identify as completely with the protagonist. Third person distances the reader from the
characters in the story. Depending on the story, that may be a price worth
paying.

It can be worthwhile to experiment with changing the "person" of
your story. On my second novel, I tried rewriting the first few chapters as
first person with two protagonists in alternate chapters. I found first person too restrictive for a novel that spanned eight years, several continents, and the lives of millions of people; but in writing from the personal
perspective and in the voice of two of the major characters, I gained
insight into their personalities, which I incorporated back into the third-person narrative. I consider the time spent on the experiment worthwhile.

Getting Tense

Just as there are three persons you can write in, there are also three
tenses:

1. Gerald walks round the corner and sees Gertrude waiting there.
2. Gerald walked round the corner and saw Gertrude waiting there.
3. Gerald will walk round the corner and see Gertrude waiting there.

Present tense, like first person, adds to the immediacy of a story. Since the story is happening right now, there is a sense of anticipation. Rather than the narrator telling a story, the story is occurring as we read. Any person can be used with present tense, but third person can feel strained. The second-person story I wrote was in present tense, and that added to the reader's identification with the character. First person, present tense, is fairly common, especially in young-adult books. The extremely popular *Hunger Games* was written in first person, present tense.[4] The combination of intimacy and immediacy makes it ideal for young adult writing.

Present tense requires that the story be viewed in a linear manner (unless the story involves time travel). Flashbacks must take place as expository dialogues, which can feel strained, or in the mind of the point-of-view character, who is forced to stand around musing on the past. That level of navel gazing can be tiresome for the reader, especially children and young-adult readers. You can't move about the time line as you can in past tense—starting in the middle, moving back to the beginning, and jumping to the end, for instance. The very first novel I wrote occasionally jumped back in time several hundred years to fill in the backstory. You can't do this writing in present tense.

Past tense is the default in English. Past tense is the story-telling verb tense. If you were to sit by the fire and share stories, those stories would be phrased in the past tense; they might be in either first or third person, but definitely past tense. Past is so ubiquitous that we move to it almost automatically. It's familiar, comfortable as a broken-in pair of shoes, and there's nothing wrong with that. My prize-winning story was written in first person, past tense, as are most memoirs. When I wrote the first book of a series of young-adult novels, I started the first chapter in present tense but switched to past tense part way through. I'm now left with the decision of how to handle a shift in tense that could be jarring to the reader.

Past tense distances the reader from the action. The events of the story are already over in past tense rather than happening now as in present tense. Most readers don't mind that small distance and find the familiarity of past-tense narration reassuring.

I can't say that I have ever read a book written in future tense or, for that matter, even a short story; however, I'm told some children's stories are written in future tense. From the 1930s to the 1950s, commercials would occasionally be presented in future tense: "Tomorrow you will commute to work in your aircar." Another use is for prophecy: "They shall beat their swords into plowshares." Stories written by children about what they will do in the future may also use future tense. Overall, use of the future tense is rare.

Choosing

Which combination should you use? Examine your story. Is the number of characters limited, or does the story include many, disparate individuals? For a story with one or at most a few major characters whose point of view are essential, first person may work. If the number of point-of-view characters is more than two, third person is your best option.

Do you need a sense of immediacy? Present tense will give you that, but you'll be limited to a linear presentation. Past tense loses some immediacy and gains flexibility.

Are you feeling wildly experimental? Try second person or future tense. Second person, as I found, can work well for short pieces.

PERSONAL CONSIDERATIONS

Now Write!

The best advice that any writer can give another writer is to write. The one thing that distinguishes a writer from a "wannabe" is the act of writing. Don't spend too much time contemplating the merits of the various points of view, persons and tenses—get the story down. Don't stop midway to revise—finish your draft. First drafts are always bad, so don't be discouraged. You'll polish it up in the editing phase.

As with any other skill, the more you practice, the better you get. What you bring to writing that younger authors do not have is the depth of experience that only years can bring. Mine it for every wonderful, quirky, and spectacular moment, and it will enhance your stories. As is also true with any skill, early efforts are rough and unpolished. Don't worry about this; think of your early works as practice efforts, a means of honing your skills. You'll have plenty of revision time to put it into shape. You may even experiment with person and tense during revisions. When you do, keep a copy of the old version; you may want to revert. Also, when working on a computer, keep backups of your work. Hard drives do not last forever, and far too many writers have lost their oeuvre to a crash. Back up daily if not more often to a flash drive *and* the cloud. Free storage in the cloud is available from many sources.

ALL ABOARD

The key thing is to write: write often, write consistently. This is a process that takes time—lots of time, time that others might think would be better spent in "more worthwhile" pursuits. A chorus of naysayers can derail your best plans and reduce your enthusiasm for this retirement pursuit. Try recruiting your partner, friends, and family as supporters. Make them your first readers. They'll give you an entirely different perspective from your fellow writers.

Express your enthusiasm for your new pursuit. Take classes in writing to show your commitment. Go to writing conferences to meet other writers, learn, and spark your enthusiasm. Join a writing-critique group; this will improve your writing and give you a support group. If there isn't an open critique group in your area, try recruiting people at writing classes and conferences to form your own.

But also make sure you set aside time for the other people in your life. Writing is a lone, isolated activity that can, if we let it, turn into a compulsion that takes up the entire day, leaving our partner and friends feeling abandoned. Schedule time away from the computer. Interacting with others will make them feel better about your writing and improve your characterizations. If the people who care about you know you'll make time for them, they'll be more tolerant of those times when you're "in the flow" and just have to keep writing, so make sure you schedule quality time with family and friends.

Writing Can Be a Pain in the Neck

You're retired, so you're no spring chicken. Injuries, stresses, and strains don't heal the way they did in your youth. You're going to be sitting at your computer for hours on end, so you need to consider the ergonomics of your work area to make sure that your writing time doesn't impact your health. First, don't skimp on the chair you use. Think of it as an investment in the health of your back, neck, and legs. Find one that adjusts and is supportive. It may be cheaper to buy one online, but go to a store and actually test the chair out first. It's the only way to tell if it's going to work for you. Sit in the chair for long enough to figure out whether it will cut off your circulation over time. Don't ignore pressure points. Adjust everything. And don't get a chair that leans unless you can lock it in place. Chairs that lean lead to bad posture. If you're really going to write, you'll be spending many hours each day in that chair. Don't let it be the reason you don't write.

I use a keyboard that allows my wrists to remain straight. They're sometimes called *natural* or *ergonomic* keyboards. The keys are displaced slightly, or the entire keyboard bows upward in the middle. Keeping your wrists straight reduces the kind of repetitive stress that leads to carpal tunnel syndrome. I position the keyboard in my lap, which puts my arms in a more natural position. with the elbows bent at a larger angle and less strain on the shoulders.

If you have a laptop, you're not restricted to using its keyboard. Most aftermarket keyboards will plug into a USB port on a laptop and work just fine. Like your chair, your keyboard is something you'll be using a lot; don't skimp on it, or you may end up unable to type, which puts a major kink in your writing.

A final ergonomic consideration is the placement of your monitor. Conventional wisdom says that if you're working with a computer at a desk, the monitor should be directly in front of you so that you are looking straight ahead.[5] But think about reading: where do you hold a book? The answer is about 30 degrees below eye level. Research by the late Dennis Ankrum showed that two factors in vision—accommodation and convergence—improve if the individual is looking down rather than straight ahead.[6]

Accommodation is the process by which the lens of the eye is minutely adjusted to keep objects at varying distances in focus. *Convergence* is the process of rotating the eyes to ensure that the image falls on the same portion of the retina of both eyes. If accommodation is off, the image is blurred. If convergence is off, we see double. Lowering text to where the eye is looking down by 30 degrees reduces the distance at which the eye is able to accommodate and also reduces the distance at which the eyes can converge by nearly 30 percent. Ankrum recommended lowering your monitor at least 15 degrees below eye level to reduce eye strain. In my office setup, I removed the base from my monitor to lower it and set it on an adjustable stand so that I could change the angle. If you're working with a laptop, you can accomplish the same thing by placing the laptop in your lap, but always set the laptop on a lapboard. The bottom of the laptop will be uncomfortably warm, and there may be vents on the bottom of the laptop used to cool the processor, so if you place the laptop on a soft surface, it will overheat.

One last tip: carry a small notepad and pen with you. Ideas come at the most inopportune times, and, let's face it, at our age we won't remember them when we finally get home. So have that notepad ready to jot them down immediately.

Writing can be a fulfilling way to enhance your retirement. May it bring you the enjoyment it has brought me.

NOTES

1. Emily Brontë, *Wuthering Heights* (London: Thomas Cautley Newby, Publisher, 1847); and F. Scott Fitzgerald, *The Great Gatsby* (New York: C. Scribner's Sons, 1925).

2. Barbara Kingsolver, *The Poisonwood Bible: A Novel* (New York: HarperFlamingo, 1998).

3. Jay McInerny, *Bright Lights, Big City* (New York: Vintage Contemporaries, 1984).

4. Suzanne Collins, *The Hunger Games* (New York: Scholastic Press, 2008).

5. "'Conventional Wisdom' vs. Current Ergonomics Thinking," Workplace Ergo, Inc., http://office-ergo.com/current-ergo-thinking/#wisdom, accessed May 23, 2013.

6. Dennis R. Ankrum, "New Visual Considerations at Computer Workstations," http://www.allscan.ca/ergo/vangle2.htm, accessed May 23, 2013; and "Humanics Ergonomics Visual Ergonomics by Dennis Ankrum," Dennis Ankrum, "Humanics Ergonomics: Visual Ergonomics," http://humanics-es.com/viewing.htm, accessed May 23, 2013.

Part III

Finding Your Niche

THIRTEEN

Compiling an Anthology

Don Mulcahy

The *Encarta World English Dictionary* describes an *anthology* as "a book that consists of essays, stories, or poems by different writers." However, the content can consist of short stories, excerpts, plays, and even songs and can also be used to describe a collection of a single author's selected or previously published works, previously published works by several authors, new writing by a variety of writers, or a combination of old and new works. More recently use of the word has been extended to include TV programs, movies, comic books, and other similar media creations.

In a way an anthology is a sampler that exposes the reader to a variety of works, styles, and literary voices without the necessity of having to buy the works of several writers. It also brings together writers who have a common interest, enabling members of the group to express their variations on a theme.

WHY COMPILE AN ANTHOLOGY?

There is scope for a multitude of creative purposes behind anthologies, so it is difficult to generalize, but some suggested reasons follow:

- You belong to a social group, workplace group, or a group with similar creative interests or at least you see the possibility of readily accessing a group of potential contributors.
- The prospect of sharing views on a subject of common interest appeals to you.
- You are prepared to do the necessary legwork, including networking.

- Your literary ability is sufficient to enable you to appraise the written work of others.
- Your computer skills are up to the task of editing the work of others and of incorporating the submitted works into a combined collection.

FUNDING FOR YOUR PROJECT

If your project is to be any more sophisticated than a straightforward desktop-publishing job done on your home computer or the one at the office, there will be expenses involved, and it would be wise to think about funding earlier than later. Few expenses will be generated in creating the master manuscript, but the publishing phase will be costly. Consider the following:

- Visualize your book: will it be an inexpensive desktop job, a softcover professional product, or a more costly hardcover book?
- If the project is more serious than a hobby project, you might consider submitting a proposal to a publisher in an attempt to get them to underwrite the publishing costs, with or without an advance.

If applying for funding, there are a few cardinal principles to keep in mind: the subject matter should appeal, as closely as possible, to the known interests of a potential backer (also those of a possible publisher), and the most persuasive factor is often the collective caliber of the writers in the anthology. Make sure of funding, and have a signed contract with a publisher before asking for submissions.

GENRE AND TOPIC

You may have decided on a topic early on, but if not, finalize it as soon as possible; this is what will bring the contributors together to create a joint publication. The possibilities are almost infinite, but the subject must be one that enables contributors to write about it in some original, knowledgeable, and creative way. Concerning subject matter:

- It can revolve around a single theme.
- It can be a miscellany of different, though related, topics on a prescribed theme.
- Or it can encompass a fairly broad swath of varying opinions on a topic.

If a literary endeavor, the genre could be prose (fictional or factual), poetry, creative fiction (as opposed to market-based), historical, spiritual, inspirational, crime, science fiction, juvenile literature, pulp romance, gender-orientated, fantasy, or one of many topics related to literature itself, as well as to literary criticism. And the theme or subject matter within a genre might relate to history, sports, travel, biography and auto-biography, and various life experiences and stories. Almost any subject matter would be valid for an anthology.

RESEARCHING SIMILAR TITLES

When you think about all those stacked shelves at your library, local Barnes & Noble, or wherever, it becomes evident that millions of new books may be appearing on the world's bookshelves daily, and statistics suggest that the possibility of someone else having used your intended subject or title is very real. Repetition needs to be avoided in the interest of originality and sales appeal, unless of course your subject matter is presented with an original slant.

To research previous titles you can get help at your library or using a variety of resources that list book titles, such as WorldCat. You can also Google your proposed subject and title to check originality or browse Amazon for similarities to your own ideas.

WHO WILL THE WRITERS IN YOUR ANTHOLOGY BE?

If you don't have a ready-made roster of writer friends or colleagues on hand, you will need to do some creative networking by e-mail, letter, or fax and perhaps a little research as well. The research would be aimed at finding writers who have previously written on your topic so that you can try to induce them to come onboard—providing, of course, that you intend to include previously published works or a combination of old and new. The more precise your description of the topic, the more relevant the submissions will be.

A letter of invitation to prospective participants should:

- be diplomatic in tone and not patronizing
- indicate why you want their personal participation
- include a precise description of the anthology's theme
- be clear regarding payment, monetary or otherwise
- and include, if possible, brief mention of the book's layout, the method of submission (e-mail being preferred), and whether or not acceptance of submissions will be competitive or guaranteed.

How many participants will you want to include in the anthology? The size of the roster of writers will depend on many things but mostly on your judgment and the size of the book you visualize. You can estimate the final length of your manuscript using a simple formula:

number of writers x *number of pages of each submission* = *number of pages in*
book

One manuscript page will not equate to a typeset book page, in word content, so you may have to work out a ratio for yourself, based on the proposed font and text-block sizes. So decide where you want to go, size-wise, and set the number of submissions and the article lengths accordingly. Study the size of other, similar, anthologies to get ideas. If you have a publisher, the length will be determined for you, and the word or page count might be set for you by their editor.

A call for submissions can be distributed via LISTSERVs, journals, posters in libraries and other public places, mailings, announcements on local radio stations, writer newsletters, and a dedicated website. You can also contact writing groups, colleges, universities, and other educational institutions with the information. Aim for a good gender balance in the roster of writers in your book. Sometimes editors only write a preface, but they might also contribute a piece of their own work to the body of the anthology.

WHO WILL BE IN CONTROL OF THE PROJECT?

You may intend to be sole editor of this book, but there are other options so as to share responsibility. If you go it alone you will be solely responsible for making the final cut regarding article selection—for sorting the wheat from the chaff, so to speak. You will be the sole supplier of those unsettling rejection slips, creating friction and perhaps bad feelings in the process. You will have to adjudicate on allowing second chances and major revisions.

WRITERS' GUIDELINES

Be specific. No matter how brilliant your writers might be, misunderstanding is always a possibility, and the person a misunderstanding will most impact is you. So do the following:

- Insist, firmly though kindly, on uniformity of a word-processing format that suits your computer.
- Have each contributor spellcheck and proof their material before submitting it to you.
- Insist on your right to edit—judiciously, of course—and that your final decisions be binding.
- Indicate font, layout, general formatting guidelines, and word and page counts in clear terms.

- Include a submission deadline and whether or not an extension is possible.
- Previously published articles must be identified as such; all publishing data must be provided, and the writer must indicate who owns the rights to reproduction of the article and where permission will need to be obtained from, if it is other than from the author.
- Get signed permission slips from the participants, agreeing to the reproduction of their work in the anthology in the finally edited form decided on by you.

WILL A CONTRACT BE NEEDED?

If your anthology is an informal project among friends or colleagues, a contract will likely be unnecessary, but if it's going to be a more serious undertaking, commercially or creatively, then a contract is necessary. If working with a publisher, they will supply it. Contracts are discussed in the *The Writer's Market*, an annual publication on the subject.[1] And, as ever, a quick Internet search will yield a trove of information.

Whether your project is an informal one or a more serious undertaking, a contract needs to deal with remuneration, if any, rights and other legal issues (who gives or obtains permission concerning current and previously published articles), and authenticity.

PROOFREADING

This is the process whereby one reads through a manuscript, checking the grammar, looking for typos and other errors. Initially this will be the collection editor's task. As editor, you are the last line of defense before the manuscript is sent to the publisher. An additional detailed, final proofreading will occur at the publishing house, but effective scrutiny by the anthology editor is necessary. In the writers' guidelines it should be mentioned that writers are expected to proofread before submitting, but the people most likely to miss discreet errors are the authors themselves.

"BUILDING" THE ANTHOLOGY

By its very nature, an anthology, like many things, is composed of its individual pieces—its building blocks, in a sense, consisting of its chapters or parts, which in turn are composed of individual articles or stories. And without a computer and its obvious benefits it would be difficult to imagine how an anthology could be conveniently constructed. Although there might be a slight risk of importing a virus or other malware, electronic submission—as attachments or in the body of e-mails—is the best option for submitting documents. It has been said that the first three articles in an anthology should be the *hooks*, and therefore the three best in the book.

Copy each submission into your master document; insert page numbers; compose a title page, dedication, and forward, preface, or introduction, and a numbered contents page—and you've almost got a book. Consult a text on the formatting of each of these features; again, the *Writer's Market* may come to the rescue if you are unsure, and there are so many other published books to consult as examples. The references used for each writer's work will appear at the end of each individual article or story.

AUTHORS' PROFILES (OR CONDENSED BIOGRAPHIES)

When reading a book, essay, story, or article many people like to know something about the identity and background of the author. It often helps to put the text into perspective, establish better understanding between author and reader, and resolve much curiosity about the origin and orientation of an author's *voice*.

These cameo-like descriptions need only be around seventy-five to one hundred words, but it is essential to specify in the writers' guidelines the length required, or you may receive extensive autobiographies.

The scope of these descriptions could contain information such as the following:

- the author's birthplace and present residence
- a brief reference to their literary interests—prose, poetry, biography, crime novels, etc.
- a brief statement about their education, if significant and applicable
- past and present positions held in the workplace, if relevant to the subject matter
- any literary prizes and awards won
- and a list of books or other major publications, anthologies participated in, and journals or magazines in which the writer has been published.

ACKNOWLEDGMENTS AND PERMISSIONS

When previously published works are reproduced in an anthology it is customary to indicate this in a list, which usually appears on the page just before or after the authors' profiles. If all the submissions you receive are new, original works, then an insert such as this would not be needed. The options vary, but a typical line in this section of the book might read something like,

A Prison Called Home, by Beverley Rowland, was previously published in *Gliss* (February 2008) and is reproduced here by kind permission of the Allmouth Publishing Corporation, Newport, Rhode Island.

Permission to reproduce a work may be obtained by either the author or the anthologist, and if you eventually submit your anthology to a publisher, written confirmation of approval from the original publishers of all previously published works will have to be cleared (for sound reasons related to copyright) before the publication process can proceed.

COPYRIGHT, RIGHTS, AND CONTRACTS

Concerning copyright, the general belief seems to be that immediately one puts pen to paper, or certainly once a written piece is completed, the law will recognize you as the sole writer, and will grant you complete power over how your work is used or reproduced. It will also guarantee your entitlement to all rights and benefits originating from that work. Additionally, the common assumption is that such protection will exist for the author's lifetime, and seventy years beyond that.

One can assume that, even though an anthology contains the works of more writers than just the anthologist, it is nevertheless a single, written composition in itself and that it too should enjoy similar protection to that mentioned above.

The word *rights* refers to the control you have over the use of your written work. A piece of writing, no matter how large or small, can be used in many ways, and the goal of a writer should be to retain as many rights as possible relating to how their work can be used. The issue of rights, like all legal matters, is complex, so if you intend to sell your work to a publisher, or even to publish via vanity press, you may need legal advice and should consult a lawyer.

Publishers have ready access to legal guidance, whereas you probably do not, but you will likely need an expert to interpret the small print in any contract offered to you. Again, this issue is complicated, so be cautious about signing any papers before you have properly digested and understood their content. *The Writer's Market* and various other books and websites dealing with publication can be helpful in providing a basic understanding of copyright, rights, remuneration, contracts, and related matters.

PUBLISHERS

Publishing and publishers exist to make money, and unless work submitted to them holds the promise of profit, and perhaps advancement of their reputation, it will be rejected. Only the best will make the cut in the highly critical, profit-orientated world of publishing, and a further disadvantage for the unknown writer is the fact that the industry is presently under huge financial pressure, originating with the multitude of new publishing possibilities that now exist for writers.

If you decide to publish your anthology privately, there are many options open to you, and that might give you more control over the destiny of your work. Options in the private market include:

- publishing privately, with you or you and your anthology colleagues footing the bill
- cooperative publishing, where you pay part of the cost and a publisher pays part
- and e-book publishing on the Internet through outlets like Kindle, Kobo, and Amazon or through e-publishers who handle one or more of these, in addition to offering other options.

REVIEWS, NETWORKING, AND MARKETING

If you are serious about marketing your anthology, as either a money maker or as a meaningful item of literature, it would be advantageous to get it reviewed. This can be done in newspapers and relevant journals or through magazines, the radio, TV, and a dedicated website. A lot will depend on your personal and professional contacts and how much you are able to afford. If the reviewer is truly unbiased and not obligated to you in any personal way (as it should be) you must be prepared for a negative review, and its consequences, if the reviewer is unimpressed by the work.

Networking, by the anthologist and contributors to the anthology, can be done through similar outlets to those mentioned for reviews, and e-mails to personal contacts can be one of the most effective tools available. Marketing the final product is often an arduous and thankless task, but if you are working with a publisher, most of that work might be done for you. Also, some private publishers will handle a certain degree of networking and publicity on behalf of your book. In addition, though, you may be expected to have display tables in malls, libraries, book stores, and other public locations and to go on tour to sell your book.

CONCLUSION

An anthology is a wonderful device for bringing writers with similar interests together so as to create a book. The purpose of the project will vary, but it will always result in great satisfaction for the contributors, and several viewpoints on a topic might have a greater impact on readers than a book by a single author. And if all the items in the book have been previously published, then the work takes on a new identity—that of a showcase. It is a digest and a truly collegial endeavor that will bring as much pleasure to its compiler and its writers as to the fortunate readers who have the convenience of, as it were, visiting so many authors under one roof.

REFERENCES

Harvard Guide to Using Sources, "Books," http://usingsources.fas.harvard.edu/icb/icb.do?keyword=k70847&pageid=icb.page363224.

Chuck Sambuchino, "Hearing Voices: 6 Steps I Used for Creating an Anthology," *Writer's Digest*, September 16, 2010, http://www.writersdigest.com/editor-blogs/guide-to-literary-agents/hearing-voices-6-steps-i-used-for-creating-an-anthology.

Scholars Publish, "How to Compile an Anthology of Original Essays," http://scholarspublish.com/publish-dont-perish/part-ii-the-conventions-of-academic-discourse/how-to-compile-an-anthology-of-original-essays/.

Dorothy Thompson, "How to Compile a Successful Anthology That Sells," Absolute Write, 2002, http://www.absolutewrite.com/novels/successful_anthology.htm.

Brenda Warneka and Arlene Uslander, "The Art of Assembling Anthologies," Writing-World.com, 2005, http://www.writing-world.com/publish/anthologies.shtml.

NOTES

1. Robert Lee Brewer, ed., *The Writer's Market* (Cincinnati: Writer's Digest Books, 2013).

FOURTEEN

Discover and Make Sense of Yourself by Writing Poetry

John Presley

I'm addicted to writing poetry, even more so now that I'm retired and can write more often. I'm addicted to writing and revision and discovering meaning in my own life and memories and to finding meaning in the lives and memories and words of others. I especially like the act of revision, when the sudden light of recognition shines and I find a meaning I didn't know that I knew or even meant at first take.

Many people think of poets as sitting in a dark garret room waiting for inspiration to jolt them into action and to write a whole poem in one fast pass, wiggling the pen as fast as they can to keep up with the pace of some spirit that is dictating the words too fast for a human to follow.

And what is this inspiration?

I believe it is the subconscious mind of the writer himself or herself and that the subconscious mind, with all its more acute observations and connections between experiences, its creativity and its therapies, can be teased into helping us and revealing itself to us by the simple act of writing that first draft of ideas that we hope to make beautiful and engaging.

I love putting pieces of words and sentences together that at first glance seem not to mean anything by themselves but that seem to present a productive mystery when they are later considered together. I revel in discovering cosmic irony or the like when I put one piece of paper near some other scrap I've been hoarding for months or years, back when my time was occupied in too many other ways. For example, I have a sheet of paper with words I overheard in the Dayton airport, when a woman in a

125

wheelchair was pushed by. When I heard her say, "Well, the first two were bipolar, and the third had a tail . . ." I knew I had to find my pencil and pad and follow her. I did, and those sentences will one day work together with others when my "inner therapist" decides to trump me or join me or play that yearning for discovery, to show me how and what these mysteries mean.

It's that love of writing and revising and what I might learn from it that keeps me writing poems—there's no fame, no money in it, now no longer even a "merit" raise every year—it's just me and my addiction to discovering meaning. Hey, some people are addicted to crossword puzzles. And I'm willing to admit that revising poetry drafts and working hours at a crossword puzzle or even a jumble have a couple of aspects in common. (But I gave up crossword puzzles when I learned that knowing too much was a disadvantage in the competition. I know the names of two "gods of war, 4 spaces, ends in *s*," for example). But while my revisions may not give me the voice of a legislator of the world, I am highly entertained by moving the pieces around until a mystery is solved and something is built.

Now, don't misunderstand: some poems of mine have "fallen from the sky" (actually, of course, from my subconscious) almost complete, and astonishingly, even sometimes in the form of near sonnets. Like Robert Graves, I try always to have paper of some kind near me in case that happens, and, like most compulsive writers, I can exhibit a bit of obsession with a particular kind of pen, a particular kind of paper. (Sometimes, when Graves forgot his paper, he had to resort to scratching on the backs of dry-cleaning receipts. Once when he was completely out of paper and a poem started to fall from the sky, he was reduced to writing on the back of a flattened-out ice cream carton! Graves called this source of ideas The Muse—but he also revised his work constantly, sometimes producing up to eighteen drafts of a single poem!) This month, I like writing on the texture of expensive drawing paper. But I am mainly addicted to the act of writing and revising, not to the paraphernalia, so most of the time I'm happy to "get an idea" and work at it, revising slowly and trying to solve the mystery of the meaning of my memories, words, phrases, and to see how they all have changed and adjusted themselves to new contexts.

Sometimes I write phrases and sentences down to hoard them, and it may be years later when I discover that the image or the stanza about the peacocks in the park in Vienna and the sentences about the old man stoically putting up and then removing all the umbrellas from the guest tables will mean more than I thought if I also allude to, or plagiarize from, E. E. Cummings. And it will be fun to put all this in one stanza. I once worked for ten years on a poem about Doubting Thomas, only to learn from the poem finally that it was not one but two poems about Doubting Thomas. Once my inner therapist finally solved the mystery, I realized that I had been deluding myself for quite some time about what I knew and how much I knew about Doubting Thomas. No wonder it took ten years.

I enjoy throwing form and structure into the mix, too. That's like really inviting your inner therapist to toss new meanings at you. The restraints—and possibilities—of form force my subconscious work to consider more alternative ways of saying the meaning I think I mean, and it makes revision just that much more surprising. Take a poem that in first draft seems to slam together two fragments I thought were unrelated to each other: the image of a halogen lamp creating the illusion of a halo and the story told to me by a friend—honest, it was a friend, and not me—about his long-ago visit to the free health clinic. Who knew that the free-clinic story, originally told to me as a joke, and a good one, would work so well with the admittedly rather strained halogen-halo figure? Or that the banal complaint of "This just isn't working for me" used here to end a relationship would be ironically illuminated by the threat of violence from the new boyfriend? Or that the poem's speaker would be as disinterested in the outcome of any fight as the "she" with the halogen halo was disinterested in the outcome of the relationship? Well, I didn't know any of these things—not until I wrote the words, and not finally until I went through the revision process with all the lines in place.

Minimalist

This is no sainted sixth century but
The halogen lamp behind her new cut
Makes her look German, religious, art.

This just isn't working for me, she says.

The old Navy doctor with his cigar
Volunteers at the new bright-lit clinic,
Mumbles, these are your red corpuscles here
And these are your white. Those other things there
The long black rods, well, they mean something else,
And reaches behind for a clean syringe.

Her new friend is ten years younger than she.
It's clear that he wants to fight me for her,
But I am deathly afraid that I'd win.

And, I am surprised that I am not surprised.

So, the poet learns what all these pieces mean, and, to some degree, the unpredictable collaboration with the unconscious and its unforeseen meanings is made just that much more enjoyable and surprising by the demands of form. I had no idea that "The long black rods, well, they mean something else / And reaches behind for a clean syringe" would make such very nice, sloppy, and surprising lines of pentameter (lines with ten syllables in each—no matter the rhythm), and I certainly didn't know that all this now-discovered boredom with love and its complications would make a nice sonnet (a poem of fourteen lines of pentameter—modern sonnets do not always follow previous rules of either rhythm or rhyme). Well, mine is a near sonnet with the sestet in the middle. (Sonnets are usually *Elizabethan*, meaning four separate four-line stanzas followed by a two-line stanza, *or* a sonnet is a stanza of eight lines—the *octet*, followed by a *sestet* of six lines). Some poems are in *free verse*, with virtually no rules of order, but I enjoy following—and sometimes breaking—the rules of so-called *formal verse*, because making words do their work inside these forms is another way of forcing more meanings and discovery.

As a teenager I once wrote a very puerile poem claiming "Poems / are words with / noises happening between." Though the *New Yorker*, *American Poetry Review*, and even *Poetry* are dominated by such "language poems," I no longer want to focus on the odd word, or the difficult and unusual syntax, the how-clever-is-this techniques of such poetry. In a recent poem I used the image of leaves blown up in the air by a passing car to represent the ideas and memories and facts that would later be reordered into a poem. But it is not a random, chaotic reordering that makes a poem—it is the act of will, the detection, the sudden appearance of the unconscious that reorders those leaves into verbal art that fascinates me now. John Updike described the way art can "sidestep mortality with feats of attention, of harmony, of illuminating connections."[1] It is those feats of attention and those illuminating connections that I want to detect and that keep me working at the mystery of writing and revising.

When I began writing "Steps," I thought, after two decades of remembering a British poet I once knew, that I might be able to "detect" a meaning, a significance, simply in my memories of him. I had been so impressed by his great talent as a poet that I'd long wanted to write a poem in which he'd be Mozart to my Salieri and in which I'd be shown surprisingly, ironically correct in my modest estimate of my talents compared to his. But my poetic Mozart had a lot of other issues: he may have been a thief, he was certainly a liar, and he was so abusive in all his relationships with women that he was the only modern, actual person I'd ever called a cad. But the act of drafting, of pressing poetry from my pen, reminded me that my poet-friend claimed to be descended from one of the executioners of Joan of Arc, and he seemed to be proud of this connection.

Steps

He claimed that he was descended from the
man who burned Joan of Arc at the stake.
How sure that guy had to have been, that she

was a different species, communed with Satan,
to be able to feed that flame after he
saw her eyes. Imagine the anger that lit
his heart, the strength of vivid conviction.

Maybe that explained why my friend was an
asshole, treated women so badly that
even I looked away. Living with me then,
he was engaged to one beauty back in
England—with a complexion like the sun
after clouds—and he cried to her on the
phone, left hand stroking his next sacrifice.

I began to detect a possible truth. As I struggled to find new words for *fire* and *glowing* and ground away at making the fourteen lines work, I was struck not so much by his hostility toward women as by his distant and unthinking assumption of superiority to women that explained these two behaviors, his and his ancestor's.

Perhaps what makes a cad is the cad's sense that no relationship is important enough to invest one's energy and time in continuing it. And what linked the image of the cad in my mind to the image of his executioner ancestor may be the "burning" complexion of the betrayed lover back in England. I didn't know about the possible existence of any of these connections—I didn't even know that I knew things I might connect—before I began to write and revise. Writing poetry, I remind myself, is submitting one's preliminary, vague, partial, or even incorrect ideas to the revelatory work of composing, revising, matching form and idea.

And the ambiguity in the last line? Just what is the next sacrifice? Well, sometimes the Poet Making Meaning may be surprised by his or her inner self—imagination meeting memory in the dark, as Annie Dillard has said. Sometimes the poet in me decides to go with the alternative presented by the inner mind, especially when the result is a productive ambiguity (think of the endings of *The Maltese Falcon* and *The Big Sleep*).

You will not be surprised to learn, I'm sure, that sometimes the act of writing can quite literally serve as a sort of therapy. A friend once set out to write a poem about his becoming separated from an uncle in a strange town one afternoon after helping his uncle with work. The speaker in the poem was about twelve years old; the poem was very true to my friend's remembered reality. The poem grew in length and in complexity; editors read the poem and expressed interest and pointed out places where the poem was ambiguous. The poem, originally focused on the man who found my friend and took him home, began to describe that man's car as dark and foreboding and the drive home as silent, empty. It was then that the ambiguous and general words his creative subconscious had suggested, especially during his revision of the poem, began to reveal their double meanings. My friend understood, finally, that he was writing a new truth, that he had been molested by a stranger, that he had never been able to remember any of the details, and that this unremembered violence had caused so many of his parents' attitudes and behaviors. And these were attitudes and behaviors that had caused him much pain and embarrassment, none of which he had ever before been able to explain or understand.

Sometimes writing poetry is entertaining. But more often it makes sense of our lives for us.

I wrote "How My Interview Went" after losing out in an interview for a college presidency. I was angry, fixated, ranting about the unfairness of it all when my wife Katherine told me to shut up and write a poem about it. I began writing the poem in a fever of wounded ego.

How My Interview Went

What the hell was I thinking?
When they said "historic home,"
I should have thought: sharecropper.
When they said "automobile of your choice,"
I should have thought: company store.

When that chinless corduroy jacket
At the inevitable Faculty Forum
Started in with his smirking quiz,
I should have put on my face
That look used by aging bird dogs
When they have to squat in the field:
I'm not here, you're not here, I'm looking
Behind that bush over yonder.

What the hell was I thinking?
My sympathies are with those who buy used,
Whose shirts are Sunday, then work,
Then painting, then grease rag.
No, I am not Prince Hamlet, nor was meant to be,
Rather, a gravedigger . . . maybe
Someone who'll do to tow a car or two,
To spend a day with duct tape under someone else's house.

When they said "mutual goals set with the board,"
I should have thought: small town lawyers and preachers,
Fifty of them, and each one thinks he's boss.
When they said "golf"
And I said: bursitis,
And they said "faith community"
And I said: What's that,
What the hell was I thinking?

Slowly, I found the act of writing uncovering for me a meaning I'd not suspected—and certainly not experienced and didn't know I knew—solving a mystery of which I was barely aware. Flinging the refrain "What the hell was I thinking?" in my face caused me to begin to think that I might have dodged a bullet when the trustees decided they liked the last interviewee, the Lutheran air force general, much better than they had liked me. When I discovered the pattern "When they said X, I should have thought Y," I began to realize what a constant strain it might have been, this posing as a college president. And when working to clarify the synecdoche of the "chinless corduroy jacket at the inevitable Faculty Forum," and then finding that figure followed, surprisingly and immediately, by the rather chagrined bird dog "squatting in the field," I knew that my subconscious memories and its detective skills had uncovered for me the idiocy and the humiliation of the usual beauty-pageant presidential interview, once and for all. My inner self had been thinking and perceiving while the interview had been in progress, noting details and drawing inferences! (In fact, I believe so strongly in this "revealed truth" my inner mind discovered during the act of my composing this poem that I went on to lecture about the absurdity of this sort of interview process many times during my time-draining career as a college administrator).

The really interesting part of writing poetry is not the rational, conscious work of trying first this alternative and then this one and adjusting all the other ideas when these two seem to click and so on. The poet feels in control, the poet is rationally testing, tasting, all the possibilities that he or she can think of. But then there is the other even more entertaining side of the work—intuition, serendipity, inspiration, the ideas that seem to fall from the sky, and the sudden thought that entirely reverses the meaning of the piece. The searching by the intellect may have started the process, but sometimes suddenly the subconscious, creative part of the mind intrudes. And these frequently ironic and playful intrusions are always illuminating!

Finally I'm working right now on a comic poem about a literary tour of Boar's Hill, the area south of Oxford, where so many British poets have lived. I felt it come together when I "suddenly realized" that the bus we had been touring in was huge, grey, with big side mirrors that stuck out like an elephant's ears as it nosed around the curves on narrow English roads. And my ideas and I were off and running.

I have another poem in draft about sleeping upstairs while a beach house is torn apart by a storm. At this point I don't think it's going to be very good at all. My inner self hasn't discovered a mystery to be solved in the draft yet.

NOTE

1. Foreword to *Updike's Collected Early Stories: 1953–1975*, New York: Random House (Ballantine), 2003, p. xvi.

FIFTEEN

Grant Writing in Retirement

Nancy Kalikow Maxwell

If you seek a retirement filled with meaning and money (and who doesn't?), consider grant writing—or, as the profession calls it, grant development. No matter what you call it, the process of preparing proposals to fund nonprofit organizations can be personally and financially rewarding. At least it has been for me. Before I retired from my thirty-year library career, I had developed and administered several successful federal grants. Hoping to put this experience to use when I retired two years ago, I opened a grant development–consulting company, Kaliwell, Inc.[1] The venture has been ideal, providing me with intellectual stimulation, social contact, and creative challenges. And money. More money than I even expected. If you possess the skills, background, and personality all discussed below, grant development may be just the right retirement job for you.

GRANT DEVELOPMENT FULFILLS BOOMER NEEDS

"Retirement job" is no longer an oxymoron. As Marc Freedman discusses in *Encore* (his term for this phase of employment), many boomers want to work after retirement. But they want to make a difference while pursuing something different. Retirees of this generation seek jobs that provide not only money but also meaning and a sense of contributing to the greater good.[2]

Developing grants for nonprofit organizations fulfills this requirement perfectly. Virtually all types of charitable groups prepare grants to better their communities and improve the health, education, income, and housing of citizens. Churches, colleges, hospitals, cities, and nonprofit organizations all use grant developers to seek out additional funding. Just about any worthy purpose that can be imagined needs grants.

Grant writing also meets the other top requirement of boomer retirees: a flexible schedule. Especially with many retirees caring for aging parents, sometimes in combination with helping grown children, the ability to freely choose hours and location of work is crucial. As a Sloan Foundation study found, a mismatch exists between the work world and this need. Many older workers are forced to choose between a full-time job with a rigid schedule or a low-wage Wal-Mart greeter–type of part-time job, none of which provides flexibility in work schedules.[3]

But for grant developers, a variety of work options is possible. Grant development can be performed on a freelance basis, as is evident from the fact that more than 10 percent of professionals work as independent consultants.[4] Grant writing can also be done part-time, on a contract basis, through a retainer basis, or as a subcontractor. Many of these options allow for a choice of when and where to work.

No geographical boundaries limit the grant developer, because much of the work can be completed online or by phone. Though some face-to-face meetings may be required during the grant-development process, finding the funding source, researching the need for the project, gathering supporting data, and writing the grant can be done from home.

In addition to developing the grant proposal, conducting research to locate grant opportunities or find data to support a proposal's narrative can easily be done on a freelance basis. Evaluating funded-grant projects is another ancillary career path available that is often done by a freelance consultant.

THE GROWING FIELD OF GRANT WRITING

Grant development is a thriving industry, having grown in recent years from a small subset of nonprofit fund-raising to its own specialty. With the proliferation of government, corporate, and foundation grants, many nonprofit organizations now employ an individual or an entire department specifically charged with identifying grant opportunities, preparing grant proposals, and implementing and evaluating grant-funded projects. In the past an organization's fund-raiser or development officer would prepare grant proposals as a sideline to their primary duties of donor solicitation, alumni relations, planned giving, and prospect development. But the process of applying for government, foundation, or corporate funding has become so complex that a need has arisen for individuals possessing specialized knowledge about grant-proposal development.

Most large organizations such as hospitals, school systems, colleges, municipalities, and museums maintain departments staffed with full or part-time professionals. External grant developers are hired to expand these institutions' grant-producing capacities. Small organizations such as environmental groups, faith-based organizations, and human-service organizations can rarely support their own grant staff and exclusively use external grant professionals to identify and seek additional funding sources.

GRANT-WRITING PERSONALITY, QUALIFICATIONS, AND SKILLS

After more than ten years of grant-writing experience, I have come to characterize grant development as the bureaucratic version of foxhunting, minus the red jackets and yapping dogs. To me it is exciting and great fun. I am not the only one who sees grant seeking in this light. Another grant writer reports getting an "ego boost of adrenaline" from grant awards.[5]

I will grant (no pun intended) that it does take a certain type of person to view grant development as exhilarating. A former academic colleague once told me she would rather kill herself than write a grant. Which leads me to the type of person best suited for the job.

Grant writing requires a peculiar type of person: someone who enjoys searching for the percent of people in Miami-Dade County on food stamps (23.8 percent) or who rises to the challenge of summarizing the need for a family-literacy program in 250 characters or less. Though I'm not aware of any research on personality traits common to grant development, the field requires the kind of person who enjoys finding a massive amount of information and boiling it down to a few cogent sentences. Grant professionals must be exceptionally detail-oriented (some would call it obsessive-compulsive—or refer to a certain part of the human anatomy).

EDUCATED, OLDER WOMEN'S WORK

Though I am loath to engage in gender stereotypes, judging from the profession's demographics it appears that women possess this type of personality more than men. Females make up 86 percent of the profession. More than one-third of grant professionals are over fifty, and those over sixty make up more than 15 percent of field. Only 3 percent of grant writers are under twenty-eight.[6]

The profession is a highly educated group. More than half (57 percent) hold graduate or professional degrees, and one-third hold BAs. The most common graduate degrees are MBAs (12 percent), masters' in education (13 percent), and masters' in public administration (5 percent). Grant professionals are predominately white (88 percent), with 6 percent Hispanics, 4 percent blacks, and 2 percent other.[7]

EASY ENTRY INTO THE FIELD

Few grant developers as children answered the question "What do you want to be when you grow up?" with "A grant writer." Most grant professionals entered the field through grant-related responsibilities assumed in other positions. Coming to the profession from another field is not only expected, it is preferable, especially in fields requiring technical, specialized knowledge. Grant-related experience in one area can usually be put to use in other areas.

Many grant professionals come to the field from nonprofit administrative positions. For instance, one high-level grant executive started out with the Girl Scouts. The owner of a multi-million-dollar grant-writing consulting company began as a college English teacher who had a U.S. Department of Education grant "dumped on her." One firefighter was tasked with submitting a Homeland Security grant and ended up as a grant professional.[8]

Those lacking any grant experience can learn the craft by taking classes, studying for certification, or working with other grant developers as discussed below.

MORE THAN WRITING

To develop grants, you must be a good writer, but the ability to express oneself in writing is only part of the job. The oft-repeated adage in the profession states that writing is the smallest part of the job. As grant professionals Jerry Dillehay and Sharon Skinner note, the term *grant writing* is insufficient because data gathering, researching, planning, budgeting, and fact checking take up as much, if not more, of a grant developer's time than grant writing.[9]

The educational background of grant writers underscores this reality. Less than 3 percent of grant writers have degrees in creative writing. The ability to craft a lyrical poem or suspense novel is not called for in grant writing. Rather the writer must be able to succinctly present a compelling case for a project within the constraints of a proposal's guidelines, which requires a different kind of creativity.

More than the ability to write, grant developers must have the patience and tenacity to scrupulously research and document detailed information as required by grant proposals. For instance, the following paragraph taken from a grant request for proposal (RFP) exemplifies the type of writing required by grant writers, requiring that applicants "describe the background of the program, its goals, and need in the proposed

geographic area. Describe how the applicant will meet the program requirements, the recruitment process, [and] enrollment procedures, and
explain how stakeholders will be engaged. The application must be dou-
ble-spaced, use a font size no smaller than twelve-point, and not exceed
seventy pages."[10]

If the paragraph above makes you hurl the proposal across the room,
grant writing is not for you. But if you are detail oriented (your friends
would say to a fault) and you enjoy researching and crafting information
within tight parameters, grant writing may be the perfect endeavor for
your retirement career.

THE INCOME AND EXPENSES OF GRANT WRITING

Grant development can be quite lucrative. Though many people think
grant development is done on a commission basis, grant developers
should be paid for their work regardless of whether or not the proposal is
funded. Producing proposals on a commission basis is considered a violation of the profession's ethical standards. The Grant Professional Association's code of ethics states that "members shall not accept or pay a
finder's fee, commission, or percentage compensation based on grants
and shall take care to discourage their organizations from making such
payments. Compensation should not be written into grants."[11]

According to Preethi Burkholder, author of *Start Your Own Grant-
Writing Business*, the average rate for a beginning grant writer is anywhere from $40 to $80 per hour, with experienced writers commanding
$100 per hour or more. Some grant professionals charge more per hour to
develop a grant than to research grant opportunities. Grant writers working on a per-project basis are paid anywhere from $1,000 up, with many
projects paying $10,000 per proposal. In my experience, most federal-
grant projects pay about $5,000 to $6,000 per project, depending on the
complexity of the required documentation and proposed project.[12]

Few retirees seek full-time work, but those who do will find that grant
positions pay anywhere from $50,000 to $300,000 per year. The most
recent Grant Professionals Association survey found a salary range of
$24,000 to $175,000, with an average annual salary of $61,927.[13]

Many independent grant writers work from home, so no office expenses are required (unless your spouse or dog creates such distraction
that you need to get away). But even if that is the case, you can always
head to a local library with your laptop and work in peace and quiet (just
stay clear of the children's section).

ANCILLARY GRANT POSITIONS

Those lacking the ability or desire to craft proposals could contribute to grant development through other avenues. Along with writing, grant-proposal development requires extensive research, which may explain why my background as a librarian has drawn me to the field. Searching for the best funding opportunity, locating data to support the need for the project, organizing information, and keeping track of proposals are all central elements of grant development. One job ad for a grant position required someone with the ability to "research and disseminate information, retrieve data from the Internet, and compile information."

Evaluating grants once funded and implemented is another avenue of grant-related work available on a freelance basis. Many large government grants include funds for an outside, independent review of the project to assure funders that the program is meeting stated objectives and spending funds appropriately. Hired as independent consultants, these external evaluators review details of the program, meet with key project and institutional administrators, analyze relevant documents such as financial transactions and progress reports, and then write a report summarizing their findings. Those with experience with federal or state grant programs or with programmatic evaluation may want to consider becoming an outside grant evaluator. Details on this aspect of the profession can be obtained from the American Evaluation Association (see below).

GRANT-PROFESSIONAL CERTIFICATIONS

Though not required, many professional-certification programs are available for grant professionals. One advantage to obtaining certification is that it automatically establishes one's credentials within the profession. Preparing for the certification exam also provides an excellent avenue to learn the craft. Several of the grant-professional organizations listed below offer certification programs. Many colleges and nonprofit organizations offer their own fund-raising certificates, but they usually bestow certificates of completion rather than formally recognized certificates.

WHERE TO FIND ORGANIZATIONS NEEDING GRANT WRITERS

Opportunities can be found in virtually every type of public institution and nonprofit organization. In these tough economic times, virtually all of them identify, develop, and submit grants. And those that don't have a grant program probably want one. As mentioned above, grants are developed by all types of nonprofit organizations, educational and medical institutions, and local governments. Those large enough to maintain grant departments often contract with outside grant writers to supplement the capacity of their grant-related employees. Many nonprofit organizations retain a freelance grant writer to perform over a specific time or for specific projects. Others hire grant developers to identify grant opportunities or to prepare all or part of a grant proposal. Along with word of mouth, institutions often turn to one of the organizations of grant professionals listed below to locate a grant writer.

HOW TO GET STARTED WRITING GRANTS

The best way to break into grant writing is to write a grant. Though that sounds facile, it is serious. Nothing can substitute for the experience of preparing a proposal. For those lacking experience, workshops on how to write grants are available through community-education programs, nonprofit organizations, and college business courses. Some offerings are free, while others cost hundreds of dollars. Almost all of these trainings will require participants to write a grant. In the doing, the real learning takes place.

Another method to gain experience is to volunteer for a grant-development project currently underway. Grants are often developed by teams and include not only a primary writer but also individuals knowledgeable about the project and representatives from partner agencies or service recipients. Often team members will research, edit, proofread, or prepare the budget. Volunteering to craft the entire proposal or helping out with any of these functions would provide valuable experience to grant-writing novices. Shadowing a grant writer is another avenue to seeing the various stages in proposal development.

ESTABLISHING THE CONSULTING BUSINESS

SCORE, the national organization of retired executives, is the best source of business advice for beginning a company.[14] I sought out my local SCORE organization for assistance in marketing my fledging consulting business. The mentor I was assigned provided me with invaluable assistance, and the exercise of preparing a formal business plan that he insisted I undertake allowed me to sharpen the focus and direction of my company.

DISADVANTAGES OF GRANT WRITING IN RETIREMENT

I am reluctant to end this piece on a negative note, but I must be honest. There are drawbacks to grant development, especially for retirees. First and foremost, the time frame for preparing grants has shortened recently, especially following the release of stimulus funding. The compressed schedule rarely allows enough time to prepare and submit a quality grant. All too often grants must be prepared at the last minute. Anyone having trouble working under pressure may want to consider other aspects of grant writing, such as evaluation or research.

Frustration over not being provided information needed in a timely fashion is another problem experienced by many freelance grant developers. Throughout the proposal-development process, specific information will be needed that can only be provided by the employing organization. Combined with the tight deadlines mentioned above, this information is often needed immediately. When the individual within the organization does not provide what is needed on time, which unfortunately happens all too often, the grant developer has few viable options. I was once forced to report the lack of cooperation to someone's supervisor. Another time I simply guessed at the information I lacked. Neither of these ended up with happy outcomes.

Another disadvantage could be termed "having too much of a good thing." The flipside of being a burgeoning profession is that there may be too many opportunities presented. I, and fellow independent grant writers, can attest that it is hard to turn work down when offered. One strategy to avoid this is to team up with other grant writers. Such an arrangement will keep you from saying no when offered work. Instead you could share sections of developing a proposal or delegate the entire project to a colleague. Having others to rely on when faced with too much work is vital. You don't want to end up working all the time. After all, you're supposed to be retired.

RESOURCES AND RECOMMENDED READING

Professional Associations

American Evaluation Association (http://www.eval.org/)
American Grant Writer's Association (http://www.agwa.us/)
Association of Fundraising Professionals (http://www.afpnet.org/)
Grant Professionals Association (http://grantprofessionals.org)
SCORE (http://www.score.org/)

Grant Resources

Foundation Center (http://foundationcenter.org/)

Foundation Center's online directory of private foundation websites (http://foundationcenter.org/findfunders/foundfinder/)
Grant Space—Foundation Center's online tutorials (http://www.grantspace.org/classroom)

The Grantsmanship Center (http://www.tgci.com/)

Service Clubs and Civic Organizations

Michigan State University (http://staff.lib.msu.edu/harris23/grants/servicec.htm)

Blogs

Charity Channel Forum's online discussion groups (http://charity-channel.com/articles)
Grants Champion's blog (http://www.grantschampion.com/blog)
Library Grants' blog (http://librarygrants.blogspot.com/)
PND Philanthropy News Digest (http://www.philanthropynewsdigest.org/)

Grant Sources

Council of Foundation's community-foundation locator (http://www.cof.org/community-foundation-loca-tor?menuContainerID=34&crumb=2)
Grants.gov's list of grant opportunities (http://www.grants.gov/web/grants/home.html)
Institute of Museum and Library Services (http://www.imls.gov/)
National Assembly of State Art Agencies (http://www.nasaa-arts.org)
National Endowment for the Arts (http://arts.gov/)
National Endowment for the Humanities' grants page (http://www.neh.gov/grants)
National Endowment for the Humanities' list of state humanities councils (http://www.neh.gov/about/state-humanities-councils)
U.S. Department of Education's list of discretionary grant competitions (http://www.ed.gov/grantapps)

Grant-Related Publications

The Chronicle of Philanthropy (http://philanthropy.com/section/Home/172)
Foundation Center's Marketplace—a list of digital grant guides (serial publications, dates vary) (http://marketplace.foundationcenter.org/Publications/Digital-Grant-Guides)

Grants for Children and Youth
Grants for Information Technology
Grants for Libraries and Information Services
Grants for Women and Girls
National Directory of Corporate Giving

National Guide to Funding in Arts and Culture
National Guide to Funding for Libraries and Information Services

Grants for Libraries Hotline (Boston: Quinlan Publishing Group, 2002–)
Institute of Museum and Library Services' newsletter, *Primary Source* (http://www.imls.gov/news/primary_source.aspx)
National Endowment for the Humanities' magazine, *Humanities* (http://www.neh.gov/humanities)
PND Philanthropy News Digest's RFPs and notices of awards (http://www.philanthropynewsdigest.org/rfps)

FURTHER RECOMMENDED READING

Annual Register of Grant Support
Joseph Barbato, *Writing for a Good Cause* (New York: Simon and Schuster, 2000).
Daniel M. Barber, *Finding Funding: The Comprehensive Guide to Grant Writing*, 2nd ed. (Long Beach, CA: Bond St. Publishers, 2002).
Larissa Golden Brown, *Demystifying Grantseeking* (San Francisco: Jossey-Bass Pfeiffer, 2001).
Beverly A. Browning, *Grant Writing for Dummies*, 4th ed. (Hoboken, NJ: Wiley Publishers, 2011).
———, *Perfect Phrases for Writing Grant Proposals* (New York: McGraw-Hill, 2007).
Preethi Burkholder, *Start Your Own Grant-Writing Business* (Irvine, CA: Entrepreneur Press, 2008).
Mim Carlson, *Winning Grants Step by Step*, 3rd ed. (San Francisco: Jossey-Bass, 2008).
Cheryl Carter and James Aaron Quick, *How to Write a Grant Proposal* (Hoboken, NJ: John Wiley & Sons, 2003).
Alexis Carter-Black, *Getting Grants: The Complete Manual of Proposal Development and Administration*, 2nd ed. (Bellingham, WA: Self-Counsel Press, 2010).
Cheryl A. Clarke, *Storytelling for Grantseekers: A Guide to Creative Nonprofit Fundraising*, 2nd ed. (San Francisco: Jossey-Bass, 2009).
Cheryl A. Clarke and Susan P. Fox, *Grant Proposal Makeover: Transform Your Request from No to Yes* (San Francisco Jossey-Bass, 2007).
Sarah Collins, ed., *Foundation Fundamentals*, 8th ed. (New York: Foundation Center, 2008).
Janet L. Crowther and Barry Trott, *Partnering with Purpose* (Westport, CT: Libraries Unlimited, 2004).
Saadia Faruqi, *Best Practice Grant Seeking: Beyond the Proposal* (Sudbury, MA: Jones and Bartlett, 2011).
Robert S. Frey, *Successful Proposal Strategies for Small Businesses*, 4th ed. (Boston: Artech House, 2004).
Mary S. Hall and Susan Howlett, *Getting Funded: The Complete Guide to Writing Grant Proposals* (Seattle: Word and Raby Publishers, 2010).
Dianne Harris, *Complete Guide to Winning Effective and Award-Winning Grants: Step by Step Instructions* (Ocala, FL: Atlantic Publishers, 2008).
Victoria M. Johnson, *Grant Writing 101: Everything You Need to Start Raising Funds Today* (New York: McGraw-Hill, 2011).
Timothy Kachinske and Judith Kachinske, *90 Days to Success in Grant Writing* (Boston: Course Technology PTR, 2009).
Deborah S. Koch, *How to Say It: Grantwriting* (New York: Prentice Hall, 2009).
Judith B. Margolin and Gail T. Lubin, eds., *Foundation Center's Guide to Winning Proposals II* (New York: Foundation Center, 2005).

Ellen Marsh and Arlen Sue Fox, *The Only Grant Writing Book You'll Ever Need* (New York: Basic Books, 2009).

Nancy Kalikow Maxwell, ed., *ALA Book of Library Grant Money*, 9th ed. (Chicago: American Library Association, 2014).

————, *Grant Money through Collaborative Partnerships* (Chicago: American Library Association, 2012).

Beverly McDonough and Daniel Bazikian, eds., *Annual Register of Grant Support 2014: A Directory of Funding Resources* (New Providence: R. R. Bowker, 2014)—an annual publication since 1969).

Jeremy T. Miner and Lynn E. Miner, *Proposal Planning and Writing*, 4th ed. (Westport, CT: Greenwood Press, 2008).

Joanne Oppelt, *Confessions of a Successful Grants Writer: A Complete Guide to Discovering and Obtaining Funding* (Rancho Santa Margarita, CA: CharityChannel Press, 2011).

Mary Ann Payne, *Grant Writing Demystified* (New York: McGraw-Hill, 2010).

Andy Robinson, *Grassroots Grants: An Activist's Guide to Grantseeking*, 2nd ed. (San Francisco: Jossey-Bass, 2004).

Nancy Burke Smith and E. Gabriel Works, *Complete Book of Grant Writing: Learn to Write Grants like a Professional* (Naperville, IL: Source Books, 2006).

Karen Stinson and Phyl Renninger, *Collaboration in Grant Development and Management* (Washington, DC: Thompson Publishing Group, 2007).

Martin Teitel, *Thank You for Submitting Your Proposal: A Foundation Director Reveals What Happens Next* (Medfield, MA: Emerson and Church, 2006).

Waddy Thompson, *Complete Idiot's Guide to Grant Writing*, 2nd ed. (Indianapolis: Alpha Books, 2007).

Deborah Ward, *Writing Grant Proposals That Win*, 4th ed. (Sudbury, MA: Jones and Bartlett, 2011).

Michael K. Wells, *Grantwriting* series:

Grantwriting Beyond the Basics (Portland, OR: Portland State University Continuing Education Press, 2005).

Grantwriting Beyond the Basics, Book 2: Understanding Nonprofit Finances (Portland, OR: Portland State University Continuing Education Press, 2006).

Grantwriting Beyond the Basics, Book 3: Successful Program Evaluation (Portland, OR: Portland State University Continuing Education Press, 2007).

Otto O. Yang, *Guide to Effective Grant Writing: How to Write a Successful NIH Grant Application* (New York: Kluwer Academic, 2005).

NOTES

1. Visit Kaliwell, Inc., online at http://www.librarygrants.org/.

2. Marc Freedman, *Encore: Finding Work That Matters in the Second Half of Life* (New York: PublicAffairs, 2007), 11.

3. Ibid., 136.

4. Grant Professionals Association, "Salary and Demographic Survey Result" (Kansas City, August 9, 2011), 12.

5. Jerry Dillehay and Sharon Skinner, "Key Skills and Behaviors of Successful Grant Professionals," *Journal of the Grant Professionals Association* (Fall 2012): 74.

6. Grant Professionals Association, "Salary and Demographic," 1–3.

7. Ibid.

8. Dillehay and Skinner, "Key Skills," 72.

9. Ibid.

10. Center for Medicare and Medicaid Innovation, U.S. Department of Health and Human Services Cooperative Agreement, "Strong Start for Mothers and Newborns," (2011).

11. Grant Professionals Association, "Code of Ethics," revised October 5, 2011, http://grantprofessionals.org/about/ethics (accessed June 7, 2011).

12. Preethi Burkholder, *Start Your Own Grant-Writing Business* (New York: Entrepreneur Press, 2008), 3–4.

13. Grant Professionals Association, "Salary and Demographic," 12.

14. Visit Score online at www.SCORE.org.

SIXTEEN

It's Never Too Late to Start Blogging

Sarah W. Bartlett

Now that we're retired, we no longer need to follow anyone else's schedule or goals. We have complete freedom to pick and choose based on what matters to us, scheduling our days to best match our own personal energy and creativity levels. Moreover we've earned the right to say what we think and feel. What better time to start a blog?

BUT WHAT WOULD I WRITE ABOUT?

Consider, for a moment, what a career in health-care and social-services planning and marketing, parenting three sets of children, and establishing a successful small business later in life have in common. Other than being a thumbnail trajectory of my own life, they are, simply, life experiences. In other words, they are prompts. We all have something to say based on who we are, the choices we've made, lives we've lived.

But who would want to read about us? The answer is simple: most of us have, at one time or another, become "experts" at some parts of our lives. Perhaps when our children were young, we battled the local school system for the same kinds of programming for gifted kids that were so readily available for struggling ones. Perhaps, as a result of our crusades, we became a local resource for alternative programs, found ourselves at the center of a community of concerned parents, discovering how hungry other parents were for mutual support and guidance. We became an expert.

We do not need to believe we have a novel hidden within, the seeds of poems that would touch others, or even the urge to collect memories of

145

our children for their own future amusement or edification—although these might be present, or evolve. All we need is to have lived a number of decades, have some newfound time on our hands, and recognize that our experience is worth something beyond the structured workday and paycheck that may have sustained us to date.

SO WHY BLOG?

For some of us, writing is a personal imperative. We *must* write. Blogging offers a ready outlet for putting our words somewhere. Taken a step further, we might wish to educate others about a field to which we dedicated our lives, perhaps including calls to action or change. Or we may feel lonely, turning to blogging as a way to entertain others from the comfort of home, a perfect solution for more limited energy and a social bent. For many this is a time and an opportunity to collect the wisdom of years in one place to share or review, perhaps for the grandchildren to read someday or to turn into a blogged collection of short pieces (even that novel you didn't know lurked within!). A primary reason to blog is to connect with friends and colleagues now that you are no longer directly connected through work. And of course more inner motivations might include entertaining yourself, learning or trying something new, stretching yourself beyond previous experience.

WHERE AND HOW TO BEGIN?

As of April 2011, I had a Facebook profile to which I had never posted in the five or more years since I created it. I had started a LinkedIn account because that was what a small-business owner was supposed to do. I had created a languishing business website, which I was in the process of changing so that I could be in charge of its design and updates. Then, in April 2012, I learned about Robert Lee Brewer's Platform Challenge, which popped up simultaneously with the annual April poetry challenge, of which I have been a regular participant.[1]

I was immediately intrigued. This was a chance to push myself into new territory, to learn something about social media by wading right in without time to grab a life vest. I would be guided by Robert's wisdom and held by the community of also-adventuring souls eager to learn the ins and outs of posts, comments, linking, optimizing, editorial calendars, feeds, sharing . . . in short, creating a presence and a persona via my own blog.

It was a trial by drowning of sorts; I'm not going to lie.

The very first step is to make an inventory of your interests, those passions or hobbies or life learnings that uniquely define you. What do you have to say about those things from your own unique point of view?

To whom do you want to say them? How? Why? Who do you want to be in the blogosphere? How much energy do you have to put into this whole venture? How will it benefit you, and what will you be giving to the world? What are you even *thinking*, jumping into this strange new world at this stage in your life?![2]

IMPORTANT THINGS TO CONSIDER ABOUT PRESENTATION

- After you have answered the self-discovery questions above, you are ready to develop a personal code, style, and brand. What do you want to be known for? What tone do you want to use? What is your voice? Here of course you have leeway to adopt a persona entirely other than the one you have cultivated all these years, should you so desire.
- Whatever voice you choose, the most frequently offered and best piece of advice out there for bloggers is to *be authentic*. Avoid being coy or obscure. Be yourself. After all, you are putting yourself out there, presumably hoping to connect with like-minded folks. Do you come across as someone *you* would like to meet and interact with?
- Due to the high volume of blogs out there, it seems advisable to focus your content on a handful of ideas, skills, and experiences that are yours. You will be stretched enough just getting into the fray; so if you try to blog about something you do not know well, your voice will come across as inauthentic, and you will have negated these first three pieces of advice.
- Blogging wisdom recommends consistent posting as the best way to create a known presence. This can take months, if not years. Yes, you will ask your parents, children, best childhood buddies, and former colleagues to follow your blog. But nothing will keep readers coming back like consistent and compelling posts. *Consistent* does not necessarily mean *frequent*, which leads directly to the next point . . .
- Know your limits. Blogging only works if you choose a posting schedule that fits your lifestyle and interest.

WHICH BLOGGING SITE TO USE??

For recreational blogging, there are two extremely user-friendly options that require no technical knowledge to set up or use, are hosted, offer a variety of templates and options to customize your blog to make it your own, and are free. Tim Brookes recently provided a terrific comparison of these two popular options.[3] If you are inclined to dig more deeply, his post is a must-read. Otherwise, here is the short story:

- *Blogger*—This easy and accessible blogging home, acquired in 2003 by Google, has two obvious advantages: people with Gmail accounts are automatically set up to create a blog. And because Google is the most-used search engine on the Web, users will have an advantage in being found. It offers a limited number of templates with unlimited and free customization options.
- *WordPress*—This platform comes in two flavors. Simple to use, with literally hundreds of templates, responsive help forums and community, and topic-by-topic help pages, *Wordpress.com* is ready to roll with your few decisions. It does, however, cost a modest amount to add customizations. It offers downloadable software that requires self-hosting. While offering unlimited flexibility, it is best used by those with programming experience seeking a highly professionalized site with all the bells and whistles.

In much the way shopping for a home or car involves a series of personal preferences, I would encourage you to go onto each site and poke around. You will quickly get a feel for some of the differences in appearance and ease of use. It is also possible to start with one and move to the other. They do not, however, "talk" to one another. So if you like the WordPress community but the feel of Blogger, you will need to choose. The bottom line is that you are going to decorate your blog home in your own style; just find the options that feel most compatible, and take it from there.

CONNECTING WITH OTHERS AND BUILDING READERSHIP

Most of us blog for two reasons: we want to write; and we want to connect with others. The mores of the blogosphere are about completing the circle. I read and comment on your blog, and you reciprocate. So the most effective way to build readership is to become an active part of the blogging community.

Reach out to others, and they'll reach back to you. To avoid instant overload, break your efforts down into bits that are manageable. To you. You might start out reading and responding to just one to three other posts per week, leaving substantive comments on each. You can find blogs to comment on in a number of ways:

- Surf the WordPress Reader; click on interesting posts, or peruse *offbeat topics.*
- Look at the blogrolls or visit commenters of bloggers you already enjoy.
- Become familiar with WordPress's Freshly Pressed features.
- Ask your readers to leave links to their favorite posts in your comments.

- Seek out like-minded online communities.
- Read everything: the news, posts, other blogs. You both contribute to those sites and enrich your vocabulary, refresh your perspective, and possibly even broaden your horizons.

Once you find a post that resonates with you, leave a real comment. Name what you enjoyed, ask a question, offer a different view, or share a related experience. Help move the conversation along.

The entire social-media experience is about building community, connections, and presence. Consistently. Depending on your level of commitment (read: time!), you might want to consider joining other social-media sites in order to have a ready avenue for connecting. These would include Facebook, Twitter, LinkedIn, and Pinterest, to name the most popular.[4]

You can set your posts to link automatically to these other social media sites. Just consider how many you want to manage actively. You decide: Do you want to put your content out there and see what happens or proactively build a following by commenting on others' posts? And, having commented, do you want to follow that blog?

The beauty of the blogosphere is that everyone is doing the same thing. Others will see and click on *your* interesting comment, which ends up bringing you more traffic and more readers. Like anything else worthwhile, it will take time to build your readership, just as it will take time to establish your unique voice and presence.

Connection with other bloggers thus provides

- a great source of support and encouragement for the act of blogging itself
- connection with those who have lived similar situations
- the notice of readers who challenge your beliefs, often sparking interesting exchanges
- opportunities to learn new and interesting things, including ideas for your own posts
- and, ultimately, readers

TIPS FOR NEW BLOGGERS SUMMARIZED

- Be yourself, sharing who you are with your authentic voice and point of view. The best posts tell a story, engage with, and connect with your intended audience.
- Write about what fuels you. If you want visitors, write strong, concise, helpful content.
- Include links, pictures, and videos with your posts. They provide interest, break up text, and bring in readers who look for different forms of expression.

- Write consistently and *at least* once a week.
- Engage your readers with questions, polls, and a blog that is unified in theme, look, and language.
- Your visitors are people. Take time to appreciate their attention, responding to them from an attitude of abundance and gratitude.
- Start small. Remember that it takes time to build an audience and find your groove. If even one person is reading what you have to say, you're off to a great start!
- Set your blogging goals, and find your niche. Does your blog reflect why you are here, help guide readers through, and encourage readers to respond and return?
- Above all, your motivation is your greatest resource. When you feel less than inspired, experiment and try a feature, a series, a roundup of links. Or simply turn to one of the many idea sites to reinvigorate your posts.
- And remember: your blog is a body of work. Treat it that way!

FINDING INSPIRATION

Presumably if you have chosen to start a blog, you have something you want to say. On the other hand, as any writer knows, there are days when the thread feels broken, the mojo is diminished, the juice just isn't flowing. Ways to reconnect with the writer within run the gamut from examining personal style to exploring myriad offerings online.

- For some, physical activity does the trick. Take a walk, clean a closet, do yoga.
- Writing sites abound, and some of them devote their posts to rounding up prompts and writing suggestions from other sites. These are worth subscribing to.
- The WordPress community provides daily and weekly prompts and challenges. In the course of responding to them, you are invited to connect with the larger community. A twofer, this gets you increased readership and exposure to other blogs while jogging your own writing.
- Blog posts aren't just about writing. Graphics, photos, artwork, polls, and video and music clips are all fair game. Your imagination is the limit. When time is short, you can just post a status, a one-line update, a favorite quotation, a burning question, or an image or gallery of images.
- Do a Creative Commons search for an image that will jumpstart an idea.
- Look at draft posts you never completed; read them all, creating a new post from that material. Or create a found poem from favorite lines from each of them.

- Run a writing challenge by posting a draft and asking your readers to finish it. They can publish the finished product on their own blogs and link to their submissions in your comments.
- Ask for help! Insert a poll at the bottom of your post, asking for feedback on how to improve or complete it.
- Write about why you cannot write. You might be amazed at what comes out!
- As a writing facilitator myself, I have hundreds of prompts on my computer. Perhaps you will create a document to which you add interesting observations, overheard snatches of conversation, unusual street signs, seeds of a story you want to develop. When your well is dry, you have your own resource at hand to quench your thirst.

FINAL WORDS

Pick and choose. In this way, you can stay true to your own purposes while reaching out and connecting in ways that enrich without draining your resources of time, energy, and interest. Be unafraid to experiment. Unlike life, you can always go back and redo a blog post! Above all, approach blogging with an open heart and a spirit of abundance. Your efforts will be returned manifold. As blogger Jon Morrow suggests, "Imagine a newsletter where all the issues are stored online, people can leave responses to your articles, and they can share your articles with their friends. Imagining it? Great. Now you understand blogging."[5]

APPENDIX I: FOUR WEEKS OF BLOGGING

1. *Define yourself*—There are questions every writer should ask before building a platform.[6]
2. *Set your goals.* Goals provide you a purpose and a finish line. A smart writer has long-term and short-term goals.
3. *Start a blog*—Starting a blog is easy with the help of Blogger's or WordPress's templates.
4. *Post on your blog*— Remember to use tags.
5. *Read a post, and comment on it*—Most importantly, link back to your own blog. Leave thought-provoking comments that will help you build connections.
6. *Add share buttons to your blog*—Even if you already use share buttons, you may find others you like better.
7. *Find a helpful article, and link to it*—Part of being social effectively is being helpful and not just in promoting yourself.
8. *Write a blog post, and include a call to action*—This is a great way to involve your reader.

9. *Post on your blog* — Remember, part of the drill is building routine!
10. *Make three new connections.*
11. *Add an e-mail feed to blog* — Your blog may already offer this, so be sure to use it, as it's important to building traffic and keeping readers engaged.
12. *Think about SEO* — Search-Engine Optimization makes it easier for people to find you on Google, Bing, Yahoo, and other search engines.
13. *Write another blog post.*
14. *Create an editorial calendar* — This tool is one of the most important for improving content on your blog.
15. *Sign up for social-media tools* — Many social-media superusers swear by Facebook, Twitter, and LinkedIn.
16. *Pitch a guest blog post* — Don't have any experience? That's fine. You can pitch relevant blogs anyway.
17. *Post again* — And this time add a poll as another way to get interactive.
18. *Check out one of the blogging communities* — Join in a conversation, and ask a question.
19. *Create a time-management plan* — Smart people realize that time is often more valuable than money.
20. *Contact an expert for an interview post* — This is nowhere near as intimidating as you might think.
21. *Create a new post based on a daily challenge.*
22. *Write a blog post, and link it to social networks* — What once was spread across two days is now done in one. Welcome to optimizing your time and efforts.
23. *Join another social-media site* — Whether it's Pinterest, Goodreads, RedRoom, or something else, keep the pedal to the metal on the social-media-hopping thing.
24. *Read a post, and comment on it* — Routines are good, especially when you're connecting with other like-minded bloggers.
25. *Make a task list* — Always think about your strategy in the bigger picture going forward.
26. *Check out one of the many writing challenges that abound on the Internet* — Become a regular participant in following prompts from one or two sites.
27. *Start reading and following other blogs outside your own area of interest for additional inspiration.*
28. *Spend a few minutes looking back at what you have learned and done with your new blog over the past four weeks* — Give yourself credit for stepping out there and creating something for yourself.

APPENDIX II

A big part of a blogger's day is networking and reading other bloggers' pages so you can link to them and talk about them. But a person looking for fresh blog content to read and link to will only find your pages if you put them in the places where they are looking in the first place.[7]

So here are six essential sites that will help you get your blog noticed if you're setting up a blog for the first time:

- *Google Webmaster Tools*—Webmaster Tools has some gems such as Web-diagnostic tools and visitor statistics. Being registered on Webmaster Tools gets you indexed on Google quicker and easier, and you can see at a glance if Google has a problem with any of your pages.
- *Del.icio.us*—Del.icio.us is becoming a search engine in its own right, and Yahoo is integrating Del.icio.us results into their regular search index. Bookmarking your links into Del.icio.us is therefore a fast track into Yahoo and from there into the other search engines.
- *MyBlogLog*—Owned by Yahoo, MBL is basically your own mini blogging network and is really good if you have multiple blogs, as it allows you to join them up on your MBL page so visitors can see the other blogs in your network.
- *Digg*—Every blogger should have a Digg account. For a start, if you're writing good blog content, it won't be long before your content reaches Digg. If that happens, you'll need a Digg account to respond to comments and to network with other users.
- *Stumbleupon*—Likewise, every blogger should have a Stumbleupon account. Ask blogging friends to stumble your posts and check the reviews often. Network with others in your niche, stumble often, and leave *lots* of comments. I find Stumbleupon to be a much better traffic generator than Digg, and the community is *much* nicer.
- *Twitter*—If you have collected a lot of followers on Twitter, setting up Twitterfeed can lead to an incredible amount of traffic being sent to your blog if the post title is enticing enough. But don't just use Twitter as a blog-post promoter; otherwise you'll find yourself being pretty unpopular *very* fast.

RESOURCES FOR GETTING STARTED

Robert Lee Brewer, "How to Build (or Improve) Your Platform in 30 Days," *My Name Is Not Bob*, http://robertleebrewer.blogspot.com/2012/05/how-to-build-or-improve-your-writer.html, May 8, 2012. This is a recapitulation of the original 2012 April Platform Challenge in 30 steps, most of which are relevant to starting a blog and are presented in abbreviated form in appendix I.

———, "Twenty-five Ways to Increase Blog Traffic," http://robertleebrewer.blogspot.com/2012/01/25-ways-to-increase-blog-traffic.html, January 24, 2012. A thorough list that puts everything in one place with helpful links.

Susannah Gardner and Shane Birley, *Blogging for Dummies*, 4th ed., (Hoboken, NJ: John Wiley and Sons: 2012).

Jane Freidman, "Get Started Guide: Blogging for Writers," http://janefriedman.com/2011/08/24/blogging-for-writers/, August 24, 2011. Includes nuts-and-bolts issues of blogging plus a downloadable PDF, "Blogging 101," which includes a linked list of some of the best blogging advice you'll find.

RESOURCES FOR STAYING INSPIRED

Robert Lee Brewer, "Best Blogs for Writers to Read in 2013," http://robertleebrewer.blogspot.com/2013/02/best-blogs-for-writers-to-read-in-2013.html, February 1, 2013. An extensive listing of resources to help start or improve your blog. It includes a list of many, many blogs for writers that is updated frequently with good learning content.

Kim Stiglitz, "Content Idea Secrets from a Content Marketing Team," http://www.verticalresponse.com/blog/content-idea-secrets-from-a-content-marketing-team/, March 22, 2013.

The Daily Post, http://dailypost.wordpress.com/.

Freshly Pressed, http://wordpress.com/fresh/.

Jane Friedman, http://janefriedman.com/. Always has superior content about social media, not just blogging, and often about the interactions between them.

NOTES

1. Robert Lee Brewer, "How to Build (or Improve) Your Writer Platform in 30 Days," *My Name Is Not Bob*, http://robertleebrewer.blogspot.com/2012/05/how-to-build-or-improve-your-writer.html, May 8, 2012.

2. See appendix I for detailed steps to follow in the first month of the creation of your new blog.

3. Tim Brookes, "Blogger vs. WordPress.com: A Complete Comparison," http://www.makeuseof.com/tag/blogger-vs-wordpress-comparision/, April 25, 2013.

4. For more sites specifically designed to increase your visibility, see Appendix II.

5. Jon Morrow, "Why You Shouldn't Create a Newsletter (And What to Do Instead)," http://boostblogtraffic.com/create-a-newsletter/, June 12, 2013.

6. This section is adapted from Robert Lee Brewer's April 2012 Platform Challenges. Robert Lee Brewer, "April Platform Challenge, Day 1," http://robertleebrewer.blogspot.com/2012/04/april-platform-challenge-day-1.html, April 1, 2012.

7. This section is an abbreviated adaptation of Mark O'Neill, "6 Essential Websites to Help You Get Your Blog Noticed," http://www.makeuseof.com/tag/six-essential-websites-to-help-you-get-your-blog-noticed/, April 2008.

SEVENTEEN

My Niche, My Way

B. Lynn Goodwin

Sometimes I feel sad that my parents never got to surf the Net. The Internet has opened up my world and given me numerous opportunities to reach out and help writers. I like calling myself "technically retired." It raises questions and gives me a chance to explain that retirement isn't what it used to be.

I feel more justified in calling myself a professional writer because I've worked under contract for Caregiver Village and for StudySync, which has stopped using freelancers, and Story Circle Network, which pays its instructors.[1] I've also marketed and taught an online workshop on journaling for caregivers, conducted through e-mail. I continue editing for clients who've found me online.

I sometimes still volunteer when I'm offered a nonpaying opportunity that could increase my business or exposure, but I always ask to be paid for my editing. As part of my promotion for *You Want Me to Do WHAT? Journaling for Caregivers*, I've given presentations about journaling for cancer patients and caregivers, the Santa Cruz Alzheimer's Association, and several senior centers and retirement homes without charge. Sometimes I sold a few books. I continue to write reviews and judge contests for Story Circle Network because I respect the organization. I blog for Inspire Me Today when I have time, and I continue to run Writer Advice, an e-zine that started as an e-mail newsletter fifteen years ago.[2] The "About Us" page tells readers that

> We have grown from an e-mailed research newsletter for writers into an e-zine that invites reader participation and celebrated our ten-year anniversary in October 2007. Our quality fiction, poetry, interviews, reviews, and articles reach readers around the globe.

155

The primary focus has always been author interviews, and editor B. Lynn Goodwin has had the privilege of corresponding with over ninety well-known and debut authors who have shared their experiences, insights, and inspiration with readers. Recent interviews are archived.

Today Writer Advice not only promotes authors through its interviews but also publishes both experienced and emerging writers, showcasing fresh ideas and high-quality writing. Click on *Guidelines* to learn more. We accept book reviews, prose, and poetry. Because reading onscreen is 25 percent harder than reading on paper, we prefer shorter pieces.[3]

Writer Advice always focuses on helping writers, whether we're interviewing an author, reviewing a book, editing a manuscript, or answering a question. We grew page-by-page and project-by-project as I developed ideas to meet the changing needs of writers. We now have both a Flash Prose (fiction and memoir) Contest and a Scintillating Starts Contest, in which I put myself in the role of an agent and explain to the writer why an opening might or might not interest me. I give creative-writing majors the opportunity to intern and get an inside look at how a small e-zine reaches out. I continue to be open to projects that enlighten and empower emerging writers.

I created my unique writing niche one day at a time, and the whole process began evolving after I left my tenured teaching job. I'd been a high school English and drama teacher and a freeway flyer commuting to several local community colleges to teach a class or direct a job. Six days after the end of the spring semester in 1995, though, I got a call from my mother. It shifted my life forever.

I knew something was radically wrong when she told me she'd traveled from the kitchen to the dining room and back without her hand ever leaving the refrigerator door. She'd had a stroke and was in the early stages of Alzheimer's. I became her caregiver and continued in that role for the next six years. To process this bewildering new commitment, I wrote in my journal almost every day. I also joined an online critique group so I could get some feedback on a young-adult novel I'd written years earlier. Okay, that was the official reason, but the truth was that I joined for companionship. Writing was a form of escape back then. I relished my time at the computer and the fictitious worlds I immersed myself in.

When I wasn't with my mother, I spent a lot of time exploring AOL. I found an ad for an editor for Haven's List, which was a newsletter giving research tips to writers. Three months after I took the job with Blue Shingles, which hosted the newsletter, the site disbanded. They let me keep their thirty-five-person mailing list. I was thrilled. I loved the empowerment. Online I felt encouraged.

Haven's List gave me a place to publish the author interviews I wanted to do. I didn't understand why no one was scooping up my young-adult manuscript, and I thought maybe published authors could give me tips that would explain the mystery.

This was before e-publishing, Facebook, Twitter, and other forms of social media. Web presences were just starting to emerge. With nowhere to turn, I hung out in AOL's chat rooms for writers. No one there knew I was a caregiver living in a strangely twisted world.

My surfing led me to the Other Side of Creativity (OSC) and the Electronic Writing Group (EWG). Both site owners welcomed my writing. I published articles in EWG and at OSC, and I hosted a weekly chatroom interview with an author every Sunday night, sponsored by OSC. My online presence grew as my mother's world was crumbled.

Sadly, I didn't feel like an author, even after the owner of a website called The Other Side of Creativity offered to publish two short books, *From an Author's POV: Tips on Writing* and *From an Author's POV: Tips on Marketing*, which I compiled from the interviews I was running in Haven's List. I compared answers to questions like, "How do you allow a character to take on a life of her own?" and "What advice do you give to people marketing their novels?" The advice is old now, but someday I might revise those books using current authors and contemporary answers.

I didn't feel like a writer because I was operating under the illusion that writers got paid. I thought there must be some value to sharing knowledge and insights with the writing community, but I didn't know yet about freelance jobs or asking for pay. Though I found plenty of information about writing online, I wasn't sure whom I could trust.

I followed another ad—a post, actually, on a message board—and started reviewing books for a website called Inscriptions. The editor, a competent woman who later took a job at the *New York Times*, gave me confidence when she published my reviews without corrections. So I used them as samples of my reviewing work when I read that Lifetime TV was seeking movie reviewers. They liked what they saw, and when they sent me a VCR tape to review I believed I'd entered the world of experts.

About that time, I also entered a contest at The Well, a subsidiary of Salon.com, and won an Honorable Mention for a piece about the day JFK died. They gave all winners a six-month free membership in their chat rooms, but my Apple IIE with its dial-up Internet connection could not access their chat rooms. I have no idea what opportunities slipped away because of that technical difficulty.

The joys of having my writing accepted were often overshadowed by changes in my mother's needs and requests. With no one to talk to, I turned to a Snoopy notebook my mother had given me and began doing the Daily Pages, which I'd found in Julia Cameron's wonderful book *The Artist's Way*.[4] I wasn't always sure how to write what I was feeling, since I couldn't label the confusion I felt around caregiving, so I copied passages I liked in the books I was reading. Sometimes I'd write about those passages, and soon I'd wallow, vent, spew, make discoveries, reevaluate my contributions, accept myself, and find hope. Not all on the same day of course. Writing begets writing.

As I wrote, I had no idea that those journals would inspire a book after my mother passed away. I was thinking about the insanity my mother's undiagnosed Alzheimer's caused one day when the phrase *journaling for caregivers* popped into my head. I knew from firsthand experience that all caregivers needed a place where they could talk without interruption, process their frustrations, analyze their thoughts, and assess their truths. Journaling was the tool that would allow that.

A writer is someone who writes, but I knew caregivers might protest. "I don't have anything to say," was a complaint I'd experienced first-hand. I solved that by writing a book that contained encouragement, simple instructions, and over two hundred sentence starts so that writers would never have to face a blank page again. "Finish my sentence start. Write another one, and you're journaling," I told them in the instructions. That was the beginning of my third book, *You Want Me to Do WHAT? Journaling for Caregivers*. This time I decided to find a real publishing company, since the Other Side of Creativity had folded, and I'd use my own website and my increasing knowledge about social media and guest blogging to help with promotion.

Haven's List had also gone through a transition with the help of a site called Novel Advice, which is also no longer in existence. Novel Advice's owner, Jeanne Marie Childs, took Haven's List into her expanding network and gave us a huge burst in subscribers. I asked for a list of all of them and added them to my mailing list after Novel Advice closed.

Once that happened, I published Writer Advice through AOL, cutting and pasting my interviews and tips into one of the web pages they provided for members. I then sent out notices to all the people on my mailing list. For six years I lived two lives. In real time I was a teacher who quit her job and became a caregiver for her mother. Online I was a writer shaping a unique path as I gave writers opportunities.

When I became frustrated by AOL's Web pages, I hired a webmaster who began placing our various sections, book reviews, contests and markets, website reviews, announcements, writing advice, and of course the interview on separate pages. He was my first paid employee, and his design was better than his ability to work with a nontechie like me. One night I searched Craigslist at midnight and found an ad for a webmaster who didn't suffer from ego issues. Paul Goulart and I have met face to face twice, but we've worked together for ten years.

Another advocate who took Writer Advice to a new level was Ron Shoop, a sales rep for Random House, whom I met when he networked with Project Second Chance, the Contra Costa Library's adult-literacy program, where I worked. He looked at my site and liked what I was doing, so he put me in touch with a number of Random House publicists.

I started reading and reviewing a better class of books, and many of the publicists I worked with were happy to arrange interviews for me. I continue to work with Random House publicists today. I also get interviews and books to review directly from authors with contact information on their websites. A couple of weeks ago, I asked Robert Dugoni, who spoke to the California Writers Club's Tri-Valley Branch, if I could interview him about his latest book, *The Conviction*.[5] He said yes, and his book arrived in the mail last week. Opportunities abound.

Last spring I spoke about journaling at the Story Circle Network conference in Austin. I sold a few of my books there and was able to take my transportation and room off my taxes. That wasn't the point though. The joy for me was in presenting a workshop that offered writers new ways to get inside their characters' heads. I loved the approval I got from the writers who attended.

I earned the same approval when I worked as a host at Caregiver Village. I wrote blog post after blog post about journaling, caregiving, and life after caregiving. People wrote back, learned to trust the writing process, and sometimes bought copies of my book from Amazon. I was proud to see journalers I'd worked with in my own online classes a couple of years earlier contribute their thoughts, and I was saddened when the mom of one passed away. Though I've never met this woman face to face, she was a friend. We'd developed an online relationship because of the experiences she'd shared in one of my journaling for caregivers classes online, and I loved seeing her reach out and take on new roles. For a while I got a respectable monthly honorarium from Caregiver Village, which reminded me I am a working writer. On the other hand, the connections with writers and caregivers offered me friendships I cannot put a value on.

My other paid writing job that year was with StudySync. I found that opportunity on Craigslist. While I was working for StudySync, I wrote critical-thinking and essay questions for passages suitable for students in grades seven through twelve. It took me back to my teaching days, allowed me to look at more books, gave me new ideas for characters and stories, and gave me an opportunity to open up young people's thoughts. I lost the job when they decided they did not need freelancers any more. I've seen firsthand that freelancing is filled with ups and downs. It's fine for a part of my life, but I wouldn't want to make my income that way.

At this moment I have editing clients, I run Writer Advice, and I'm reading the entries in Writer Advice's eight Flash Prose (fiction and memoir) Contest. I'm still a guest blogger, I contribute to Story Circle Network, SheWrites, and occasionally RedRoom. In the back of my mind, I've never lost sight of the fact that I'd like to publish my young-adult novel, *Talent*; I'm currently drafting a major revision. These days I use my journal to write about my first husband, whom I married a little over a year ago when I was sixty-two and he was sixty-seven. I hope those journal entries will lead me to a memoir that only I can tell.

I've built my writing career one writing opportunity at a time. Today I know that a writer is someone who writes and doesn't quit.

Writer Advice gives me a platform for my work. I've gone from being hesitant about both my work and my purpose to delighted in the fact that I'm creating my own unique path. In the process of promoting authors through interviews and book reviews and encouraging emerging authors through writing advice, editing, blogs, and articles, I've created a unique niche for myself.

I've learned to follow my heart without having to worry about earning an income. Instead I seek validation, and I have it every time someone thanks me for an interview, a review, or a contest opportunity. I get it every time someone publishes a piece of my writing.

I've also learned that writing groups don't work for every writer. I've learned to value my unique voice and journey rather than offer it up for judgment. I listen to the suggestions of others and measure it against my intentions. I experiment bravely, but I keep the older copies of my work, because writing is a process.

I'm happy to run Writer Advice in exchange for the opportunities it gives me, and I'm grateful that it's been in circulation for almost sixteen years. I'm willing to donate my time to judging contests. I'm delighted to say yes whenever almost anyone asks me to share an article, write a review, or speak. I take pride in being of service to writers. Whenever I falter, I remind myself that a writer is someone who writes. Whether I'm writing or editing professionally or venting in my journal, I know I fit into that category.

Writer Advice comes out quarterly now instead of monthly, but it is still online because I continue to organize and publicize it. I make enough money from contests and editing to pay my webmaster, cover my office supplies, and have a little left over for gas and an occasional conference. When I sent acknowledgments to each contributor to the current contest and asked how they learned about it, many said they found it through a Google search. I know next to nothing about search-engine optimized writing, so I have to assume the contest made it into the search because of my efforts to get the word out. I'm not an efficient computer guru—I'm a woman following her passion.

I like writing in retirement, and I enjoy saying I am partially funded by State Teacher's Retirement. I've considered applying for grants and using them to offer classes to those who cannot afford them, and maybe I will someday. Turning Writer Advice into a grant-funded nonprofit that offers classes online is an idea I've kept on the back burner for years. It sits right behind the young-adult novel I'm revising and the memoir about marriage at sixty-two that I'm brainstorming.

I hope I don't run out of retirement before I've finished all the projects I have underway. I've slowed down physically, and I respect the arthritis and fibromyalgia that require me to take breaks from typing.

I keep going because I love my online presence. I get lots of respect from readers, contest participants, writers I interview and review, and those who seek my editing advice. My PayPal account remains active.

All my life I've believed that a career was something you were paid for. Now that I'm technically retired, I no longer think that way. Writing is not about the money. It's about sharing ideas and digging for my truths. It's about finding a purpose and fulfilling it. For me it's about finding my niche as I help other writers. I'm building a career that gives me joy with almost every new opportunity.

I know it's wise to have a business plan, but frankly I prefer the wandering path my writing has taken. When I started Writer Advice, it was unique. Now the Internet is filled with writers' blogs and sites that celebrate the written word. Self-publishing and independent publishing have become a viable alternative to traditional publishing. Many of us are charting new territory in writing and publishing.

There's joy in writing about what matters to me, in helping others, in making contact with published writers, and in carving a path toward an unknown but promising destination.

NOTES

1. Caregiver Village's online presence is currently being redesigned as of this writing. StudySync is found online at http://www.studysync.com/ and Story Circle Network at http://www.storycircle.org/.

2. Inspire Me Today is found online at http://inspiremetoday.com/ and Writer Advice at http://www.writeradvice.com/.

3. B. Lynn Goodwin, "About Us," Writer Advice, http://www.writeradvice.com/about_us.html, n.d.

4. Julia Cameron, *The Artist's Way: A Spiritual Path to Higher Creativity* (New York: J. P. Tarcher/Putnam, 2002).

5. Robert Dugoni, *The Conviction: A Novel* (New York: Touchstone, 2012).

EIGHTEEN

Using Life Experience

Memoir Writing

Rita Keeley Brown

Memoir is but one window into your life. It is not the whole house or your entire life. It is about a particular period, situation, or event in your life. And, most important, it is a truthful account of what you experienced during that window of time.

This window I chose for my memoir, *Good Luck, Mrs. Brown . . .*, would describe a painful, stressful, and dangerous period in my life that I was not anxious to revisit. In this period my husband, after years of a happy family life with our six children, had a complete mental breakdown. His illness was very similar to that of John Nash in the book and movie *A Beautiful Mind*. The movie removed one of my biggest excuses for not writing our story—that being, how I would explain the illness. Very little has been written about the impact of mental illness on the family and loved ones of the person who is ill. They are the ones who must face it and deal with the sadness and perplexity of it every hour of every day. I began writing this memoir about four years after my husband was no longer part of our daily life. The thought of revisiting those painful years was not an especially welcome one.

My "inner critic" was having a field day with the prospect of writing about what happened. There were an endless number of considerations on my yes-buts and what-ifs list:

- What will our families, relatives, friends, and neighbors think if I write about all that?

- Will this complicate the children's lives? How will they feel toward me for writing it?
- Never having written anything longer than lesson plans, letters, or business memos, what makes me think I can write a book?
- Mental illness is a subject no one welcomes in this we-don't-talk-about-it world.
- Do I even want anyone to know about it?
- Could it actually be of help to anyone?
- I will have to relive it to write about it with any depth.
- It has to be accurate, and I'm terrible with dates and orders of events. There were so many.

I felt compelled to write our story whether I wanted to or not. The strongest compulsion came from a remark my oldest son made to me: "You know, Mom, when we were going through all that with Dad, if I had known other families had gone through that and came out O.K., it really would have meant a lot to me." His comment seriously changed my vision and catapulted me off to the store for a stack of legal pads and packs of pencils—"erasers and sharpener included."

WHERE TO START?

My next problem was what to do about my "fuzziness" with those dates and accurate order of events, especially when these are things you prefer to forget. The children were better with dates and sequences of events than I. They connected them with someone's birthday, their school basketball tournament, or some important event in their life. However, I had to get these things clear in my brain so I could write accurately with information in the right context and make the story flow smoothly. What do you do when you need to remember past dates, events, and so on? I dug out all of the documents, letters, receipts, appointment calendars, diaries, journals, photographs, and whatever else I could find to help create a time line. I opened Excel on my computer and built a time line of events ranging from when my husband and I first met, through our marriage, and on to the end of the situation. I set it up in increments of five-year periods and entered everything that happened in those periods in chronological order. This time line showed me clearly that the most difficult years occurred during a span of approximately ten years, from 1976 to 1986. I realized that this ten-year window would be my focus, and it gave me the confidence of knowing I could present things accurately. (It also made me aware that I am very definitely a visual learner.)

The children were very supportive and anxious to help in any way. This brought a huge decrease in my angst, but I was still unsure about my ability to put it all together in a memoir. My minor in college was English, so I knew how to write a decent sentence and was a pretty good storyteller, but this venture involved much more than that. Since I had recently retired, my financial status was wobbly. I couldn't afford to enroll in any comprehensive writing programs, but what worked for me was going to libraries and used bookstores for books, magazines, and anything I could find anywhere on "How to Write." I also took several affordable classes in college-extension programs. These classes were invaluable to me. Not only were the teachers and the material presented extremely helpful, but almost as valuable was the reaction and encouragement I received from classmates. All this took place over a period of many months. It was an intriguing search, and I am still doing all these things.

As you can see, some items were getting checked off my yes-buts and what-ifs list by now. Those biggies that won't even let you get started were now dwindling.

JUST DO IT! START WRITING—FACTS, ANECDOTES, SCENES . . .

In writing classes they tell you to beware of "your darlings"—those parts you write that really sound great to you but are not essential to the story—and be willing to get rid of them. I wasn't too sure what to think about that as yet. If they are great, why should you get rid of them?

I began by writing a three-page preface to set the stage for the story. I then followed that with a six-page introduction to explain what the story was about. Later on, I realized that the six-page introduction had really been for me, not the readers. It had given me clarification and shaped the story. It was that teacher in me that wanted to be sure the assignment was clearly understood and everyone was prepared for what was to come. Eventually I sent the teacher on sabbatical, edited the preface down to two pages, and cut everything else. It wasn't bad writing—it just delayed getting into the story. I did, however, save all those pages I cut, and they became very useful later on in giving talks about the book. I had "killed my first darling," but it took time and deliberation before I understood and could do it.

As I moved on writing the story I was still plagued by my remaining yes-buts and what-ifs and a few new ones. My inner critic was working overtime:

- What if people think you are a lousy writer?
- What if they think you were a rotten mother for keeping your children in that situation for so long?
- What if no one believes it because you never told anyone about what was going on? Did you ever think about that?

After a bombardment like that I admit I was a little shaken in my commitment. What astounds me is the way something would always happen in some totally unexpected way that would speak to my soul, saying, *Do not listen to that negative stuff!*

FINDING YOUR STYLE

What helped me get back to writing was to imagine myself sitting on a comfy couch telling the whole story to a trusted friend. This removed that paralyzing tension. I felt more relaxed mentally, and the story just poured out over the next few months. There were periods when I had to get away from it for a few days or even weeks. During that time away from it I discovered that my subconscious continued working on it, and when I went back to writing I could pick up right where I had left off.

Have you ever had recurring thoughts or happenings that were not at all what you had in mind but they just sort of hung out there, staring at you, not going away? What interesting turns your life can take when you finally give them your conscious attention. When you finally stare back at them, it becomes clear what path brought you to where you are, what doors have been opened to you, and what new paths are available.

As I completed the time line and became so vividly aware of that ten-year window of time, 1976 to 1986, I was still in a state of waffling that would have put the Pancake House out of business. In my mailbox later that day was another of those "Refinance-with-us" letters that proliferate in all homeowner's mailboxes. I usually tossed them in the trash, but one was from a company with whom I'd formerly had my mortgage. I heard that they were under investigation by the government for some kind of financial shenanigans. My curiosity said, *See what they have to say,* so I tossed the envelope on my desk instead of the trash. When I got around to open the envelope I discovered it was not a letter, it was a check! Years ago they had overcharged me on closing costs and now had to issue a refund. This came at a time when I had just quit working and welcomed any spare dollars from any source. It was a large check, and it was made out to me! I was ecstatic. When I looked closely at the amount of the check, I had to grab a chair for support. The amount written on the check was $1,976.86—1976.86, the same numbers as that ten-year period I was trying to write about. I just sat for a while, pondering this, then grinned, raised my eyes, and said, "Okay, I get the message. I'll write the book. No more waffling." I ask you, what are the chances of those numbers coming up in that way at that time?

WRITE ON!

I continued writing, and the chapters seemed to flow from one to the next. Well, that isn't quite true. There was one chapter I simply could not bring myself to write until the very last. It was about a particularly painful incident when my husband, in one of his psychotic episodes, injured our youngest son. I could not write about that until everything else had been written. It was the final missing piece and the toughest one to write. The chapters now went 1 to 13, then 15 to 21. After several long deep breaths, I began to write chapter 14. I imagined being in a dark theater, watching a movie of the incident. This helped give me some needed emotional distance. Of course, tears flowed, but I kept on going. When my youngest son read it, he said, "Yeah, Mom. I still remember all that really well. I remember everything that happened that night and afterward." I cautiously asked, "Would you want to write down what you remember?" He said, "Yeah. I can do that." And he did. When he gave it to me, I was mesmerized. It was such honest writing and gave a very personal picture of all that happened to him physically and emotionally. I asked him how he would feel about having what he wrote in the book for others to read. He said, "Sure. That'd be cool." It became the powerful finale of chapter 14.

When I finished writing all that I intended to cover, there before me was the rough draft of our story. Any early draft is never a finished product. This is just for you. It proves to you that you can do it. All the material is now out there to take a close look at and work with. The next draft exists after you have read it again and checked it for correct dates, spellings of names and places, and other information to be fact-checked and then have made all those corrections. The following drafts are for editing and improving your work. Did I mention that most of writing is rewriting?

ANY MISSING PIECES?

There were seven people—our six children and me—living in the same situation; however, the experience was not exactly the same for each of us, based on age, personality, position in the family, and relationship with the parents. I wanted to have my children contribute their thoughts, too, but some of them would not have been comfortable writing something to be published in a book. I devised a method that I thought might work well for them and would give insight into what they had experienced. I wanted their individual responses, not a group consensus. I came up with four questions and asked each of them to answer with whatever popped into their mind as they read it. I told them not to give any thought to sentence structure and the like, because that didn't matter in this case. I asked them to take an hour or so with no interruptions to write their responses. I asked that they return them within two weeks and gave a deadline date. (I know I always work better with a deadline.) These were the questions:

1. What emotions pop into your mind when you think about your childhood, and what things or events are associated with these?
2. What do you remember most of your father? Your mother?
3. What were the most significant things/times in your childhood and growing up?
4. If you could, what would you like to have changed about your childhood?

When they e-mailed their responses to me, I was amazed. These were such valuable insights but more of an after view of the story. These had to be in the book. I decided to put them in a separate chapter in the addenda. Trying to spread them throughout the book would have lessened the impact. I did not edit them; I wanted to publish them just as the children had expressed themselves. The only manipulating I did was to group all the responses to each question in order from oldest to youngest child. It showed how the experiences of each child were not quite the same. We all learned a great deal more about each other through this experience of writing, and, to my delight, two daughters also wrote wonderful vignettes about times significant to them that added so much to the book.

Now that the story has been written, what about a title? While I was writing I had used a working title. It seemed to hold the manuscript together for me, keeping me on track, but I wasn't sure it was the right title for publication. My working title was *The Tap Dance*. This symbolized what I'd had to do to keep peace, some degree of normalcy, and safety for the children and myself. Gene Kelly would have been jealous of all the steps I had to come up with to accomplish that. This was about keeping things stable until I could figure out what bigger steps I could take. That title didn't quite address the core of what the book was about. The children had mixed feelings about it. I said I wasn't sure about it either but that the only other idea I'd been able to come up with was *Good Luck, Mrs. Brown*. My oldest son said, "Mom! That's it! That's what they told you every time you tried to get help for Dad when he wouldn't come in voluntarily or you didn't have enough money for treatment even if you could get him there. That hits on what our story is about." He was right. And so the memoir became *Good Luck, Mrs. Brown* . . .

It is important to have a few other sets of eyes read through your final draft for feedback, preferably some of whom are familiar with writing. It is usually recommended that they be from outside your immediate family for more unbiased comments. You do not have to make any of the changes they suggest, but you are sure to be shown things that were unclear to the reader, typos you had read over many times but hadn't seen, ideas you had not thought of, and the kinds of reactions your work brings. I have found this process to be of great value. If you intend to publish your manuscript, after the reader feedback it is time to have the work edited professionally. But publishing is not a necessity; you may have written it just for your family or only for yourself, and that is admirable.

FORGET-ME-NOTS REGARDING MEMOIR

- A memoir is *your* perception of *your* experience, of your involvement in a particular situation in your life. It is not your sister's; it is not your father's or anyone else's. There will always be someone who will say, "That's not how I remember it." Their experience of it may have been different, but, for you, what you are writing is *your* experience of the situation. It is true and accurate to the best of your ability. It is hard not to worry about what others will say about what you have written, but many times people do not react at all in the way we expected they would. Telling truth with love and consideration is the key to writing your story. An honest account of what you experienced is what memoir is all about.
- Understanding memory is another critical element in memoir. Aristotle talked about two types of memory, so this is not a new revelation. He spoke of *simple memory* and *reminiscence*. Computer memory, another type of memory—is the exact preservation of whatever was input and saved. Our memory is more akin to reminiscence about what happened. We remember feelings, atmosphere, and most often a sense of what was said, though not necessarily the exact words spoken. Computer-type memory is of exact details— dates, order, and structure. Human-type memory recalls the impact on our senses, the emotions felt, the general details, and its lasting effect. Many people hesitate to write memoir because they say they cannot remember the exact words someone said. They know the who, what, where, why, when, and how of what happened, but exact details are not so clear, and the more time that has transpired since the actual occurrence or situation the less precise they are. Recall can be heightened through old photographs and other research materials but still are not likely to bring total recall. Imagination and logic come into play to help re-create as probable and accurate an account of the incident as anyone is able to do. This is a part of normal human memory that is understood and accepted because exact details can seldom be recalled in computer-like fashion. The most important and informative essentials of the story are what is being shared with the reader.
- There are legal and privacy considerations to be dealt with. Most publishers may require signed releases or permissions from living persons playing a major role in the story if you are using their real names. If the person is deceased, there is no problem. I opted to change my husband's name in the book rather than try to deal with

getting a signed release from him. We are divorced, and he has lived away from us for many years. The person he was before he became ill or even when he was in a period of remission would be pleased about the book, but there is no way of knowing how he would react on any particular day. If he were in one of his episodes, it could be a big problem. I also changed the children's names out of concern for their privacy. I wrote a statement at the end of the preface so readers were aware of this. This did not disturb the authenticity that a memoir must have, because all the facts and events were true as written.

- A memoir is not a documentary, and neither is it a biography or autobiography. You do not have to tell every single thing that happened during this window of time. You only need write what is pertinent to the story and only as much of that as you are comfortable with. The major situation should be described in as much depth as possible, as well as descriptions of the main characters and the impact of the situation on their lives. It is important to limit the number of characters to the principal people involved. Even though that young man who comes every week to cut the grass is absolutely adorable, do not include him if he is not essential to the story.

"WHAT'S IT ALL ABOUT, ALFIE?"

The sharing of stories broadens our outlook on life. People identify with and draw strength from reading about the struggles of others. Readers can try on the life of the characters in the story and see how they would have felt and reacted without having to suffer through the experience themselves. They become that protagonist, that main character, as they step into his shoes and walk through the difficulties he faces.

Story is in the soul of our humanity. Recent brain-imaging studies show that the areas of the brain that process our physical senses of sight, sound, taste, and touch are the same ones that are activated when reading a compelling story. We are there, in those shoes.

Writing memoir is a wonderful gift for the writer as well as the reader.

NINETEEN

Writing about the Body in Sickness and Health

Maxine Susman

HOW THE BODY GETS TO BE A POEM

My focus is poetry, but what I say easily applies to other types of writing.

Why write about the body? During the winter and spring of 1995–1996, my sister, a close friend, and another friend all had breast cancer. We were still in our forties. My sister and one friend had mastectomies and underwent months of touch-and-go, debilitating treatments. I had a scare of my own. The other friend, mother of my son's schoolmate, with two even younger children, died in early spring. The colleague I later showed my poems to—a wonderful poet and teacher—never told me she too had had breast cancer. She died of it a few years later. Writing was a way of understanding, enduring, sorrowing, venting, and staying aware of my own responses as witness.

I am the daughter of two doctors. I grew up aware of the attention they paid to their patients: watching over their health, noting conditions in need of care. This too feeds my interest in writing about the body. My father, a pragmatist with a sentimental streak, taught me to respect the body's abilities and its limitations. My mother, who loved poetry, taught me a sense of the body's shame and pleasures and their sometimes close connection.

You will find your own reasons. Our bodies with their glories and miseries shelter all our experiences, so when you write about the body you are also, of course, writing about the brain and the heart and the intricate, fluctuating relation among all the working parts. Since the body is always changing, the possibilities for writing about it are limitless.

HOW THE POEM GETS TO CHOOSE ITS BODY

Let's think not about "the body" but about your body, my body, the body of a loved one: the particular, individual person you are deciding to write about. We might agree that the aim is to become simultaneously intimate and objective—in other words, to observe in detail what the body is doing and to find words for how that looks, sounds, feels.

Think about what the body enjoys, because that yields much worth writing about: food, sex, warmth, nakedness, clothes, movement (what kinds?), calm, play, touch—and this list is only a start. For any of these, think where you can start a poem.

Think about what causes pain. Writing about injury, handicap, or sickness is a way to probe how you feel about it and the person involved; it's a way toward handling the sense of deprivation and powerlessness that sickness and loss of capacity bring. Especially with aging, it's a way to keep up resistance—think of Dylan Thomas's "Do Not Go Gentle into That Good Night" to hold out for at least putting into words what otherwise is not controllable.

Whose body is it—your own? That of a lover, spouse, parent, child, friend, total stranger? And when you write about this person, aren't you really writing in some way about the relationship between the two of you? Writing "cancer poems" about my sister, I am partly writing about her in relation to myself. The poems I wrote about my mother's long struggle with dementia were really about the two of us.

PROPS AND PROMPTS

I include here a few techniques and warm-up methods. The first five come from my experience teaching college classes and adult workshops, the fifth from my days outdoors.

Read Published Poems

People have been writing body poems for centuries, so you have a wealth to draw from: poems about the wonders of the body, its secrets, its ailments and embarrassments, and then poems about the inevitable, death. Graphic, comforting, erotic, gross, idealized—they reflect all the ways poets experience their own bodies or perceive the experience of others.

The website poets.org offers a long, eclectic list (with links) of poems about the body and other lists of poems on love and sex, aging, and related themes.[1] Some personal favorites of mine are

- Lucille Clifton writing affectionately to her uterus, her period, her hips
- Sylvia Plath writing about slicing her thumb and other suicidal pleasures
- Chaucer's Wife of Bath enthusing about the pleasures of the bed
- John Donne, likewise
- Carl Phillips's speculations on the fusion of physical pleasure and pain
- Adrienne Rich on "Diving into the Wreck"
- Mark Doty on dreaming his dead partner's embrace
- William Carlos Williams dancing naked in front of his mirror
- and Mary Oliver holding a grasshopper in her palm.

Take Notes

Do this on paper, on computer, even just in your head, so that you can keep track of what an experience feels like while it is happening or soon after, still fresh in your mind.

Pay attention to how the body registers sensations and stimuli. In detail. Don't rely on memory—we can remember being in pain, but it is mercifully hard to recall exactly how it feels. Can you, for example, honestly remember what childbirth feels like? From minute to minute? What's true of pain goes likewise for pleasure, and that's why good writing about sex is rarer than good sex.

Think Viscerally

How close can you get to reproducing the body's experience in words? To finding words for physical sensations?

How graphic do you want to be? How direct? You can choose to be explicit in what you write, or you can rely on inference and the power of suggestion. Both work, for different kinds of poems. Sharon Olds insists on describing her old father's naked body. If that seems too voyeuristic, think centuries back to Robert Herrick's wonderful little striptease, Julia. Details add immeasurably to a poem's honesty. What does a dying person look and sound like? What about a newborn baby?

Think Metaphorically

I'm often struck by how many things, human-made and nature-made, connect to the body in some symbolic way. When you think in metaphor, one thing puts you in mind of something very different: love is a rose.

Their meanings in some strange way converge. For example, when Yeats talks about "the foul rag-and-bone shop of the heart," we may not know rationally, but we still know intuitively, what he means.[2]

Shakespeare writes,

> That time of year thou mayst in me behold
> When yellow leaves, or none, or few, do hang
> Upon those boughs which shake against the cold[3]

comparing his aging body to a tree facing the winter of life. Metaphor.

If I ask workshop participants to think of a metaphor, a farfetched alter-ego word for some organ or limb—the heart, for example—they come up with *mud pie, canoe, jellyfish, cabbage, clock.* That's when the fun begins: putting the metaphor to work in a poem, making the comparison between a part of the body and the leap to something else—finding the surprise of a new thought or feeling.

Think of Muscle Tone

Remember that old chestnut, "The heart is a muscle: the more you use it, the stronger it gets." Apply this to a poem, where tone conveys the speaker's mood, attitude, frame of mind—the emotional surroundings of the poem—and this brings both the poet's and reader's empathy, and sympathy, into play.

Writing about the body can be difficult, since often we write when something goes wrong with it. Consider what you're feeling as you write and what you may be asking your reader to feel. Consider this again when you go back and revise. When a poem tries to force its reader to feel a certain way (sad, optimistic, inspired) it usually backfires on the poet by making the reader feel manipulated.

Let the poem's tone speak through an action, as when Jane Kenyon describes the fatigue from chemotherapy, "not to be able to button a button."[4] Or the exuberant page after page of Walt Whitman's praise of men's and women's bodies in "I Sing the Body Electric." Or through understatement, the way Elizabeth Bishop tells how the child barely hears her aunt's moan through the dentist's door.

Take a Walk

Put your own body in motion. The physicality of movement, the kinetic sensation—being aware of your body moving in space and taking in sights, sounds, smells—can focus your energies and give you a noncerebral pathway into writing.

SUMMING UP

My best piece of advice for writing in retirement: Nothing in, nothing out—do things that stimulate, engross, and please you, and somehow they will feed your writing. My equally best piece of advice for writing is to keep writing. Maybe you'll write every day; maybe you'll write in your head every day; maybe you'll think about writing every day until finally you do it. Musicians make music, artists make art, poets make poems, and chops come with practice. You will be writing about the same things people always write about. But the words can only be yours.

NOTE

This chapter is intended as a companion piece to this volume's next chapter, "Writing about Heritage."

1. Visit poets.org online at http://poets.org/.
2. From "The Circus Animals' Desertion" by William Butler Yeats.
3. From William Shakespeare's Sonnet 73.
4. From "The Sick Wife" by Jane Kenyon.

TWENTY

Writing about Heritage

Maxine Susman

HERITAGE AND ITS CONFUSIONS

I just returned from visiting my daughter and her newborn son. Most of the grandparents I know, now that I have recently joined that clan, travel a distance to see their grandchildren—to a different part of the country, even to a different country altogether. To meet my grandson I flew to Tuscany, a reverse migration for our family, since my grandparents and great-grandparents left the shtetls of Poland/Lithuania/Belorussia for the promise of America. Now my daughter is finding a different kind of promise. She married an Italian, whom she met in New York City, whose family has lived in the medieval hill towns near Florence for centuries.

My son traveled cross-country several times with his band, in every state of the lower forty-eight except Kansas. He returned to live under his father's roof through grad school and is four years into a loving relationship with an African American woman from a nearby town.

My children's father was a lapsed Christian of mixed German-WASP background. His old-fashioned grandmother's second husband was a much younger Italian Catholic. In my mid-fifties I divorced, remarried a Jewish doctor with a heritage much closer to my own. I muse about how migrating in his twenties from Minnesota to New York City was as far as traveling from one country to another.

What did it take to decide, say, to leave a shtetl in Minsk and head for a distant port, journey in steerage across the ocean, walk down a gangplank onto Ellis Island or Montreal? What if this happened when you were small? Who would you miss most, what would you find to replace what you left behind, what would most intrigue you? What were the conflicts and complications?

Whatever your background, you can think of your own questions to substitute for these. *What was it like?*

COMPASS POINTS: CURIOSITY AND OBSERVATION

Center on two compass points. The two are intertwined, recursive, and can get you into trouble—emotional, psychic trouble—which is just what you need for writing a dive-beneath-the-surface poem. Sometimes you start with one, sometimes the other. The more curious you are, the more your powers of observation are on the lookout for information; and vice versa—the more you observe, the more your curiosity grows about the information you're observing and absorbing.

You can, of course, write a poem that simply pays homage to the past, but you can also *complicate* the past, which will come closer to telling the truth about it. That requires even more curiosity and observation.

If I may use myself for an example, my first poetry collection is about my father's life as a young doctor during the Great Depression of the 1930s, when he lived and worked in Gogama, a remote settlement in the Canadian bush. I started with observation: looking through his old album of snapshots, combing through notes from conversations with him years earlier when he was still alive, recalling stories I remembered from my childhood.

> I walk the flat grid of prefabs and trailers
> that bake in record-setting heat,
> looking for traces of Dad's old photos
> cornered in my mind, their black and white
> blurred by hot swirls of dust . . . [1]

These fed and teased and fed my curiosity, which centered on his personal world, his personal experiences, and for that I had to call on a third quality: imagination. Despite what had sounded like adventure tales when I was little, years later he told me those had been the loneliest years of his life. I wanted to know why, to understand living in a two-room cabin in a cold, dirt-poor French-Canadian and Cree community, practicing basic medicine hundreds of miles from a hospital and far from his big Jewish family. What was that like? I could no longer ask him; I had to imagine it. I read and did background research, but mostly I was on my own.

> Patients crowd the vestibule,
> Spill onto the porch,
> mothers with babies,
> men from Poupore's Mill . . .

> He works alone in the one-room office,
> shelves of stoppers, starters, cod liver oil,
> giant jars of colored aspirin . . .[2]

Curiosity may start as external, but as you question what you know and don't know about your heritage, about history and the lives of people you're connected to through descent and family ties, the curiosity becomes internalized, and you start to ask other questions: How do I feel about this? What would I have done?

In my case, I'm curious about how my maternal grandfather came to New York alone in the early twentieth century as a very young man—what took my paternal grandparents to Canada instead. Beyond the factual questions, What were they thinking and feeling as they started to assimilate and, later during the war, when letters from family in Europe stopped coming? The questions start to be internal ones.

Just as curiosity encompasses both external and internal questions, so observation looks both ways to the external and internal. To begin with the external, when you start to write about a world you stem from, what are its details—what did it look like? Sound like? Taste, smell, *feel* like? What can you observe about it, and what else can you find out?

Don't be hesitant to read and do research, online or otherwise, to supplement information you already have. I wrote a poem about my mother eating cinnamon buns while cramming for medical exams. Did that happen? I know she studied hard, I know there was a bakery on her corner, I know she loved cinnamon buns. . . .

There are also the internal observations we all have that let us imagine the effect of what we observe. If you're writing about a traditional family meal, who's there, who sits next to whom, what mood are people in, who does the talking and who is reserved—why might that be? Conjure up more details. What foods are you eating? What dishes are you eating from? If you are writing about your grandmother, what is she wearing? Does she sit with the family, or is she busy serving?

In other words, trace your inner, emotional observations as well as the factual ones. Is this an occasion for rejoicing or sorrow, for optimism or regret? You may well find that your emotional observations are not so easy to sort out. A family tradition, a family meal or heirloom may send you mixed messages that take you beyond nostalgia. They can enrich the emotional life of your poem.

YOUR TOOLBOX

I offer these suggestions for finding ideas and details to use in your writing.

Memories

Use not just yours but memories of people in your life you can call upon to verify, witness, corroborate, supplement—or even contradict your own. Poke around for clarity—even if the more you probe the more incomplete or even unsettling the memory becomes. Be honest; don't go overboard with the sentimental stuff. "Cut the schmaltz," as my father would say (or might have said, or maybe it was my mother, or maybe I just made it up because, after all, it's a plausible thing to say and, to paraphrase Julia Child, you're alone in the kitchen).

Stories

Pull out the family stories—the ones you can believe and the ones too good or bad or farfetched to be true. Which are the stories that justify someone's behavior or that become the myth surrounding that person? Then there are the close cousins of family stories: family secrets, well worth your curiosity and observation.

It is perfectly fine to simply make up a story (remember, you're alone in the kitchen) if it could happen in the world of your poem *as if* it actually occurred. Anecdotes are retellings of events, and every retelling is an act of interpretation, as is every poem. I wrote a poem about my mother spending Yom Kippur in a lab class; it didn't actually happen, but it could have, and it speaks to a split between her past and present life that I imagine she would have felt.

Artifacts

A souvenir, keepsake, heirloom can lead you to a poem. When I give a workshop on Jewish Heritage, I spread out a collection of things: an awl from my grandfather's toolbox, a Shabbas spice box, a wax figurine of a Bar Mitzvah boy, another of an old-world peddler. When people see and touch and pass around these objects, they recall anecdotes, mementos, loved ones of their own.

Photos

They are visual records of our lives and of those who preceded us, of places lived in or traveled to or from, of what they considered worth documenting. I have an old dress box full of extended-family portraits taken in the old country some time in the late nineteenth century—sepia-tinged children dressed up in smocks and sailor suits, handsome matrons and family men in high collars and long sleeves. I don't even know who they are, but they have come down to me, and I am somehow connected to them. Does any of this sound familiar to you?

I wonder how storing our photos online and in clouds will change their nature, rendering pictorial records more ordinary and, oddly, more remote. Will it shift how we recall our visual memories, think about them, write about them? I am thinking of my father's album.

Published Poems

The more you read, the more ideas will come to you for your own work. Li-Young Li evokes a whole history of his parents and siblings in a short poem about a family meal. Lucille Clifton writes about visiting a plantation and honoring the unmarked graves of her African American foremothers. Gary Snyder writes about showing his little boy how to make an ax handle to teach him about heritage. Enid Dame uses Midrash, the tradition of retelling/reinventing stories from Torah, to imagine the Jewish women she descends from. Victoria Redel links her life to her mother's through old pocketbooks she collects. Edna St. Vincent Millay describes an heirloom brooch left by her mother as a link to her New England ancestors.

Other examples abound of poets who draw from of memory, story, artifacts, and photographs to trace their heritage in their poems.

ZOOM IN, ZOOM OUT

Allow yourself the full range of responses you may have, even if they are troubling or contradictory. Your poem may veer toward a positive feeling of pride, say, or gratitude or inspiration drawn from the values and experiences embedded in your family past. Or it might want to delve into a more complicated and ambivalent feeling, say of being trapped by the past, or embarrassed, even irked, by what seems like an outgrown template you don't fit into any longer.

In either case, follow your poem, and see where it takes you. If nothing comes to mind, just free-associate, and take notes—start writing, keep writing. Then you can go back and sift through whatever has shown up on your paper or screen, for flashes and moments that can form the beginnings of your poem.

A last piece of advice: When the words first start to flow, don't have an idea fixed in your mind of where you will end up. A good poem about heritage is both recovery and discovery.

NOTES

I hope you'll read this chapter together with chapter 19, "Writing about the Body in Sickness and Health." Both draw from my career as a college professor, from my experiences giving poetry-writing workshops and teaching adult education, and from my own writing as well.

1. "Sighting" from Maxine Susman, *Gogama* (Kennebunk, ME: Sheltering Pines Press, 2006).

2. "Dispensary" from Susman, *Gogama*.

TWENTY-ONE

Writing for Literary Magazines after Retirement

Barbara Kussow

When I retired from my full-time job at a state agency in 2002, I had no intention of being idle. I wanted to go back to work part-time when I found something suitable and to have more time with my three young grandchildren and my elderly mother who was then living with us. I was also determined—though perhaps less vocal about it—to spend more time writing and to initiate a serious, sustained effort to publish some of my poetry and short stories.

In doing research to find suitable venues for my own writing, I noticed that there were few magazines that paid attention to older creative writers. This discovery planted a small seed.

What if I were to start a literary magazine devoted to the writings of people over age fifty? I did some research on starting a literary magazine, much of which was not encouraging. In a *Poets and Writers* article, Dennis Held had this to say: "First, one word of advice: Don't. No, I mean it. Of all the myriad ways you could squander your time, starting a literary magazine is—or editing an existing one—is the worst."[1] An online wikiHow article mentioned a quotation attributed to poet E. E. Cummings to the effect that running a literary magazine is like trying to push your head through a straw.[2]

I formed some general ideas about what I wanted such a magazine to be like. I wanted fresh perspectives that challenge patronizing, sentimental, and stereotypical attitudes toward aging. I wanted thoughtful pieces that reflect the rich inner life of people over age fifty, but, overall, I

wanted it to be upbeat. Above all, I wanted material that was well written.

By all means, I wanted it to be online. I was fortunate in technology,
for I have a son who works with computers. He agreed to be my webmaster. Submissions would be made via e-mail but also via paper by old-
fashioned snail mail. However, the magazine would be distributed in
print—a copy for each contributor and subscriptions or single copies
available for purchase.

An appropriate title was a big decision. I considered serious-sounding
titles, like *Reflections* or *Encore*, but, then, thought about *Still Crazy*—as in
Paul Simon's song, "Still Crazy after All These Years." I liked it, not
because I wanted to publish only wild and crazy things, but because it
evoked the creativity and rich inner life that exists in all of us even as we
age.

I published the first issue in January 2008. I designed the cover (which
seems amateurish now) with a lavender background and the title centered in large red letters edged in yellow, using Microsoft WordArt.
Those were the colors that have stayed predominant in covers to the
present. Why did I choose them? I admit to being influenced by the
opening lines of the poem "Warning" by Jenny Joseph:

> When I am an old woman I shall wear purple
> With a red hat which doesn't go, and doesn't suit me.

Going on six years later, I view *Still Crazy* as something between a
hobby and a very small business. When planning the magazine, I was
concerned that writers might not want to contribute to a publication that
identified them as "over fifty." I need not have worried. The submissions
rolled in. Once, when the magazine was mentioned in *Poets and Writers*, I
was deluged with so many submissions that I had to suspend them for a
while.[3]

I feel that I have been able to publish many talented writers and pieces
that might not have been published otherwise. The writers represent virtually all areas of the United States and other countries as well—China,
England, and Canada. I have been amazed and gratified by the quality of
the submissions I receive.

So this has been my journey. I have been immersed in over-fifty writing for the past dozen or so years both as a writer myself and as an editor
and publisher of other writers. What have I learned from this editor-
writer combo that might be of value to people who want to write after
retirement? I have distilled some information into six subject areas that I
hope will be useful.

TYPES OF OVER-FIFTY WRITERS

What types of over-fifty writers have been published in *Still Crazy*? I came up with the following categories:

- *College or university English teachers*—Creative writing is part and parcel of their identity and enhances their reputation and their professional standing.
- *Freelance writers*—These are people who earn all or part of their living writing nonfiction. Sometimes, though, they have a side calling for creative writing. They submit poetry or short stories to the magazine.
- *Writers who have "day jobs" or professions but have the urge to do creative writing on the side*—These include attorneys, doctors, psychologists, and elementary and secondary teachers. Some of these people have published books or articles in professional journals. Example: a doctor who had published medical books submitted a short story to the magazine.
- *Retirees*—Often they are people who now have the time to pursue long-dormant interests. They might gather late-life courage and hone their writing skills through writing groups or creative-writing classes.

Writers run the gamut from very experienced to relatively inexperienced.

THEMES IN OVER-FIFTY WRITING

Were sociologists to sift through the pieces in *Still Crazy*, they might come up with a pretty good snapshot of the joys, sorrows, hopes, and fears of people over fifty.

Many of the themes are universal to literature—but, of course, with the special twists of the age group. Take, for instance, romantic relationships. Here are two very different views of the contentment of "old love" from the pages of *Still Crazy*. Both offer vivid images.[4]

In Autumn
J. J. McKenna

all that April racket's gone—
begetting, begotten, born—
the dawn a madcap swarm
of cries from birds that warn
the others: this space is mine.
But our love is another kind

of thing that visits, welcomed, this
special time of year. The mistress
of our souls, it speaks, "Share
with me your garden, the care
you take to grow the perfect rose
like love that blossoms in repose."
In September a couple come to love,
but softly, with nothing left to prove.

Every Saturday Night
Ray Greenblatt

Every Saturday night
my wife and I tromp and glomp
around the living room
our shadows clinging doggedly;
makes no difference if it's
atonal Prokofiev
silly creaky waltz or
last week's heavy metal,
we dance the same pace—
do the same weaves and dips
break or spin here or there—
we did years ago
which fits us perfectly.

Other themes in *Still Crazy* include grief and loss, adjustment to aging, memoirs, retirement, seniors as heroes, veterans' stories, special interests or hobbies, and writing and creativity. Topical themes are found in short stories portraying men who become unemployed after age fifty and an essay about an older couple taking on parenting responsibilities by adopting an infant.

In short, older writers have a wealth of experience they can mine for writing topics.

I would offer some special advice in the following areas: writing about grief and loss and incorporating humor into your writing. Polarities, you might say. First, take care when writing about grief, separation, and loss. Done well, this type of writing can be cathartic for writers and their readers. In the past several years well-known writers have written popular books about grieving loved ones. Examples are *A Widow's Story* by Joyce Carol Oates, which is about the author's grieving her husband of many years, publisher and editor Raymond Smith. And *The Long Goodbye* is Meghan O'Rourke's examination of her mother's prolonged illness and death.[5]

In an online discussion between Oates and O'Rourke, "Why We Write about Grief," O'Rourke says that "memoirs and movies about loss . . . create a public space where we can talk safely about grief."[6]

Honesty, directness, eloquence, and arresting imagery are characteristic of these two authors. For less-talented mortals (myself included), this type of writing is difficult to do effectively and perhaps harder to get published. Rejection from editors may also seem more personal.

Of course people can experience traumas at any age, but many older writers have experienced sadness and loss because of their longevity. They have seen loved ones die or become disabled, and they feel the aging decline in themselves. It is natural to write about these themes. *Still Crazy*, perhaps because of its focus on over-fifty writers, receives many of these submissions. Sometimes they don't get published because of the writing and sometimes because including too many of these pieces would make the magazine too grim. That said, I do not disregard the darker aspects of aging; I just do not want to overemphasize them. I have the feeling that that is the case even for magazines that do not focus on this age group.

Here is one of my favorite poems on loss that *did* get published in *Still Crazy*:[7]

A Quieting
Michael Harty

Every day she spoke of the wind,
always the wind, constant as her presence,
molding every tree to point
a steady northeast, scouring paint
from the south wall, decorating
barbed wire with tumbleweeds,
mesquite with candy wrappers and rags.

Familiar as a bedtime book:
the chinks never sealed,
dust mopping twice a day, still the skids
on powdery linoleum, still the jokes
about grit in the sandwiches.

Every day, until the day
you walked through a house full of silence,
stepped out a screen door, leaned
into a wind that wasn't there,
staggered, almost fell.

At the other end of the spectrum is humor. In writing as in life, humor can be a great asset. Few writers are humorists, but I think it is possible to learn the art of slipping in sly or subtle touches of humor. To get some tips on humor writing, writers might turn to the Internet. When I Googled "using humor in writing," I found several good articles.

Here is a *Still Crazy* poem that takes a wry, self-deprecating look at what it means to have a collection of one's poems on the shelf of the local public library[8] :

Local Branch

Richard Luftig

Having your book of poems appear
at the local library branch
is much like being named
Pork Queen in the festival parade.
Like in football when you forward pass
and two of the three possibilities
are bad, the reasons why
your book shows up on the shelf
might be considered suspect.
"He's not selling well
and the least we can do
is help out." Or
"He's not that great,
but still and all, he's ours.
Besides, he might draw
a little more traffic
to the 800's stack.
That can't be all bad."
Anyway, it's patrons' comments
that count the most, the consistent
clucking of tongues collected
by the librarian like overdue fines—
"Go figure. And all this time
I thought he was a regular guy."

PROFICIENCY IN THE TECHNOLOGY NEEDED TO PREPARE AND SUBMIT DOCUMENTS ONLINE

- Know how to use a word-processing program to prepare your document in a form commonly accepted by magazines.
- Have an understanding of the file formats associated with word-processing programs.
- *Format* refers to the way a computer stores data. Some of the common formats are .doc (Microsoft Office Word), .rtf (rich-document format), .docx (Microsoft Office Word, 1997), and .txt (text file). Magazines usually stipulate the types of formats they will accept in their submissions guidelines.

- Many magazines accept submissions via e-mail. Some will require that a submission be in the text of the e-mail itself. In that case, the writer needs to know how to cut and paste from the word processor into the e-mail. Other magazines will accept submissions as attachments to an e-mail. In this case, the author needs to understand how to attach the file from the word processor.
- The latest technology for submissions is the use of electronic submission managers. This means understanding how to upload a file. *Still Crazy* began by accepting submissions both by snail mail (postal mail) and via e-mail attachment. In its third year, we changed to a submission manager (developed by the webmaster). Although most people use the submission manager successfully, a small percentage of people have problems. Most of the problems, though, are due to people uploading files in unacceptable formats. (They have not read the magazine's guidelines.) Submission managers are wonderful organizational tools for editors. They keep track of submissions, maintain bio information, generate statistics, and send automatic messages (accept, decline, and, in the case of *Still Crazy*, problem with file). Submission managers also allow the author to withdraw their submissions if they wish.

LEARNING ABOUT A MAGAZINE
BEFORE YOU SEND YOUR SUBMISSIONS

Common advice from editors to writers is to read the magazine before making a submission. Many magazines have selected material available on the website. You may find poems and either excerpts from stories and essays or, sometimes, the full text. It is true that reading the magazine does not always help you decide whether your writing will fit, but it is still a good idea.

Reading submission guidelines is very important. Guidelines can usually be found on the magazine's website. As indicated previously, they will likely tell you about acceptable formats or other instructions for electronic submissions. They will no doubt give length restrictions. (It is a pet peeve of this particular editor to receive materials that exceed the length given in the guidelines.) Often the editors will give a general idea about the themes or types of writing they do or do not want.

REVISION

Truman Capote said that "Good writing is rewriting." In other words, revision *is* writing. It is an integral part of the writing process. I revise my own writing constantly.

Revision may come as a request from an editor, in which case it is sometimes difficult to figure out what the editor has in mind. The best revision, I believe, is self-initiated. Writers know what they have in mind. The trick is to be able to look at one's writing dispassionately. Another famous author, William Faulkner, said, "In writing, you must kill all your darlings." In other words, remove the phrases, description, etc., that might have sounded wonderful to you at first but do not really accomplish what you wish to accomplish.

On a more mundane level, your word processor can be immensely helpful in revision. Cut and paste, delete and insert, find and replace, and other features can make revision much more efficient.

REJECTION AND ENCOURAGEMENT

Rejection hurts. There's no getting around it.

I have been on the receiving end and the giving end. Both are hard. When a piece of my writing is rejected, I nurse my disappointment for a couple of days and then try to put it behind me. I decide whether the piece might benefit from revision. If so, I start thinking about changes I might make. If not, I look for another magazine to which I can submit. Two of my short stories found homes this year after a few rejections.

Remember, rejection is not necessarily a judgment on the quality of your writing. It may be that the piece was well-written but not quite what the magazine needed.

Magazines receive many, many submissions but have limited space. (*Still Crazy* is published biannually. Each issue includes a dozen or so poems, two to four short stories, and three to five essays.)

Subjectivity is also a factor; editors differ in tastes.

We've all heard about well-known writers whose work got turned down numerous times before they got published. George Orwell's *Animal Farm*, Anne Frank's *The Diary of a Young Girl*, Stephen King's *Carrie*, and Margaret Mitchell's *Gone with the Wind* are just a few of many examples of books that have been initially turned down for publication.[9] If you're feeling particularly stung by rejection, surf the Web. A slew of sites list famous authors who received rejections, some of which came with rather nasty putdowns.

More often than not, though, editors do not offer comments. It simply takes too much time.

If you receive criticism, consider it carefully, but don't be crushed by it.

On the other hand, be sure not to diminish any encouragement, recognition, or positive feedback you get. I think the instructor who encouraged me to write in an undergraduate course in short-story writing was instrumental in my finally having the courage to become serious about writing. Heck, I even remember a short essay I wrote that was chosen to appear in a high school English-class publication.

CONCLUSION

My after-retirement writing has not made me rich or famous, but I can say that it has given me a great deal of satisfaction. To use a psychological term, it's been self-actualizing. As editor and publisher of *Still Crazy*, I am pleased that I have been able to publish other older writers. It is enriching and rewarding for me.

To all people who want to write after retirement, I say persevere. If you were an experienced writer before retirement, you may want to consider different themes or topics to pursue now. If you are changing genres, there will most certainly be a learning curve. To new writers, I say learn all you can about writing in your genre. I leave you with that timeless quote from George Eliot (Mary Ann Evans): "You're never too old to be what you might have been."

NOTES

1. Dennis Held, "So You Want to Start a Literary Magazine? Seven Steps to Lit-Mag Mania," *Poets and Writers* (January/February 1999): 70–75.
2. wikiHow (to do anything), "How to Start a Non Profit Literary Magazine," http://www.wikihow.com/Start-a-Non-Profit-Literary-Magazine (accessed August 13, 2013).
3. "Literary MagNet," *Poets and Writers* (May/June 2010): 19, http://www.pw.org/content/literary_magnet_45.
4. J. J. McKenna, "In Autumn," *Still Crazy* (July 2011): 12; and Ray Greenblatt, "Every Saturday Night," *Still Crazy* (July 2011): 12.
5. Joyce Carol Oates, *A Widow's Story: A Memoir* (New York: Ecco, 2011); and Meghan O'Rourke, *The Long Goodbye* (New York: Riverhead Books, 2011).
6. Joyce Carol Oates and Meghan O'Rourke, "Why We Write about Grief," *New York Times*, February 26, 2011, http://www.nytimes.com/2011/02/27/weekinreview/27grief.html.
7. Michael Harty, "A Quieting," *Still Crazy* (July 2011): 17.
8. Richard Luftig, "Local Branch," *Still Crazy* (July 2010): 3.
9. George Orwell, *Animal Farm: A Fairy Story* (London: Secker and Walburg, 1945); Anne Frank, *The Diary of a Young Girl* (Netherlands: Contact Publishing, 1947); Stephen King, *Carrie: A Novel of a Girl with a Frightening Power* (Garden City, New York: Doubleday, 1974); and Margaret Mitchell, *Gone with the Wind* (New York: Macmillen Publishers, 1936).

Part IV

Publication and Marketing

TWENTY-TWO

How to Become a Successful Romance Writer in Retirement

Lori Leger

March 4, 2014, marked my two-year anniversary as a full time writer, and it has been an absolute joy. After years of designing road-construction plans with an office full of civil engineers and other technicians, I retired.

First and foremost, no one is born knowing how to write, so educate yourself. There are hundreds of books out there on writing—pick a few. With e-readers, it's so simple to download books right away. If you're like me and need a physical book to fill with tabs and sticky notes, they're available at your local bookstore.

Online workshops are fabulous ways to take advantage of the knowledge of successful authors and are priced reasonably. Local writers' groups contain a plethora of information, so if you aren't a member of one, think about joining. Then write, write, and write some more! It is the best way to master the craft.

I went to my first Romance Writers of America conference. All I had were my manuscripts, a handful of rejection letters, and a dream to write books that people want to read.

One of hundreds of articles I scoured for suggestions offered the best advice. It urged me to act like a serious writer, regardless of whether I had already been published or not. I suggest you do the same.

That will entail securing

- business cards to hand out to everyone you meet
- promotional items such as bookmarks, pens, postcards, and so on (this is optional but a huge step in the right direction for marketing purposes)

- a blog
- and a website.

While the first two items represent the physical aspect of marketing, the last two would establish what every author needs in this digitally electronic age of ours—an online presence with a great personality.

This list may have terrified another person, but with fifteen years of technical training in computer drafting and the use of programs such as Word, Excel, and Adobe, I wasn't a complete novice. I should mention the real motivation for overcoming any lingering technophobia: my rapidly advancing age.

The first step is to develop a platform and a brand. I'm from southwest Louisiana, deep in the heart of Cajun country. I based my series of books on characters who shared the same French and Acadian ancestry as mine. Some do, anyway.

I wanted my writing personality to encompass three specific things:

1. the French Acadian/Cajun culture
2. the fleur-de-lis, which is a symbol of my Christian French heritage
3. and a catchy brand line, in my case, "Contemporary Romance with a Cajun Flair."

My first stop was the Vistaprint website, where I downloaded my own business-card design, something I came up with using Microsoft Publisher, and ordered one thousand business cards. That turned out to be the easy part.

When it came to choosing a host for my own website, I again turned to Vistaprint, since I was already somewhat familiar with their operating procedure. At that time, I had zero experience with designing websites, so even the slightest familiarity was a comfort. I started with a basic package with five pages and paid for it monthly until I realized, quite some time later, it was more affordable to pay by the year. I know professionals who charge five to six hundred dollars a pop to design websites, so the money I saved by doing it myself was well worth the week I put into it.

There are companies that offer free websites, with very basic designs and little in the choice of modifications, but I preferred to pay extra to get what I wanted, along with my own dot-com domain. I modified the website's page headers to match my business-card design by using the same colors, text style, and tagline.

After doing some comparison shopping, I found the following prices to be typical for most sites, within a few dollars.

I started with five pages.

- *Home Page*—A short personal bio with a description of the type of books people could expect to see from me. I included a picture of myself, a snapshot that I eventually replaced with a professional

Basic Package	Standard Package	Premium Package
$4.99/month	$14.99/month	$24.99/month
Use drag and drop tools	Basic Package, plus:	Standard Package, plus:
Edit professional designs	Custom Web address	Search-engine optimizer
Unlimited pages	Show up on search listings	Create a Facebook page
Mobile-optimized Website	Includes a shopping cart	

portrait. I also included contact information, such as website URL, blog site URL, e-mail address, and P.O. box mailing address.

- *Books*—I included the titles of all my manuscripts, both completed, and works in progress, along with a synopsis of each.
- *Inspiration*—Physical descriptions of each manuscript's hero, the challenge he faces, and the name and picture of an actor I used as my inspiration. (Example: My inspiration for Sam Langley is actor, Ed Harris. I show a picture of Ed Harris, followed with an excerpt from my book *Some Day Somebody*, in which Sam has an interesting interaction with Carrie, the heroine.) This page is divided into two sections, one with the headline "Beef from the Bayou State," which includes all the male characters that hail from Louisiana. The second section is headed "Prime Texas Beef," with similar inspirations, synopses, and book excerpts for a few of the Texas-based heroes.
- *Lagniappe* (French for *extra*)—This page is dedicated to fun facts and photos, such as a list of Cajun French surnames used in my books and their pronunciations, local artists, and facts about the state of Louisiana. It also includes photos of a manuscript signed by a country singer at a concert I attended and a subsequent article about said singer and the book I named after one of his songs. That turned out to be excellent publicity for both of us.
- *Sign-In*—A form provided for all website visitors to leave their names and e-mail addresses.

Later on I added a few more pages.

- *Cajun Eats*—Since I'm quite accomplished in the kitchen, I love sharing my years of experience as a good Cajun cook. I include tips on seasonings, recipes, variations, and color snapshots of the finished products that are sure to make anyone's mouth water.
- *Events*—A list of upcoming events, such as contests, conferences, workshops (and, later, book signings) I attended or plan to attend. I also include brief write-ups of past events, along with snapshots.

- *What's New*—Changes in series names, logos added, book covers, etc.
- *Songs*—Songs or poems I've written for specific uses in books or otherwise.

None of this is set in stone. You should update your website at least once a year to keep up with changes and trends. Vistaprint, as well as other sites (such as Intuit.com, Webs.com, Web.com, Wix.com, gybo.com, Weebly.com, just to name a few), have extremely easy site-builder tools, complete with toolbars to enable you to add, edit, and format text and images and insert links, widgets, maps, pay buttons, and social-media buttons. They also have update tabs in case you decide you want to change your design or page order, your page colors, or your layout. With a little time and effort, anyone can design a basic website. If you get stuck, simply click on the universal sign for help—the question mark (?). I can't vouch for any other website hosts, but I've always been able to contact Vistaprint personnel with technical issues easily enough.

So you've got your pages in order and formatted the way you want. All you have to do is preview them and then hit the *publish* button. As simple as that, your website is up and running.

Now what? Two words, people. *Social media*. If you don't have a Facebook account, open one. If you already have a personal account, start up a fan page. Facebook is the easiest way I know to build your fan base. Are you working on a manuscript? Post a paragraph or two to build interest in the book long before you publish. Do whatever you can to drum up interest in your work, whether you are planning to self- or traditionally publish. Are you looking for a name for your new book or series? Post about it—or, better yet, ask for suggestions. You would be surprised how many great ideas I get from readers and FB friends. Facebook is the bomb, but it is only the beginning.

Twitter is huge right now, and just like Facebook it is free, so take advantage of it. Start up an account, and get tweeting! I can admit that though I know the basics of tweeting, I have not mastered it, by any means. Before I had the chance to delve too deeply into the world of tweets and retweets, a friend had already talked me into opening a Pinterest account.

Honestly there are so many ways to network out there, it boggles the mind. The bonus is that you can connect them all together in one easy step by incorporating Share, Facebook, and Twitter buttons on all your sites and pages. With one or two clicks of a button, whatever you post on Pinterest will show up on Facebook, as well as Twitter, or vice versa.

It is all so overwhelming that I almost forgot Digg, Reddit, Goodreads, and LinkedIn, all excellent ways to get your name out there and network with other people who have the same interests, both personal and professional. The most amazing thing about social media is that by the time you read this chapter there will probably be a couple of new social-media interfaces climbing their way to the top of the heap. It is a good example of the digital age we live in. Just like with computers, by the time you master one, it becomes obsolete and you have to start with an entirely new one.

You would think with all of those sites I mentioned that would be the end of it, wouldn't you? If you did, you would be dead wrong. I have barely touched on the biggest online presence of them all . . . blogging! The reason I left it for last is that I am so awful at it—not so much at my actual blog entries but at the frequency, or infrequency, of said entries. Blogging isn't nearly as time consuming as Facebook. Maybe it's just me, but I get terribly distracted on FB with all of the friend requests, notifications, likes, dislikes, and adorable pictures of babies, bunnies, and, occasionally, hunky man candy. Blogging isn't nearly as much fun, and it's seriously more work, in my opinion.

I admire those members of my ACAngel blog group who find the time to faithfully post once a month. I nearly always miss my turn. I'm also a member of the Beach Read Author blog group with several other authors. We take turns posting once a week. I'm truly respectful of anyone who can find the time to blog once a week. To those of you who manage to contribute more than once a week—or, horror of horrors, every single day—I bow down to thee! I only wish I were as dedicated in my own blogging ritual.

I have professional blogs. Two of them, actually. At the time I started my website, Vistaprint didn't have the capability to add an actual linked blog to the site. Now they do, of course, but by the time they got around to it, I had already established one through Wordpress.com. Here are just a few sites that offer free blogging:

- Wordpress.com
- Blog.com
- Blogspot.com
- Blogger.com
- Thoughts.com
- Freeblogit.com
- LiveJournal.com
- Blogs4Me.com
- SimpleSite.com

Honestly, I started out at a steady pace with my blog. For the most part, I had managed to keep up with current events, new manuscripts, proposed book covers, conferences attended, and latest character inspirations. It was only after I decided to self-publish, and did—three full-length novels (averaging 90,000 words each) in a period of six months, that I turned into a blog slacker.

When I first began, I had my blog's and website's headers match the design of my business cards. It seemed important at the time, but I've since revamped them. The only thing they have in common now is my name and brand somewhere on the header.

Just as with the Vistaprint website, WordPress has different packages, ranging from free to less than $8 per month to a high-price package for business purposes. These prices should not be used as quotes but as approximate guidelines, and comparable to prices of most of the sites I've mentioned above.

Let's go into some details of the options listed above.

- *Themes*—All of the blog host sites that I've mentioned offer dozens of themed blogs to go along with the feel you're trying to attain. They come in all designs, from floral and butterflies to high tech and art deco. The number of themes you have to choose from depends on the package, just as with the website. The free package comes with a limited number of themes, still in the dozens, though, and that is nothing to sneeze at. Some themes repeat among the different blog sites, while some are exclusive, with host organizations who obtain their own designers.
- *Blog address*—With most free blog sites, you will have to share your blog address with the name of the organization.
  - Cajunflair.Wordpress.com
  - Cajunflair.blogspot.com
  - Cajunflair.LiveJournal.com, etc.
- *Site name*—If you choose a paid-option plan, your blog address could omit the host site's name. Of course if you want three different blogs featuring entirely different subjects, it would serve your purpose to come up with uniquely suitable names.

Basic ($0/life)	Premium ($99/year)	Business ($299/year)
Free blog	Free blog	Free blog
WordPress.com	.com, .net, .org, or .me address	.com, .net, .org, or .me address
Basic customization	Advanced customization	Advanced customization
No premium themes	No premium themes	50+ premium themes
No video storage	Store dozens of videos	Store unlimited videos
3 GB of space	13 GB of space	Unlimited space
Community support	Direct e-mail support	Unlimited space

- LoriLeger.com
- GenerallySpeaking.com
- LoriCajunWriter.com
- PoliticsAside.com

As far as the customization goes, the basic packages generally include a dozen or so fonts, with capabilities for text styles such as bold and italic, size, and coloring. The paid packages will offer hundreds of fonts to choose from with a bigger selection of colors and headline formatting.

Let's discuss space. The above example offers three gigabytes, thirteen gigabytes, and unlimited gigabytes. Do you need a blog with video-storage capabilities? I guess that depends. Do you have book trailers you've made? Do you have videos of conferences you've attended and met your favorite author? How about traveling? Have you been to any inspirational places lately? If the answer is yes, you may want to spend a little each month to have the capability to store several dozen videos. Obviously videos will eat up a lot of space, so if you decide you want to add them to your blog you'll probably want to purchase an upgrade. I am so far from being a computer guru, it's ridiculous, so I can't tell you how many videos and picture files you can store in twenty-five gigabytes of space as opposed to thirteen. A lot more? I recommend starting with the free one, as I did, and if you run out of space, then upgrade.

Last on the list for blog options is the type of support you get.

- *Community support*—FAQ (frequently asked questions) sections and forums where you can send in a question and wait for a reply from someone who's had the same problem.
- *E-mail*—E-mail specific questions to members of the support team and wait for a response.
- *Live chat*—The best and coolest option, of course. Click on a button, a window pops open, usually with a blinking cursor, asking for your name. After you type it in along with the question or problem you have and hit *send*, someone will respond immediately with a solution or an answer.

Okay, so you've published your own website, as well as a blog. You're out there, on the World Wide Web, floating around in space, just one of millions of https and wwws in the world. In conclusion, once you have taken the time to set up your website and your blog, along with the social-media sites, such as Facebook, Twitter, Goodreads, Pinterest, and LinkedIn, you can sit back and spend all day writing.

Not so fast.

Now that these sites are established, you have to maintain them. Set a schedule for yourself if you must, but it's good to check them once a day, at the very least, to keep things from piling up. The problem is that once you've checked in with Facebook, accepted friend requests, replied to messages, made your own posts regarding your works in progress, checked and answered your e-mail, tweeted, updated your website and blog and Pinterest account and Digg, Reddit, LinkedIn, and anything else you've signed up for, half your day is gone. Social media and networking, if not taken in moderate doses, can rapidly eat up large chunks of writing or crafting time.

As a result, I've come up with my own ritual for putting my writing first and foremost by establishing a word count for the day. I silence my smartphone so that the ding of notifications doesn't tempt me to check my Facebook and Twitter pages. I open Microsoft Word on my notebook, ignoring everything but my work in progress. At the halfway mark, I figure I've earned the right to check e-mail and the website for messages. By noon I'm checking all the social-media sites and then close them up immediately afterward. Once I know that I have met my word count for the day, I can afford to play a little more. It's vitally important to reign yourself in, especially if you're like me, easily prone to frequent side trips and flights of fancy. It's funny, but I didn't suffer from Attention Deficit Disorder until Facebook, Pinterest, and Twitter came along.

I'm nearing the end of my wealth of personal experience on this subject, but there is one more item I'd like to throw out there. For all you novice writers looking for experience that counts, please don't disregard entering the occasional contest. My first was an annual writing contest for unpublished authors at a romance-review website. It was both terrifying and thrilling to put my writing out there for others to see for the very first time. There is something about seeing your own work displayed on a contest website; it makes you feel like an author. It seems more real in the light of day.

The downside is that the slightest typo seems ten times bigger. As a result, you become more diligent when it comes to self-editing.

The upside is that when readers and judges like what they see, they let you know. There is nothing quite like getting your first positive review from people who simply read for the pure enjoyment of reading. After all, writers are the same as anyone else who creates something they believe in. The occasional word of encouragement and a compliment every now and then can motivate us all to greater achievements.

I hope I've given you all a few tips you can use to get yourselves out there in the digital world, now that you've retired from the working world. Just because you don't have to drive in to the office every day doesn't mean you can't have a new fulfilling career. Trust me when I tell you again that I knew nothing about websites and blogs when I started doing this. Experience has been a great instructor and given me the confidence to connect with thousands of people I would never have otherwise.

My first two years of professional writing have brought in an income in the lower five figures—not too bad as a supplemental income for a beginning writer. With more books published this year, I hope to surpass that. I have also found more ways to add to that income by hiring out my formatting services. Since I occasionally need my own editor, I was thrilled when she came up with a brilliant idea to trade services . . . she edits my books, and I format her e-books so she can self-publish them.

Most writers have their own networks. Please don't miss out on the benefits of joining in on that camaraderie simply because you've never done it before. You can do this with patience and perseverance, just as I did.

On the plus side, writing is doable from the comfort of your home. If you're one of those special people who can be perfectly productive in your jammies, without a trace of makeup on your face, it is an ideal situation. If, like me, you function even better curled up on the couch with a laptop and a cup of hot coffee or tea, it is absolute paradise.

TWENTY-THREE

It Won't Work If You
Can't Work with Editors

Katie McKy

Editors are busy people. They're a mother of quintuplets times a Fortune 100 CEO times an emergency-room doctor. If they were jugglers, they'd be juggling a bellowing hippo, a flaming and fleeing falcon, a greasy bowling ball, and two tussling wolverines. If you don't get to the point, your pursuit of publication will be pointless, because they won't listen to you.

This applies to both book and magazine editors. Book editors have offices with piles of submissions. If they only accept electronic submissions, their hard drives have cyber piles. Magazine editors have deadlines stacked like planes over O'Hare during a blizzard.

If you want an editor's door, charm isn't the key. Keeping it curt, compact, and clean is key.

WORKING WITH MAGAZINE EDITORS

For example, if you wanted to pitch (a query) a magazine article to an editor, here's how to do it the right way and the wrong way:

> I would like to profile Bill Wallace of Eagle River. Wallace reclaims the components of local homes about to be bulldozed, from floorboards to fireplace mantels. Wallace, who is passionate about reclamation, has agreed to be interviewed, as have two of his customers, who've integrated Wallace's recycled finds into their home renovations. His photogenic salesroom is a massive, century-old former-lumberyard horse

barn. I can submit up to two thousand words of copy within two weeks.

Note what's missing in this query: There's no mention of articles I've written. There are no clips or samples of my writing attached. When I first started writing, I read books where the authors asserted that editors need to see clips because clips are the definitive proof that you can write. I've found otherwise. Editors are too busy to open and read clips. The quick, essential proof that you can write is in the well-crafted, professional query, and variants of this query work because:

- I led with the lede, which is the who, what, and where of the story.
- By describing the barn, I've shown that this story lends itself to photographs, which are essential components of most magazine articles.
- I've delineated how I'll flesh out the article by interviewing two customers.
- I've promised to be prompt and to produce whatever word count is needed.

I know this query works because I used versions of it to sell this story to four magazines, although I've changed the name and location of the architectural antique dealer. Now here's a version of what wouldn't work:

> I'm a longtime fan of your magazine, and now I want to be a regular writer. In recent issues, you have had articles about going green in your home, such as the one about using bamboo for flooring because it's a rapidly growing grass rather than a slow-growing tree, and then there's that one about replacing older appliances with Energy Star appliances and incandescent bulbs with CFLs. Well if you want a verdantly green story, I have one for you. It's as green as Augusta the week of the Masters! It's as green as the Hulk eating split-pea soup! I'd like to write an article called "Red Is the New Green," and it would be about Bill "Red" Wallace of Eagle River, WI. "Red" goes into homes that are about to be bulldozed, and he removes everything of value. These "treasures" might be old wood floors, which are scuffed but still fine, and fine, old light fixtures. Sometimes he even finds stained-glass windows and fireplace mantels! "Red" takes his "treasures" back to his big barn, which serves as his shop. I wrote "treasures" because Red's shop is called "Red's Architectural Treasures." In the story, I could write about all the wonderful things "Red" has found. Your readers would love to read about "Red's" finds, I'm sure! Plus, "Red" is quite a character!"

This wouldn't work because:

- It's too long.

- "I'm a regular reader of your magazine, and now I want to be a regular writer." In your first sentence, you present yourself as a sycophantic minion rather than a serious writer.
- "In recent issues, you have had articles . . ." You might think that you're showing you've done your homework by delineating what was in recent issues, but the editor edited those issues. He/she read every word of every article in every issue. The writer's intent is to show how the piece will synchronize with the magazine's themes, but that's not the writer's job. That's the editor's job. Here's every writer's job: *Get to it.*
- "It's as green as Augusta the week of the Masters! It's as green as the Hulk eating split-pea soup!" This is not the place to play with words. That comes later. For now, get to it. Also, exclamation points merely punctuate your unprofessionalism.
- "I'd like to write an article called 'Red is the new Green,' and it would be about Bill 'Red' Wallace of Eagle River, WI. 'Red' goes into homes that are about to be bulldozed, and he removes everything of value." The writer has buried the lede in the middle of the query. Lead with the lede.
- "Your readers would love to read about 'Red's' finds, I'm sure!" The only certainty is that you're not landing this gig.

Terse, tight communication isn't just required at the beginning of an article. It's also required upon submission of the manuscript. What follows are first a professional and then a poor example of submitting the article about the architectural antique dealer. First the good:

"As Green as It Gets," the article about Bill Wilson, the architectural recycler, is attached. It's for the spring issue of *Midwest Homes*. Thanks for the work!"

This works because:

- In just three sentences, it conveys the essentials, which are the name of the article, a summary, the issue, the magazine (many editors work on multiple magazines.), and your gratitude.

My e-mail's subject heading would read: "As Green as It Gets, *Midwest Homes* Spring issue, McKy."

That way the editor doesn't even have to open the e-mail until needed.

Now here's how to brand and tattoo yourself as a bumbler and time vacuum:

Well, it's done, and what a journey it was! I had so much fun chatting with Bill and following him around. I spent so much more time with him than I had expected, but it was time well spent, as you'll soon see. Bill is a character times two and maybe three! I'm sorry it took a little longer than I expected, and I expect submitting a day late isn't that big a deal, but once I got into it, I realized that there was so much more to this story than I'd first assumed, which is why I'm over the word count by just a couple hundred, but don't worry, because I won't be expecting you to pay me any more for the extra words. If you must tuck and nip, I'd like for you to consult me first, as I've grown rather attached to the story. Anyway, *enjoy!*

Why doesn't it work?

- "Well, it's done, and what a journey it was! I had so much fun chatting with Bill and following him around. I spent so much more time with him than I had expected, but it was time well spent, as you'll soon see." Forty-three words that convey nothing essential. Just get to it!
- "I expect submitting a day late isn't that big a deal." Wrong. Submitting late is a big, bad deal, just as submitting early is a big, very good deal. If you want to write full-time, you have be timely. At the very worst, submit on time. To be at your best, submit days, weeks, or even months early. You won't be able to hear it, but trust me: Your editor will sigh when you submit early.
- "I'm over the word count by just a couple hundred." You should have written, as it would be more honest, "I don't care enough about your time to protect it, so I've exceeded the word count."
- "If you must tuck and nip, I'd like for you to consult me first, as I've grown rather attached to the story." A magazine editor doesn't have time to consult you.

WORKING WITH BOOK EDITORS

The rules for communicating with book editors are the same. Here's the full list:

1. Get to it.

This comes with one caveat, which is that books don't sell themselves. Magazines have established readerships. Just as billions of folks are familiar with rice and buy it, tens of thousands or even hundreds of thousands of people are familiar with established magazines and buy them, where they might encounter your article. However, a book is like a newly developed grain, and no one is going to buy that grain unless its creator publicizes it. Even famous people have to do this, which is why, when a movie is released, its stars appear on talk shows. What follows is a cover letter for a book I've sold:

I submit the YA picture book *Wildchilds*. It is the story of a con man who steals babies and puts them into cages with wild animals. He fabricates these feral children to stock his Benevolent Home for Wild

Children. He then asserts that he rescued these children from jungles and mountains. Pretending to be their protector, rich women give him money to maintain the home. It is a love story, the story of the love these wild children have for each other and what they'll endure to be free.

If accepted for publication, I'll develop a blog dedicated to *Wildchilds*, cold call schools and libraries to arrange visits, maintain a Facebook page, develop a presence at Goodreads.com, do signings at bookstores, do radio and TV interviews, and attend any events you'd like me to attend. Promoting this book will be my full-time job. In the past, my promoting, in part, has produced worldwide book sales exceeding eight hundred thousand for my picture book, *Pumpkin Town*."

Why did it help sell this book?

- "I submit the YA picture book *Wildchilds*." Again, I led with the lede.
- "It is the story of a con man who steals babies and puts them into cages with wild animals . . . It is a love story, the story of the love these wild children have for each other and what they'll endure to be free." There's the plot in five sentences, which might be one or two too many, as I had one editor say, "If you can't make your point in three or four sentences, you don't have a point."
- The second paragraph of the cover letter is key, since it delineates how I'll promote the book. It doesn't convey an expectation that someone else will promote the book or that I can be casual about promoting. It makes clear that I'll do what will need to be done.

Now here's an example of a cover letter that covers much more than needed and reveals how unprepared the author is to live an author's life:

Have you ever thought about the editors who passed on J. K. Rowling and wondered what you might have done if you'd been in their shoes? Well, now you know, since the very manuscript in your hands is sure to be a best seller. You're probably wondering what it's all about, and I'll get to that, but first, I think you should know how this story came to be. You see, ever since I was a little girl, people have told me that I should be a writer. Well, life got in the way. The kids came, and they were three handfuls, but when the nest started emptying, I got busy and wrote this soon-to-be-best-selling book. Just so you know, my kids have read it, and they love it, and my husband too! One of my girls even gave it to a friend to read!!! You're probably dying to know what it's about, and I'll tell you now. It's about a kid who's walking through the woods, and he sees an owl with a wand in its claws, which is a good thing, because the bullies at his school are vampires! What makes it even worse is that his teachers turn into werewolves at night. Like I said, my kids *love* it, and you will too, so put some coffee on, 'cause you'll likely to stay awake all night just to read it! When it reaches the best-selling list, I'll do my best to be where you need me to be, but I can't promise you anything. Still, we won't have to worry about that, because this book will sell itself! You'll see; trust me.

This cover letter is wrong in so many ways. It's unlikely any editor would ever finish it, but it's instructive in that it's so persistently, doggedly erring. For example:

- "Have you ever thought about the editors who passed on J. K. Rowling and wondered what you might have done if you'd been in their shoes?" Rather than suggest that you'll be the next Rowling, you might as well wear a sandwich board with *rank* on the front and *amateur* on the back as you parade back and forth in front of the publisher. In the history of publishing, J. K. Rowling is a commercial anomaly. Comparing yourself to her crosses naïveté and delusion.
- "You're probably wondering what it's all about, and I'll get to that . . ." No, don't talk about getting to it. Just get to it.
- "Just so you know, my kids have read it, and they love it, and my husband too!" This means less than nothing to an editor. Even if the author's kids didn't love her story, they love her enough to say they love it.
- "You're probably dying to know what it's about, and I'll tell you now." The only thing that's died is the editor's interest in the story.
- "It's about a kid who's walking through the woods, and he sees an owl with a wand in its claws, which is a good thing, because the bullies at his school are vampires! What makes it even worse is that his teachers turn into werewolves at night." It's a mishmash of best sellers. Now, all stories borrow from preceding stories, but this isn't borrowing a cup of sugar from a neighbor. It's akin to breaking and entering and emptying their kitchen, which includes ripping the cupboards from the walls and wheeling the major appliances out on a dolly.
- "When it reaches the best-selling list, I'll do my best to be where you need me to be, but I can't promise you anything." All spurs and no horse, so this cowgirl isn't going anywhere.
- "Still, we won't have to worry about that, because this book will sell itself! You'll see; trust me." Unless your name is Stephen King or one of his few peers in commercial success, no book sells itself, and the only thing the author will see is her manuscript returned to her and stamped *Thanks, but no thanks*.

THE EDITOR'S ROLE

If you manage to sell a book manuscript, then you enter into a relationship with an editor. Perhaps the most famous editor of books was Maxwell Perkins, who worked with Ernest Hemingway, F. Scott Fitzgerald, and Thomas Wolfe. Perkins contended with Hemingway's bawdy prose, Fitzgerald's alcoholism, and Wolfe's circumlocution. Perkins was steadfast and loyal to his authors but also fierce in contesting his authors for the sake of their stories. For example, Perkins fought with Wolfe for two years to reduce the word count of his novel *Of Time and the River*.[1] Wolfe loved every word he'd written, and this is an uncommon Achilles' heel. The editor must have commercial considerations. If a book doesn't sell, a publishing house can fall. So when working with your editor, it's crucial to love the story more than the words that comprise the story. It needs to be a commercially viable story if you're to be a professional writer.

It's not your editor's job to be your buddy, but your editor can be your best friend if what you want most is to write well. Let your spouse be your buddy, or your college chums. Let your editor see what you can't see, for we aren't limited by our perspective, which is the culmination of our particular experiences. Your editor will give you a different look at your story, and if they see something you don't see, that's gold that was buried just beneath your feet. Treasure that perspective.

THE WRITER'S ROLE

Finally, be willing to do the work of revision. The writer's road isn't easy, just as the road of any artist isn't easy. Even Michelangelo spent years of his life simply quarrying stone. For some statues he had to go the quarry and extract the marble, but the toil didn't end there. He had to secure the marble's return to his studio. One time he had to actually construct a road to get it there. Yes, Michelangelo, perhaps the greatest artist of all time, spent months of his life building a road to procure his art supplies. He was willing to do it because it had to be done.

Michelangelo's travails didn't end there. Two times, after investing years in procuring the marble and transporting it, those commissions were cancelled. The good news is that editors won't do this to you. Work with them, and they'll stick with you too, as long as you don't fritter their time with superfluous syllables. That's because editors need copy, so get busy, and get to it.

FIRST CONTACT

You can't have those compact, clear conversations with editors unless you initiate contact. To begin, look locally. Every town and region has local publications. You'll often see stacks of those publications at the doors of grocery stores. The publication might have a website. If so, its URL or the editor's e-mail tend to be on the first or second page. Most importantly, many smaller publications are perpetually looking for writers. Once you've proven your reliability with editors, if you want more work, let them know. If they don't have more work, they might know other editors who want to work with you. Start small and locally, building competence and confidence, and write for larger and larger publications. There are also myriad websites dedicated to freelancing, and they can be found by simply Googling *freelance writing*. Publications like *Writer's Market* and *Writer's Digest* also list everything from current jobs to editors' e-mails to writing contests.

Writer's Market is also useful for aspiring authors, as it lists the major and minor publishing houses and their submission procedures, as well as agents and their contact info. Most genres also have their dedicated organizations with their specific publications, which contain tutorials and germane contacts, such as the Society of Children's Book Writers and Illustrators. However, as always, the most essential advice is encapsulated in three words: Get to it.

NOTE

1. Thomas Wolfe, *Of Time and the River: A Legend of Man's Hunger in His Youth* (New York: C. Scribner's Sons, 1935).

TWENTY-FOUR

Promoting Your Best Writing through Good Time Management and Persistence

Carole Mertz

A number of issues arise when we begin to address time management, commitment, and the writing life in earnest. Starting your new pursuit after a possibly long and successful career in another field takes a bit of courage. You may have asked yourself whether this new investment was feasible. You were an expert in one field and are now starting, possibly as a novice, in another. *Am I beginning this too late in my life?* you ask. *Do I have what it takes?*

In truth, you can't know the answers to these questions ahead of time. But if you make the commitment, you can establish good methods and habits to help you. You will recognize that, in order to develop as a writer, you must make an emotional investment, most likely an initial financial investment, and, most importantly, a considerable investment of your time. Pen and paper are cheap. Writing courses can be costly.

MANAGING EXTERNAL DISTRACTIONS

In managing external distractions, try to create the best circumstances for your writing. I've found the following helpful:

- Work in a location that is quiet, offers good lighting, and offers no visual or aural distractions, such as a TV playing within the same room or evidence of walkers or other distractions outside your window.

- If music helps your flow of writing, use it, especially if it covers other annoying noise distractions. (Note: Some writers use the length of a musical work to time a given writing session—i.e., your session ends when the music stops.)
- Choose a writing location you can return to as your habitual workplace. This familiar site is likely to set the scene for your optimal concentration. Normally, by working in the same spot each day, you allow the habit to work for you. Establishing your own best work space may require shifting furniture or changing the way you use certain rooms or areas in your home. When you express your needs, family members are often quite willing to make adjustments along with you.
- Try to find the best time of day for your optimal output and remain mindful that writing requires physical stamina as well as mental acuity. If possible, work at your peak hours, and plan to work during the same writing hours daily. Here again, habit plays its helpful part. (Life and family demands may cause you to alter this routine, but it's up to you to establish and honor the discipline as faithfully as you can.)
- Sometimes a change of venue for your writing sessions is warranted or even necessary. We'll consider that below.

Having established your work space, enter your writing sessions with tolerance for your varying states of mind and your varying degrees of commitment to your writing projects. If adhering too tightly to a schedule seems to constrict you, loosen up a bit, and allow yourself to follow your creative instincts. You need space, figuratively and literally. Writing mentors also speak about "getting yourself out of the way while you write."

Recognize your specific abilities and inabilities and your peculiar idiosyncrasies as a writer. I have no rituals before I sit down to write. But having a cup of coffee nearby is a must. Allow yourself the specific creature comforts you may need, so long as they themselves do not become distractions. (If you like having your Westie snoozing near your feet—what harm done?)

MANAGING INTERNAL DISTRACTIONS

Internal distractions, compared with the more easily adjusted external distractions, are often more difficult to handle. Often we simply don't know what's bothering us.

If resistance is at play, try to acknowledge it and wear it down. Writing mentors Anne Lamott, Steven Pressfield, and others have offered numerous tips to handle all kinds of resistance. They guide writers toward breakthroughs, helping us achieve our unique creative expression.

Crushing resistance may require months or hours. It's unpredictable. Pressfield, a former marine, uses a kind of "warrior code" to face down resistance. The entire book 1 of his *War of Art* identifies the "foe," and book 2 lays out his "battle plan." "Resistance will reason with you like a lawyer or jam a nine-millimeter in your face like a stickup man," he says. But overcoming it, he adds, means you are already "turning pro."[1]

Writer and teacher Anne Lamott encourages you to write terrible first drafts, an excellent way to plod through the jungle of resistance. She has penned seven novels, along with her colorful *Bird by Bird: Some Instructions on Writing and Life*. In this volume she recommends zeroing in on postage stamp–size focus rather than attempting to "describe an entire canvass."[2] Resistance often enters when we become overwhelmed by the large size of writing tasks we set before ourselves.

To minimize resistance, try to break down your self-assigned tasks into the smallest of segments. For example, if working on a chapter of a novel, do not expect yourself to write the entire chapter. Instead reduce the chapter into scenes or even fragments of scenes. I learned this from author Heather Sellers (who I'll talk about in a minute), and it's useful advice.

Ask yourself questions about the characters. Describe the clothing your character is wearing. Create brief passages of dialogue. Tell yourself, *This is only temporary. I can change this if I want to.* Just write to get the feel for the character's mood or condition. Ask yourself why he has left a question unanswered, where he would go now if he were not restrained by X, what in his past caused his current reactions to Y as revealed in the dialogue you are unfolding. These descriptions ultimately may not go into the chapter, but working on them helps you to move beyond the resistance.

Be prepared in advance for the days when writing blocks do, indeed, present themselves:

- Create a collage from pictures and lettering you tear randomly from newspapers and magazines in an effort to free your subconscious. Paste these elements onto a large sheet of paper or cardboard. Work quickly. Then study what you've made. You might want to write about a portion of the collage that speaks to you. If you sense a particular emotional response to one area or one juxtaposition of words, delve into describing that area or your overall response to the collage. Use your response as a springboard for getting words onto paper or into your computer. You selected the elements you put into your collage. Your subconscious might be trying to tell you something through those elements. Work with your collage as you try to unlock the area of resistance, even if this requires a day or two.

- Read in a genre that is totally alien to you, and use this method as a deliberate brain shock. I once turned to the *I Ching*, a philosophical thought system about which I knew nothing. In a matter of days I had composed an essay that referred to this ancient book. My essay was a response to a new stimulus.
- Select one of the many prompts you can find online or in writers' manuals, and work them diligently, even if you don't want to. (You're in resistance mode, and you probably won't want to budge. Do it anyway.)
- Ask for deliverance from your block before you go to sleep at night.
- View photos, and, in a relaxed atmosphere, allow yourself to free-associate about what you see. Describe what might have happened just prior to or following the click of the photo. Allow yourself to fantasize in this exercise.
- Record a dream. Then allow yourself to free-associate about it. Record an extension of the dream, taking note of your feelings.
- Plan a deliberate day away from books, desks, and computers. Trust me, this requires discipline.
- Call on a writer friend or friends and ask for direct help. Try to define what you are resisting.
- Write a letter to your mentor requesting help and advice.
- Create a "retreat" day for yourself—a day when no reading and writing are allowed. I guarantee this enforced restriction will reveal much to you.
- Promise yourself rewards: *After I complete this section, I may go visit my cousin June.* Or *If I write the chase scene, I'll buy myself a new wrench set or a pair of shoes.* (Save the Mercedes Benz for the day your novel is completed and selling well.)
- Deliberately use a different venue for your normal writing session(s). If you normally work alone, put yourself in a public place.

A RICH WRITING ENVIRONMENT

Maintain the best writing environment you can. It may mean you need to share relaxed time with your family or friends. Sometimes you may need to seek out the most stimulating conversationalists you know. Other times you may need time alone to think deeply about your writing.

Natalie Goldberg, in *Writing Down the Bones*, reminds us that the more we write, the better we get at it.[3] Ms. Goldberg has taught thousands of writers over the past thirty-five years. Her tips are invaluable, especially if you appreciate her Zen approach to writing and life. I viewed her recommended-books reading lists for the intensives she conducts, in her volume *The True Secret of Writing*.[4]

To stimulate your writing, allow the quiet time you need to absorb the books you value, especially those you feel are pertinent to your current writing projects or are written in the styles or genres you most admire.

- You can use various approaches to maximize your productivity. Use a timing device (a simple kitchen timer, for example) or a timing app on your computer to measure your writing time.
- At first, deliberately limit your writing time. You might plan to write a certain number of words at a setting or write for a selected number of minutes. Mary Rosenblum, author, and writing instructor at Long Ridge Writer's Group, cautions against having too much available time. (This sometimes happens to retirees.) You tell yourself you have all day, and you therefore take a lazy approach. Forty minutes of actual writing and thinking about your work will yield better results than attempting to write the entire day, especially if you are a beginner. Recognize idle dawdling when it occurs, and move away from your computer for a time. (Beginning writers can limit themselves to a twenty-minute writing session, the duration of a CD of music, or the completion of a prescribed number of words or pages.)
- Prepare carefully for each writing session. Heather Sellers has written three books and numerous essays on the writing craft. In *Chapter after Chapter*, she advises us to plan ahead for each day's work. Never end one session without having some idea of how you'll proceed into the next session. Prepare by laying out your things: papers, pens, reference books, etc. Keep the subject matter foremost in your mind. Be as meticulous as a schoolgirl who lays out her clothes and book bag the night before her school day. "Keep your book close and prepare it for its day."[5] Many successful authors stop deliberately mid-chapter because they know in advance how the next scene will unfold. They are planning for that fruitful next start.
- Be respectful of your ideas. When we treat our writing time with care, we are declaring to ourselves and others, *My thoughts matter, my writing projects matter, and my topics (themes or characters) are worthy.* When we truly believe this about ourselves, new ideas present themselves. Keep alert for the ideas that may be percolating in your subconscious as you progress.

HOW CHARTING HELPS YOUR TIME MANAGEMENT

I suggest you quantify as many aspects of your writing work as you can, especially the business aspects. Keeping good records will not only facilitate your income-tax reporting but will also make you a more productive writer.

- Keep clear records of the number of pieces you published within the year. Record your earnings.
- Record your writing-related costs. These will include the purchase of books and paper, travel expenses, magazine subscriptions, etc.
- Charts help you set goals for yourself, allowing you to easily access names and e-mail addresses of publications and editors, while providing information about your output at a glance.
- Count the number of short stories, poems, essays, or other forms of writing you've penned in the past six months. You can easily assess how you've spent your writing time.
- Document what you've written, by title, and of those titles which you've submitted and which you have not.
- Record your work to reveal trends. You may notice that your writing time has decreased, for example, while your marketing time has increased. Reflecting on these trends may help you define your future direction. It may help you select your next writing projects, project your income, or redirect some of your efforts.

In summary, quantifying often provides encouragement. And this is worth noting. Your records will be quick indicators of the progress you've made. In the past month, for example, you note that you've lengthened your daily writing time from forty minutes to two hours. You've sold more books this year than last. The digital self-published version of your novel has sold more copies than the Simon & Schuster print version. (Would that we were all so well situated as author Hugh Howey. I talk about his extraordinary publishing story below.)

MARKETING YOURSELF EFFICIENTLY

Part of your time as a writer will be spent on the business aspects of writing and on learning how to market yourself and your work.

- Efforts at self-promotion may be incorporated into your regular writing time or may be set apart.
- Self-promotion may serve more than one purpose. For example, while you are blogging, you may simultaneously be exercising your writing skills while promoting works you've written. A brief allusion to your story or essay in a blog post is a form of self-promotion. Be judicious in the way you self-promote, however. Writing well on a blog is as important as writing well in your other forms of writing. Don't bore your readers. Give your followers the quality of style and information they have come to expect from you. A loyal following soon expands your readership.

- I recommend you post to your website and blog and that you tweet at times separated from your routine writing times. Maintaining those boundaries, however, is often quite difficult.

Consider how to fit the marketing of your product (your writing, speaking engagements, classes you offer, or other product) into your regular schedule and how to market yourself efficiently and effectively.

- As you persist in your writing time, begin to set aside the time you need or want to spend marketing yourself. Consider devoting a separate day of the week to this effort.
- Keep close track of the time you spend tweeting and retweeting. Don't feel you must respond to every blog post. Tweeting and blogging can quickly become a writer's trap and steal from you your precious writing time.
- Learn how to blog well. Ideally, blogging and all forms of self-promotion should run parallel to the development of your writing skills.
- Learn how to use search-engine optimization to your advantage.
- Create a website that enables you to capture e-mail addresses. The faster your list of followers grows, the faster your readership expands.
- Use Facebook, LinkedIn, Twitter, and other social-media tools to reach your public and expand your readership.

USING VARIOUS FORMS OF TECHNOLOGY TO EXPEDITE YOUR WORK AND AID YOUR MARKETING

- Make use of writing apps such as Dragon, a popular voice-recognition app that records (i.e., prints) your spoken words. This is a time-saver, especially if you're a slow typist.
- Always back up your entire writing product. (Schedule routine backups for times when you are normally sleeping—i.e., not writing.)
- Hire experts if you're unwilling or unable to commit the time required to acquaint yourself with the various computer programs and apps you may need to use.
- Establish and maintain a website. Offer quality writing, style, and information on your website, and post to it regularly.
- If you plan to publish, you will have learned that self-publishing, or publishing through indies, can be accomplished in much shorter time than through agented big-name publishers.
- If you self-publish, learn how to convert your manuscript into the format that meets the e-publisher's specifications.

- Run comparisons of various e-publishers in order to determine the best publishing options for you. There are so many to consider—for example, Smashwords, Lulu, and BookBaby. What is the royalty rate offered? How quickly can you receive sales data? Can you set your own book pricing? Who executes the book cover? What length of time does the publisher require between your manuscript submission and its appearance in retail bookstores? Plan to incorporate this type of analysis into your schedule so you can make informed choices.
- If you're talented in the visual arts, create your own book covers. This may save time and money in the book-production process.

Many writers offer short manuscripts, or opening chapters of their longer works, as initial forms of self-promotion. Hugh Howey published serialized portions of his novel.[6] Frequently new writers offer their early work as freebies. These attract visitors to their sites. If marketing well, the author plays a hand in creating reader anticipation. Your best promotion will occur if you continue to offer the highest quality of writing. In addition, the greater the quantity of good writing you produce, the more likely you are to sell. Agents, editors, and publishers will more likely notice you if you've created a volume of output.

OTHER HABITS TO HELP YOU WORK EFFICIENTLY

- Lump all of your online research into a given time slot for your day or week. (Keep notes during the day on which topics you plan to research further. To prevent interruptions to your writing flow, do the research later.)
- Limit the time you spend in e-mail responses.
- If you reach a point of depletion while writing, shift to a less-challenging task, such as filing, recording data, (dusting your books,) or phoning an expert to ask for clarification of a point you couldn't verify through your research. If these less-demanding tasks fail you, take a nap.

Always be kind to yourself so, like a well-tended plant, you can flourish at your writing tasks. If you persist with good time management, your writing success is almost guaranteed. Persistence for the beginning writer may mean writing and publishing that first short story. For the more experienced writer, it may mean seeing a longer project through to completion as you work in tandem with your editor. If you've completed your first novel, persistence for you is moving on to your next novel. (I smile now when I think of my first mentor telling me, "I know you'll succeed, as long as you persist.")

NOTES

1. Steven Pressfield, *The War of Art: Winning the Inner Creative Battle* (New York: Rugged Land, 2002), 9.

2. Anne Lamott, *Bird by Bird: Some Instructions on Writing and Life* (New York: Pantheon, 1994), 17–18, 21.

3. Natalie Goldberg, *Writing Down the Bones: Freeing the Writer Within* (Boston: Shambhala, 1986).

4. Natalie Goldberg, *The True Secret of Writing: Connecting Life with Language* (New York: Atria, 2013), 225–30.

5. Heather Sellers, *Chapter after Chapter: Discover the Dedication and Focus You Need to Write the Book of Your Dreams* (Cincinnati: Writer's Digest Books, 2007), 65.

6. In a near first in publishing history, author Hugh Howey self-published his novel *Wool*, then sold print-publication rights to Simon & Schuster, but *retained the e-book rights*. This marks a significant shift of power in the publishing world. Howey definitely knew how to market successfully. He offered an early version of the novel as a short story in mid-2011, selling it on Amazon for 99 cents. His sales were immediate and considerable. At the end of 2011, he sold a sequel. He then released a third and a fourth installment. With readers begging for more, he published the final installment for $2.99 and then sold the collection for $5.99. By then, he was so well-positioned that he could refuse Simon & Schuster the digital rights. See Alexandra Alter, "Sci-Fi's Underground Hit," *Wall Street Journal*, March 14, 2013, http://online.wsj.com/news/articles/SB10001424127887324678604578340752088305668.

TWENTY-FIVE

Self-Publishing

A Viable Option

Kathleen Clauson

Two hundred million Americans dream of becoming writers and publishing their own books.[1] The motives fueling the drive to become a published author are many. Fame and fortune seem to be at the top of the list. Many have a story to tell and feel their life experiences may help others going through similar circumstances, giving their lives a new sense of purpose they never thought possible. For others, just seeing their own name on the jacket of a book or included in a table of contents creates an adrenaline rush that never gets old. The best reason to publish anything is because you really love writing. In a recent survey by HSBC (Hong Kong Shanghai Baking Corporation) Holdings about approaching retirement, fifteen thousand people in fifteen countries responded, of which 12 percent hoped to become writers in their golden years after retirement and 2 percent of that group identified writing a book as the most important thing they wanted to do.[2]

This chapter offers suggestions intended to help you shape your ideas for writing, to explain the difference between traditional publishing and self-publishing, to offer insight into the phenomenal growth of the self-publishing industry and growing numbers of self-published best sellers, and to highlight some important factors you should consider if you choose a self-publishing company from the myriad of options.

Landing a traditional book deal has been compared to winning the lottery. Nowadays most large publishers won't even look at unsolicited manuscripts unless they are submitted by a literary agent. Gone are the days when a publisher decided to publish a book many-times rejected by other publishers and ultimately abandoned by the author and thrown in the trash, which is the story of how Stephen King's wife Tabitha salvaged his novel *Carrie* from the garbage and urged him to finish it. It became the breakout novel that allowed him to quit his day job and the extra moonlighting jobs and write full-time.[3] There is only one thing as difficult as getting published by a traditional publisher—finding a top-notch agent to represent you. However, don't let that discourage you. Not even traditional publishers could have predicted how technology would change the book industry. Nor did anyone expect self-publishing companies to take the market by storm.

Technology has changed not only the way we communicate: it has also changed the way we search for and store information, including the way we read and buy books.[4] Many believed the e-book would never catch on, but the folks at Amazon beg to differ. As a result, getting your work into the hands of your readers as fast as possible has never been more important, nor has it ever been easier.

WHAT IT TAKES TO BECOME A WRITER

Once you have decided to take the plunge and try your hand at writing, how do you get started? Let's examine some fundamental considerations you will face as an author before you start practicing your autograph for book signings. First of all, writing is hard, tireless work that requires scheduled dedication. You need to embrace the fact that you must find the time to write every day.

After you're retired, and you hope to make writing your eventual encore career, it is important to stay attuned to what writers are saying about getting paid. Unless you have the means to pay your bills from month to month, it is imperative to understand that writers who hope to earn money for their writing are *not* writing for that reason alone. Some write for the "passion of the art" or the possibility of "discovery and revelation."[5] Publishing in literary journals and e-zines is a good way to test the water before deciding to publish your book. Look for calls for submission, which generally do not charge reading fees, as opposed to contests, which do.

How you measure your own success is usually difficult to explain to other people, but it is necessary for you to know where you stand, just for your own benefit:

- What are your own motives for writing?
- What are the specific goals you wish to accomplish?
- What is your time line for your writing?
- What will you write about?
- Will you write fiction or nonfiction?

- Who will your readers be?
- Will you start with by publishing short stories, poems, or essays?
- Will you delve right into a book? If so, what genre? What theme?
- How do you envision your book cover?
- How will you publish your book?
- Do you want your book in print or as an electronic e-book?
- Do you have plans to promote your book?
- Who will form your team for editing, design, marketing, and distribution?

If you can sit down and write out the answers to those questions in a notebook (or on fast-food napkins) then you are ready to start thinking about publishing.

TRADITIONAL PUBLISHING VERSUS SELF-PUBLISHING

What is the difference between traditional publishing and self-publishing? Traditional publishers employ editors to field offers from agents. Once a book deal is negotiated, a traditional publisher may send the author an advance check. The amount of the advance is based on what they predict in sales, and basically it is an advance on royalties. Royalties are a percentage of the number of books sold. Traditional publishers pay all expenses for publishing, marketing, and distributing the books they accept.

In self-publishing, the author chooses a publisher and pays for a publishing package ranging from a few hundred dollars to several thousand dollars. When your manuscript is complete, you will send it to the self-publishing company you have chosen. It will be formatted, sometimes within a few days, and you will receive a galley proof for your review. If there are corrections to be made, the author is responsible for submitting a detailed list of the changes. A corrected proof will be sent for your approval, and once you sign off on the book it will be sent to production. Most self-publishing companies offer packages that include several free copies of your printed books. From the time the final corrections are made, it generally takes at least a month or two before you can see the finished copy. As copies of your book sell, your publishing house will send you royalty checks.

WHY SELF-PUBLISH?

Aside from the previous discussion on the difficulty of getting a book deal from a big publishing house, the main reasons authors choose to self-publish can be classified in the following categories—time, money, and control.

The turn-around time for self-publishing is much faster than traditional publishing. If your book focuses on a hot "right-now" topic, you don't have time to wait for a traditional publisher to put it on the market. Some authors believe the cost of self-publishing is less than the cost of lost time (and lost sales) while waiting for their books to hit the bookstores.

Royalties paid for books self-published are generally higher than royalties paid by traditional publishing houses. Traditional publishers pay an average of about 10 percent, while some self-publishing opportunities, depending on the format you choose, range from 30 percent to 70 percent. However, keep in mind that the reason self-publishing companies can afford to pay you higher royalties is because they are paying a minimal amount for the production of your book and the price of your publishing package covers most of their expenses. Normally they offer print-on-demand books, which means books are printed only when they are ordered, and therefore there is no stockpile of printed books somewhere on the shelves of bookstores or warehouses

Self-publishers may offer services for editing, cover design, and marketing, but generally these are extra options that you may choose (and pay for) in addition to the cost of the publishing package. And, frankly, this is how they make their money. They don't make money by selling thousands of books written by a handful of authors—they make money by publishing thousands of different authors and selling one hundred to two hundred books each. Nevertheless, depending on the publisher you choose, the cost of your package, the popularity of your book, the format, and number of books you sell, your book could become a profitable endeavor.

TRIPLE-DIGIT GROWTH

Although self-published books were once scorned and not considered "real books," that mindset is a thing of the past. Self-publishing companies are popping up everywhere, and the number of books that have been self-published has tripled since 2006, with a growth spurt of 287 percent, according to Bowker statistics.[6] As e-books for Kindles, iPads, and other popular devices have taken the market by storm, self-publishing is expected to reach new levels in the coming years. Traditional publishing houses and authors who have long been loyal to their publishers are sitting up and taking notice. In 2011 only about 1 percent of books published in the $14 billion trade-publishing industry were self-published. However, in the first four months of 2013, 50 percent of the top ten best-selling books were self-published.[7]

MY EXPERIENCE WITH SELF-PUBLISHING

I started writing professionally back in the late 1980s. I wrote business articles and economic forecasts for the international bank where I worked as an assistant financial controller and as a freelance journalist for an international business publication. When I moved back to the States I needed a job with insurance benefits and opportunities for upward mobility, so I applied for a variety of university jobs, ranging from civil service to academic. Meanwhile I worked as an advertising representative for a local newspaper, and after continually pestering the editor to give me a chance to write I started writing book reviews, film reviews, special-feature stories, and seasonal pieces for special holiday supplements and later was named editor of another small hometown publication. A few years later I accepted a full-time position as a library assistant. I started taking classes to pursue a new career trajectory—creative writing.

The professors of my writing courses encouraged us to submit our work to journals to become accustomed to receiving rejection letters. Until I took advanced creative-writing workshops, I didn't feel I had anything seriously publishable. Many talented writers were in our group, and under the auspices of our professor several of us considered pooling funds and self-publishing a collection of stories from our workshop. We assembled a team to collect and format the stories, proofread, and choose a cover and interior design. Several of us were on board, but as members of the group graduated, got married, moved away or just got lost in time the project fizzled before it got started.

Selected by my peers as one of the top stories from our class, *Eva Galuska and the Christmas Carp*, my fictional Christmas story set in Chicago, had great potential, I felt, and I decided to self-publish it. I wanted to see my story in print, yet I wanted to retain the rights and have a say in the design. I didn't want to wait for an agent or a publisher to tell me it was publishable, so I made contact with the company we had considered for our class collection of stories. Instead of spending time trying to find an agent and a traditional publisher, I worked full-time at the library, and after work and on weekends, until the blue hours of the morning, I wrote, for five solid months, expanding my story to novella length. I finished by late October of that year. It was an eye-opening experience, and I learned writing it was a piece of cake compared to promoting it and distributing it.

For $499, I bought a two-book publishing deal, which included a marketing package. I opted for a custom cover (at no extra charge) because I wanted a colorful Christmas red and green cover with old-world appeal. By networking with an author of an ethnic-history book, I found a photographer in Chicago who was willing to shoot my cover photo for $400, which was very reasonable, and the cover was breathtaking. A former student worker of mine had taken a job as a graphic designer for a posh print magazine, and he was willing to design my book cover just for the experience and as a rèsumè builder.

After my book was published, local media interviewed me, and the photographer helped me arrange a book signing in Chicago. I promoted the book on my website and on the Author's Den, an online forum for authors. I also spent $290 on a tiny insert ad on the "New Titles" page in *Poets & Writers*. I quickly made enough to cover my entire original investment and even made a small profit. Although Oprah never chose my book for her book club, I'd accomplished what I set out to do. I still write and publish while balancing my day job. I'm one of those people who still enjoys the thrill of receiving an acceptance e-mail or letter. Seeing my own name in print is the closest thing to nirvana. There's nothing I love more than writing.

The main complaint I had with my publishing company stemmed from an unexplained number of books that showed up for sale in the "stores" of what appeared to be small online booksellers. What puzzled me was that there were no immediate records of those book sales on my quarterly sales reports from my publisher, nor did it seem I was receiving royalties for these sales. I was disappointed that I never received a satisfactory response from the publishing company, so finally I ordered a couple of my own books from two different online booksellers for retail price. After many e-mails I learned these were actually book distributors, in spite of their seller names and locations, somehow affiliated with my self-publishing company and legally able to sell my books via a drop-ship operation. The sales eventually showed up on my sales reports, months later, but I was paid a lesser royalty percentage for sales outside my publishing company. What most annoyed me was the canned response from the customer-service representatives at my publishing company who had no idea what was happening and sadly couldn't even begin to understand what I was trying to tell them.

Timing for seasonal books is critical. My book was a Christmas story, and the final manuscript should have been finalized by June, rather than October. An e-book would have been ideal with a print-on-demand option for those who wanted to give copies as holiday gifts. Although my manuscript was formatted and corrected, it took much longer to receive the first print copies than I'd anticipated. I didn't receive the first shipment until mid-November. This affected the possibility for timely reviews of my book. When you self-publish, be aware that it is your responsibility to send out review copies, and this is something you need to arrange months in advance.

What would I change the next time I self-publish a book? I would spend more time doing my homework in preparation for the actual writing by reading books in my favorite genres critically, focusing on how the story makes you feel, how the characters keep your attention, and how the author encourages you to keep reading, as recommended in James Scott Bell's *Self-Publishing Attack: The 5 Absolutely Unbreakable Laws for Creating Steady Income Publishing Your Own Books*.[8]

I would spend more time comparing the options offered by different self-publishing companies. *Publish a Book: Compare Over 50 Self-Publishing Companies*, by J. Steven Miller, is a treasure trove of objective comparative information designed to help you choose the right company for your book.[9] One preference would be to find a company that allows me to buy copies of my own books at a flat rate, significantly less than retail, regardless of the number I purchase. The company I worked with charged an average of $10 for my book, which retailed for $19.99.

Long before my book hit the market, I would have started working on marketing and promotion. Like many other newbie self-publishing authors, I was not prepared for the huge responsibility of promoting my own book. My marketing package was nice but minimal, consisting of color business cards, bookmarks, and postcards, but I received them several months *after* my book signing. For my *Eva Galuska* book, I had many good ideas that I never found the time to put into action, including a blog of my own, geared toward ethnic neighborhoods; links to the shops, the food, and the culture; some strategically placed advertising on others' blogs and websites; mass snail-mail and e-mail book announcements to everyone in the local and nearby communities; and well-timed book signings and interviews with the media.

CHOOSING A SELF-PUBLISHING COMPANY FOR YOUR BOOK

Most self-publishers use the same type of technology to print books, but they offer a myriad of packages and options. How do you choose a reputable self-publishing company that offers the services you want, will do a good job on the final copy, and will pay you the royalties you have earned? The following list, based on my experiences and market research, highlights some important factors you should consider before making any final decisions about which self-publishing company you will choose.

- Have you seen other books published by this publisher or read reviews of this company written by authors who have actually engaged their services? Blogs and discussion boards offer great insight you won't find anywhere else.
- What does the self-publishing contract say? Is the publisher willing to send you a copy of a standard contract before you actually purchase your publishing package? Things to look for include being allowed to retain your rights without being charged a fee, the right to terminate your agreement at any time without a penalty, and a contract that is short and easy to understand.

- When you ask a question, is the publisher willing to answer you in writing? Do you get a chance to talk to representatives who have the authority to make decisions and solve problems? Ask to speak to a person who will handle your book at different stages of production.
- How much control will you have in the design of your book cover? Can you custom design your book cover, or must you select from among their basic templates? Keep in mind that most people will look at a thumbnail image of your book cover on a website, and an easy-to-read attention grabber is your best choice.
- What are the prices for publishing your book? What are the differences in packages and options? Please be aware that normally this information is not available on the websites and that you will have to speak to a customer representative who will send you an author's kit. Don't be afraid to negotiate, but ask for details about all special offers in writing, and avoid being pressured to make quick decisions by telephone.
- What are the hidden costs, such as additional fees for proofs, corrections, revisions, different fonts, custom covers, and fees for after-publication revisions? Will you be charged additional fees for ISBN numbers, copyright registration, and Library of Congress classifications?
- How are royalties calculated, and how often will you be paid your royalties? Will the company automatically issue you 1099 tax forms for additional income? Are you paid royalties on net sales or retail sales? Will you be paid the same rate for book sales ordered from major online booksellers (such as Amazon) as you are for sales of books ordered directly from your publisher? What are the differences in rates for print books and e-books?
- Can you set your own retail price? Beware the company that offers high royalties but expects you to set high retail prices. If the price is too high, your book just won't sell. Think about what you would pay for a similar book.
- How much will you be charged for a copy of your own book? The most ideal scenario is a low, fixed rate, regardless of the number of books you order. Avoid companies that sell you your own books at a price discounted from the retail price. Some self-publishing companies are notorious for making money by charging the authors almost retail for their own books.
- After you have formatted your book and sent digital images to your self-publishing company, do you own the rights to them? The answer is *no* in many cases. This is something you want to ask about before you ever purchase a package, because you never know what you may want to do with your work in the future.

- Does the publishing company offer any promotion or marketing? Normally you are responsible entirely for your own marketing without any useful guidance. Is optional marketing available? Does it seem too good to be true? Are they telling you that by purchasing a special package your book will be delivered to a Hollywood director or producer? Ask for verifiable examples and statistics, and consider contacting some authors for their feedback.
- Some publishers offer "book review and/or press-release options," but sometimes they are selling the "possibility" of a review—not a sure thing. Professional press releases and book reviews, the kind you *can't* buy as part of a package, are the best promotion you can get. If you want your book reviewed, you will have to send it out yourself, and you'll have to pay for the copies and the postage to do so.

As you embark on your writing adventures, my best advice is to stick to a writing schedule every day. Follow your original goals and objectives. Do your homework; don't get in a rush. Ask the publishers the tough questions, and ask for confirmation in writing. Engage the help of editors, designers, and marketing professionals if you can, but try to keep your own out-of-pocket expenses to a minimum, and pay for extra options only if they seem justified. Be realistic about your expectations. And, most important, have fun! Writing should be a joy, not a chore.

NOTES

1. Justine Tal Goldberg, "200 Million Americans Want to Publish Books, But Can They?" *Publishing Perspective,* May 26, 2011, http://publishingperspectives.com/2011/05/200-million-americans-want-to-publish-books/.

2. HSBC, "The Future of Retirement: A New Reality," 2013, http://www.hsbc.com/about-hsbc/structure-and-network/retail-banking-and-wealth-management/retirement/life-after-work?WT.ac=HGHQ_FR_nr1.3_On.

3. Neil Gaiman, "Popular Writers: A Stephen King Interview," *Neil Gaiman's Journal,* April 28, 2012, http://journal.neilgaiman.com/2012/04/popular-writers-stephen-king-interview.html.

4. Rachelle Gardner, *How Do I Decide? Self-Publishing vs. Traditional Publishing: A Field Guide for Authors* (Santa Rosa, CA: R. L. Gardner Publishing, 2013).

5. Nick Ripatrazone, "On Getting Paid: Literary Magazines and Remuneration," *The Millions,* February 15, 2012, http://www.themillions.com/2012/02/on-getting-paid-literary-magazines-and-remuneration.html.

6. Bowker, "Self-Publishing Sees Triple-Digit Growth in Just Five Years, Says Bowker," October 24, 2012, http://www.bowker.com/en-US/aboutus/press_room/2012/pr_10242012.shtml.

7. Jeremy Greenfield, "When the Self-Published Authors Take Over, What Will Publishers Do?" *Forbes,* April 30, 2013, http://www.forbes.com/sites/jeremygreenfield/2013/04/30/when-the-self-published-authors-take-over-what-will-publishers-do/.

8. James Scott Bell, *Self-Publishing Attack: The 5 Absolutely Unbreakable Laws for Creating Steady Income Publishing Your Own Books* (Woodland Hills, CA: Compendium Press, 2012).

9. J. Steven Miller, *Publish a Book! Compare Over 50 Self-Publishing Companies* Acworth, GA: Wisdom Creek Press, LLC, 2012).

TWENTY-SIX

A Writer's Marketing Recommendations

Ann McCauley

So you've written a great book, poetry, essay, or memoir. Your sister, Jean, and your cousin, Sue, adore it, as well as the women in your book club . . . therefore, it must be good. But wait, *maybe* it needs serious editing and they don't want to hurt your feelings. *Possibly* your work is great. Most likely it is somewhere in between.

Experience has taught me that before sharing anything I must first ignore it for at least three days. Then reread it. If you try this simple system, you will be amazed at how many typos, sentence fragments, and misspelled words you missed in the first draft. Then repeat this exercise *at least one more time.*

My husband is my first reader; all writers need someone who will provide honest feedback on their work. I don't always agree with his comments, but he's on the money too often to ignore. Detailed objectivity is the sign of a good first reader.

WRITER'S SUPPORT

Join a writers' group, maybe through your local library. If that doesn't work, search online for writers' groups in your state and region. I belong to Pennwriters, Inc., and West Virginia Writers, Inc. There are many small groups available within the larger organizations, geographically as well as genre oriented. Both send useful monthly newsletters written by members with ongoing helpful hints about the writing process, the latest trends in the writing world, as well as successes of fellow members. Their successes make me feel hopeful for my own writing as well as happy for their well-deserved success.

I subscribe to two writing newsletters, *Story Circle* and *Working Writers*, as well as two magazines, *Poets & Writers* and *The Writer*. There are many more excellent resources available, but I would not be able to keep up with all the information if I subscribed to more. These publications also provide information on many contests you can submit your work to.

I'm going to jump ahead. Let's pretend your work gets published, either by an established press, large or small, or by you through self-publishing. There is such a glut of new books published each week that to get readers to notice yours is a major challenge. (And for this essay I'm not even going to comment on the numerous online sites that offer guidelines for the labyrinth of *e-books only*.)

PRESS RELEASE

After your book is with the publisher, a press release is the first thing to prepare. A press release is your best shot at free publicity, and it's often your only one, so make it count.

Marketing is a lonely journey for a writer and almost overwhelmingly so at times, though the rewards can be worthy of your efforts. Use your creative genius; it took creative talent to write your book, be it fiction or nonfiction. Your press release should include a cover shot of your book, a photo of yourself—or, better yet, one of you holding your book. It should also include a short bio about yourself with emphasis on writing, a few lines about your book's plot, and a couple positive comments or mini reviews about your book, preferably from known people in your area. Also include where your book is available. Most press releases include the publisher's name. Keep it concise and to the point.[1] If your publisher handles press releases, offer assistance and insist on rights to proof releases before they're distributed. Your book is your baby, and to the publisher it is just another book.

Prepare your press release while your book is with the publisher. This is your one, perhaps *only*, shot at free publicity, so make sure your press release is the best it can be.

BOOK REVIEWS AND PRESS KIT

You will need a press kit, hard copy as well as digital. An online press kit should include a photo of you, a photo of your book cover—front and back—a one-page author bio, a one-page synopsis of the book, a few book reviews, and contact information. A hard-copy press kit includes professionally printed pocket folders featuring a photo of the book on the cover, all of the above professionally printed on high-grade paper, as well as professionally printed business cards, including a photo of your book on postcards and/or bookmarks. Save your receipts from these for appropriate tax deductions. Yes, writing is a business.

Send your work to national reviewers, easily found by typing *book reviewers* in any Internet search engine, and remember that *reviews are free*. If they want a fee, move on to the next one on the list. Also submit to national and regional contests; these are becoming expensive, so you'll need to study and decide which ones would be best suited for your work. Don't be afraid to ask your local librarian to write a review.

Writing is a solitary occupation and requires a commitment; it demands a real chunk of time. But take note—*solitary* is not the same thing as *lonely*. Writers have their stories and characters to keep them company. And the writing process is the preferred pastime for most writers.

Endeavors required for successful marketing are clearly outside most writers' comfort zones. So what can a writer do? Plenty!

When your book is released, all of a sudden everything seems to happen at once; you will be glad you have the press releases ready. Send press releases and photos by e-mail to local newspapers. That doesn't mean only your hometown newspaper; include neighboring towns, your parent's hometown, and maybe even your cousin's hometown. (It is easy to get e-mail addresses for newsrooms by using Internet search engines.)

Send a press release to your local chamber of commerce; if you are not a member, join for $30.00 per year. They will print every bit of progress your book makes as long as you provide them with the information. If you belong to a professional writing organization, alumni association, fraternity, sorority, service club, or church, they will likely be happy to share the good news of one of their own. Place an ad for your book in a magazine or catalogue that targets libraries and booksellers. The cost would be about $200 a month, but most offer two months for the price of one several times a year.

Send press kits with your book when submitting it to media sources, prior to interviews and when submitting your book for reviews. A great press kit can be the tie breaker when potential reviewers try to decide which books to review.

MARKETING PLAN

A writer needs a documented marketing plan to stay on course. Even if you have a major publisher behind you—unless you are an established, best-selling author—*you need your own marketing plan*. Publishing houses put their maximum effort (Translation: marketing money) behind their authors who bring home the most bacon.

Even chart-topping author James Patterson spends millions of dollars each year marketing his books, in addition to that spent by his publisher.

Almost *every* chain bookstore you walk into has a cardboard almost-life-size display of Mr. Patterson and his latest book, which are coming out at the rate of at least one per month thanks to his cowriters. He wouldn't market like this if it didn't pay off, *and for him it does*. Few other writers can afford such pricey advertising campaigns.

Marketing should target readers who would most likely benefit from reading your book. Also, if there's an angle you can use to generate interest, use it! For example, for my novel *Mother Love*, I concentrated on Mother's Day for most of the promos.

For my second novel, *Runaway Grandma*, one of my target groups was fourth- and fifth-grade teachers. I visited their classes and talked to the students about the importance of reading. I also read two short children's stories I'd written. Then I told them a little about *Runaway Grandma* and challenged them to write an essay for a contest: "Why my grandma would *never* run away." It was such fun! Each event merited newspaper coverage too.

In 2007 author Lisa Genova self-published her first novel, *Still Alice*, about early onset Alzheimer's disease. She sent copies to the Alzheimer's Association, and *Still Alice* has become the only work of fiction the agency has ever endorsed.[2]

ONLINE ADVERTISING

But, writer, beware! There are many online-marketing promoters out there, with hefty fees. My experience has been that they promise more than they deliver, and some have only nominally professional staff. I had to edit ads after marketing *pros* butchered the concepts of one of my books. Realistically it's hard to write a convincing blurb about a book if the marketer hasn't taken the time to read it.

I placed an ad on a major search engine a few years ago. I do not recommend it; it cost me $300 per month, and *I couldn't even find my own ad!* Big surprise, I did not see a major jump in interest in my book. It took me more than a month to stop the ad, as well as the continued automatic deduction from my credit card. However, after ten days of Facebook limited targeted ads, thousands of people clicked *like*, and many left messages on my Facebook page. I saw a bump in sales. Fear from my previous Internet-advertising fiasco prevented me from continuing at that time, though I definitely will use Facebook again when my next book is published. Their targeted ads are reasonably priced and actually contact potential readers, whereas with the giant search engine, readers must search for books and authors they have never heard of before they'll ever come across the ad.

Limit your online time to bare necessities; otherwise, it can eat a hole in your time. And you won't be able to meet your writing deadlines.

WRITER'S PLATFORM

If you are fairly new to the writing field, you may wonder what a *writer's platform* is. I know I did. Your platform includes your writing credentials, previous publications and books, total book sales, as well as your professional presence in the writing world, which will eventually include not only the Internet but television, radio, and print media as well. It can be overwhelming to maintain your platform, but when you take it one day at a time, it is a feasible task.

I have learned to avoid big media conglomerates; they seem to deal only with big-time agents and booking companies. Have you noticed how the same celebrities tend to appear on every major talk show on network and cable television when they have *allegedly* written a book? I remember watching Kathy Lee interview a retiring syndicated talk-show host on the Today Show a few years ago. He was unable to answer any of her questions about his book. She finally leaned forward and asked, "Didn't you even *read* your book?"

LOCAL MEDIA

Send professional queries to local radio stations, and follow up by calling the radio personality you feel most akin to or the station manager, bearing in mind they have lots of air time to fill and love to interview local writers. They especially like writers who provide them with a short synopsis of their books and advance questions for the interview.[3] It also increases interest if you donate a book or two to the station to give away to callers.

Consider pursuing an interview with one of your local or regional television stations, using similar techniques as mentioned above. Public-television stations are also an excellent resource for writers. But their interviewers *actually read* the books and will not be interested in your prepared questions. These are tougher interviews but well worth the effort. These stations have wide viewerships and are open to independent queries. If no interest is expressed regarding your book, move on; never stalk media interviewers. Realize that their disinterest is their loss and that maybe the time was not yet right for you.

For your first book, until you have developed some name recognition with newspapers, you may have to make a follow-up call to the newsroom and inquire whether your press release was received. Don't be discouraged if you have to resend it.

ONLINE PRESENCE

A website, blog, and Facebook page are necessary if you want to be taken seriously as a writer. If you are at a loss as to how to do this, check with local colleges; inquire about marketing students who would be available to help set up writer websites and Facebook pages for a fee. Students are usually in need of extra cash, and they can set up these entities with minimal effort. They also teach technically challenged writers how to maintain these e-sites. Trust me—it's a good investment![4]

I had to draw a line in the sand about incorporating new Internet phenomena into my already crowded platform. Facebook and my blog require *enough* of my time, so I refuse to include Twitter. After all, I need time to actually write. Experts in the field have advised me twice a month that entries on Facebook and my blog are minimally enough.

A few years ago I read an author whose work I adored. I looked up her website from the back cover of her book, and she had not updated her website in two years. I never found any more books by this writer either. I felt a loss; it is one of the mysteries of life. I hope she is well.

Another day I looked up one of my long-time favorite prolific writers. Her website showed the same photo that is on the back of her books. Her entire website: "Thank you for reading my books. Yes, I have a private life, and I plan to keep it that way. If you are a writer, do not expect assistance from me; you are my competition." Despite her abrupt website, I still love her books; I also admire her courage to defy the demands that she have a social-media presence.

PLANNED GIVING PAYS OFF

I donated a copy of each of my books to libraries within eighty miles of my home. I included a self-addressed stamped envelope with a letter, requesting they send me a receipt for the donated book, useful for tax deductions. I also include a short bio with a letter informing them of my availability to visit libraries to talk about my books. This has helped get my foot in the door in new communities.

Developing a network of book-loving acquaintances has helped establish a following of loyal readers by word of mouth, which I believe is still the most effective marketing tool. When possible, start locally, and continue to build your base of support from where you are. If someone tells you they like your book and they are at all computer savvy, ask them to post a review on Amazon and at Barnes & Noble's website. Readers' reviews can be the determining factor in whether a future will buy your book or not.

That may sound tacky to some readers. However, back in the early days of my nursing career, the nursing supervisor encouraged new nurses to ask patients to put it in *writing* when patients wanted to thank us for extraordinary care. She said that having positive statements from patients in our employee file would help us at our annual reviews.

I buy eighty copies of my books to distribute to libraries, use in gift baskets and send to reviewers. I keep meticulous records of my writing expenses; every tax season, I am very happy I did.

PROMOTE OTHER WRITERS

My name and the names of my books are listed in bold font at the top of an eclectic list I compiled of my top one hundred favorite books and authors. It has helped me sell books after speaking, especially when the readers in the audience see that we like common authors. Interacting with fellow book lovers is *almost* always a joy; readers have much in common.

PUBLIC SPEAKING

Then there is the public speaking. You might be thinking, *Yikes, not that!* I admit that the first few times were hard, way outside my comfort zone. But the strangest thing happened . . . my comfort zone expanded. It is not as hard as it was at first, and sometimes it's actually fun. Experience has taught me to say near the end of every talk, "If you read my book and like it, please tell your friends—especially those who do not live in this area. That will help me build a larger base of readers. *However,* if you don't like it, please don't bother mentioning it!"

Olive Ann Burns, author of the Southern classic *Cold Sassy Tree*, said the difference between an author and a writer is that writers write and authors talk.[5]

Often I get paid well; other times, only a stipend. I always request that a table be provided to display my books . . . to sell after speaking. I arrive at least fifteen minutes early in order to present my books most appealingly; I bring a white tablecloth and a vase of red silk roses. I distribute bookmarks and the list of my favorite authors on each chair or at each place setting. Sometimes a friend goes with me and passes them out while I speak. I keep my talks to between twenty and thirty minutes—that's as long as most organizations designate for guest speakers. I always ask for questions and comments afterward, and those times my program has run a few minutes longer, no one has complained.

I've developed my talks by leaving out things that don't work and including more of those that do. I find reading one or two short reviews about my books holds audience attention better than reading paragraphs from my books. I'm also bored listening to other writers read from their books. In retrospect, writers' reading their own work does seem a bit egocentric.

I include humor in my presentations; I briefly talk about myself and the challenges of starting a writing career later in life. I also include a few stories about well-known writers who either started late in life or continued to write late in life.

I donate a copy of my book, some candy, and a mug with tea bags, all in a basket, prepared in shrink-wrap, with a big bow in the season's appropriate color. I ask all in attendance to sign up for a chance to win the gift basket. I buy my baskets at the local Goodwill store for a few cents each and my shrink-wrap from the produce department at the grocery store. (And, yes, I keep receipts for each gift basket and its contents.) This gesture has been appreciated by every group I have spoken to.

Genova's *Still Alice* is on my list of favorite books. It did so well that a major publishing company made her an offer she couldn't refuse. She in turn found a good agent. Now she can limit her time to writing while her agent arranges short book tours for her with each new book.

LITERARY AGENTS

Speaking of agents, my writing friends have told me for years that a bad agent is worse than no agent at all. Author Stephen King said that new writers should write and not be concerned about finding an agent. I e-mailed an agent listed in *Writer's Digest* several years ago; she immediately asked me to send her a sample of my work, and she loved it. What writer wouldn't love to hear that? *However*, she needed three hundred dollars up front to handle office expenses for representing me for the first year. At the beginning of my year with an agent, it was a relief to be able to say, "My agent is submitting my new book to publishers." At the time, my mother was losing her battle with cancer, and I was emotionally drained. It was one less thing to not have to worry about.

My writing friends had warned me *never* to pay an agent in advance; agents get their percentage out of the actual sale of a manuscript. I paid anyway, thinking this might have been an appropriate exception. Then I barely heard from her until she wanted the next year's office expenses paid in advance. I never received any proof that she'd actually submitted my manuscript anywhere. I terminated her service after one year and I realized I'd been had.

ALWAYS BE PREPARED

My husband is semi-retired, and we love to travel. We often meet new people from all over the world. If the conversation turns to books, and it often does, and *if* I feel the right rapport, I mention that I write and offer one of my bookmarks. There has been an upswing in online sales in the weeks following each of our trips. It has also led to far-away book clubs choosing my books for their discussions.

It is absolutely necessary to have your book available through the big Internet stores as both hard copies and e-books, as well as through local outlets.

Eventually most authors realize that writing the book was the easy part. Eleven years ago most of the suggestions I'm making here would have overwhelmed me. But if I could rise to the occasion as needed, you can too. It truly does get easier with time. Good luck, and please don't forget to keep writing.

NOTES

1. Refer back to the first page of this chapter for editing guidelines.
2. As an aside, *Still Alice* is also the only book I have ever read in one sitting. I started it after dinner one evening and soon told my husband, "When the dog needs to go out, you have to take him, because I'm not moving until I've finish this book." Lisa Genova, *Still Alice: A Novel* (New York: Pocket Books, 2009).
3. Interview questions should be prepared immediately after you have completed your press release.
4. It is important to find someone who is familiar with writers' needs for this.
5. Olive Ann Burns, *Cold Sassy Tree* (New York: Ticknor & Fields, 1984).

TWENTY-SEVEN

Writing Children's Books

Seventeen Steps to Success

Angela Narth

"We are pleased to inform you that we love your story for children and are most eager to publish your book for our upcoming season."

Is this a message you have been waiting to receive? Well, it certainly was my dream for the last few years before I retired from a thirty-five-year career in education, and I was over the moon the day I received the long-awaited news that someone actually wanted to publish one of *my* stories!

What followed was a year and a half of editing, working with the illustrator, making required changes, approving format, compromising when disagreements arose, and conforming to tight deadlines. In 2000, eighteen months after the manuscript was accepted by GWEV Publishing, my first picture book for children, *Simon with Two Left Feet*, was published. Much to my surprise and delight, the book hit a nerve with the young reading public; it stayed on the local best-seller list for twenty-seven consecutive weeks. Over the next few years, it went into second printing, garnering a Silver Mom's Choice Award and a Bronze Moonbeam International Medal and was short-listed for the McNally Robinson Book for Young People.

I walked around in a rosy mist after the book was released, visiting a number of bookstores to get a glimpse of *my* book on the shelves. By the time my head shrank back to its original size, I found I was involved in several months of whirlwind activity that left me happily exhausted. Q & A sessions following readings are typically about the book itself: the

243

characters, the plot, and so on. But at one Q &A, the children were more interested in the business end of things, asking questions like, Who was my manager? Shouldn't the bookstore charge more for my books? How long did it take to receive royalties? Could I claim my expenses?

Near the end of the session, one boy of about eight asked solemnly, "Are you an M?"

"An . . . M?" I echoed.

"From your writing," he sniffed. "You know, a millionaire."

He did not look impressed when I chuckled. He looked even less impressed when I pulled out the large posterboard pie chart that I had created in anticipation of such a question. As I began to pull the pie sections apart—this percentage for the illustrator, this percentage for the publisher, this much for the bookseller, and a so on—I watched as his face registered mild interest, then surprise. By the time the pie had been reduced to the author's paltry earnings, his face was the picture of utter astonishment.

"Then why," he gasped, "do you write books?"

And you must begin by asking yourself that very question. Since writing children's books is not likely going to make us rich, what is our compulsion to do it? Every writer will have a slightly different answer to this question but they will all likely center on the same theme: to affect children's lives in positive ways. And that is what children's books have the power to do: teach, touch, and inspire.

But where to start?

You already have your story idea? Good. You have a story written? Great! Now shelve it. Put it in a safe place. Go back to it every now and then as more ideas surface. But before you think about submitting, it would be best to start at the real beginning.

STEP 1: DECIDE ON A GENRE

One of the most overused phrases in writing advice is to *Write what you know.* You are a retired train engineer, so you want to write a book about trains. That's all you need. Right? Well, not quite.

While it is important to be familiar with any topic you wish to write about, the focus, form, and tone of your project will be largely determined by genre. It is vital, therefore, to know what classification your work will fall into before you get too far into your writing. And my advice here is to *Write what you like.*

If you love fiction, you might choose to write short stories or novels, and you will need to decide whether you want to write humor, drama, or romance. Maybe action or fantasy or mystery or science fiction is more appealing to you. All are parts of the fiction genre open to writers.

Nonfiction may not immediately spring to mind when you think about writing for children. But writing biographies, or providing accounts of past or current events, may provide an outlet for your creativity. It might also allow you to bridge your former career as an archaeologist, police officer, hairdresser, or basketball coach with your new one as a writer. Trivia, cookbooks, and how-to writing can also provide you with many opportunities to be published. Be assured that there is room for all of them in a writer's repertoire.

To help you get started thinking about what is possible, have a look at *You Can Write Children's Books* by Tracey E. Dils.[1] It provides clear details of the different genres, as well as excellent inspiration exercises to get the creative juices flowing.

STEP 2: SELECT A TARGET AUDIENCE

Children's literature is categorized according to age. Since category will determine theme and word choice, you will need to know the age of your intended audience before getting too far into your writing project.

A very useful and accessible resource for establishing age-appropriate themes and vocabulary is *The Children's Writer's Reference* by Berthe Amoss and Eric Suben.[2] This is best described as a book of lists—a compendium of words categorized by theme, age group, format, character, and setting.

Your audience age will also dictate acceptable word count. Although minor variations exist among publishing houses, the list below gives book lengths and word-count ranges that are fairly standard in the industry.

STEP 3: CONSIDER CURRENT TRENDS

Publishing is, in many ways, a fickle science. Trends vanish in the blink of an eye; styles can change almost overnight. The books you enjoyed as a youngster would sit untouched on bookstore shelves today, and you need to know what is currently selling.

Category	Approx. Age	Word Count	Page-Count Range
Picture books	toddler–8	0–1,000	26–30 (text)
Easy-reader books	5–9	100–2,500	15–25
Chapter books	7–10	8,000–12,000	30–50
Middle-grade novels	8–12	20,000–40,000	60–200
Young-adult novels	11–19	30,000–60,000	150–350

Spend time at your local library seeking out the assistance of the librarian to direct you to the most popular books. *Story Sparkers: A Creativity Guide for Children's Writers* by Debbie Dadey and Marcia Thornton Jones, provides lists of exemplary, award-winning books in various categories.[3]

Read as much and as often as you can in your chosen genre and category. Learn what it is about these books that appeals to audiences: How do the stories typically start? In what ways are the main characters similar? How do the main characters reflect the ages and interests of the target audience? How are story conflicts resolved? What themes are most popular today?

STEP 4: GET TO KNOW YOUR TARGET AUDIENCE

Several years ago, when my husband and I were on holiday, we got to know a lovely couple whose grandson had come to stay with them for a few weeks by the beach. When ten-year-old Brian found out that I was a children's author, he asked if I would write him a book about pirates. Heavily into another project, I declined, until his grandmother confided in me that she was afraid Brian would lose interest in reading because he was having trouble finding books about his passion—pirates. The situation tugged at my writer's heartstrings. I relented, on one condition. I would write about pirates for him, but it would be a short story, not a book.

This would be a cinch, I thought, secure in the benefit of my own childhood interest in pirates. On the weekend I had between my current project and the next, I sat at my desk ready to quickly polish off the story for Brian and got the shock of my life! I was blocked. Seriously and profoundly blocked! With four books already published and another on its way to print, I surely knew how to write. Then why wouldn't the images come? And I had been a public-school administrator and a teacher. If anyone knows how kids talk, it's a teacher. So why did the dialogue sound so forced? Why was I suddenly struggling?

Then it hit me. Although I had spent a few delightful hours on the beach with Brian, I really didn't know him. In fact, I no longer knew any boys Brian's age. My books to date had concentrated on the toddler-to-six demographic, and my public-school teaching experience was two decades in the past. I had no idea anymore how ten-year-old boys would talk, how they would dress, what upset them, or what would get them excited. Brian and his peers were a completely unknown quantity. Sadly, without the time to devote to proper research, I never wrote that story. But I don't think Brian missed anything. The story would have been a fake, and he deserved better.

So do not make my mistake. Get out there, and get to know your intended audience. If you have neighbors or family members in your target age group, you have a leg up. If not, do not despair. Approach your local school or community club, tell administration why you want to volunteer, and ask to work with children in your target population. Then get actively involved with them.

Pay attention to their speech patterns, the words they use, the way they talk to peers, the way they relate to adults. Observe the games they play and how they resolve issues with one another. Make note of what they are wearing and how their hair is cut. Check out what they are reading and what movies they see. Find out what they are watching on TV, what music they listen to, what kinds of activities they are involved in outside of school. Find out what makes them curious, what saddens them, and what makes them giddy with pleasure.

STEP 5: A ROOM OF YOUR OWN

All the ideas in the world will not get your story written if you have to pack up and move all your notes, equipment, books, and technology every time the dinner hour rolls around or the moment your cousin Howard drops in for a visit. You will need a space of your own.

Your work area should provide, at the very least, excellent lighting, an ergonomic chair, a bookshelf, access to an electrical outlet, a secure Internet connection, and a desk or table where notes and writing tools can be left undisturbed. Your new office space need not be glamorous; it need only be comfortable, functional, quiet, and more or less permanent.

You might have noted the absence of a telephone in the list of office needs. It was not an oversight. In my opinion, telephones are among the most obtrusive elements in a writer's day. They should be banned from your work area—or at least silenced while you're working.

STEP 6: ORGANIZE YOUR WORK

If you are not already using a computer at home, this will be the time to consider going digital. No doubt you will be able to write and create without a computer, but most publishers these days rely on e-mail to do business. From sending queries to submitting manuscripts to final editing, electronic communication is the norm.

Getting into the world of bits and bytes need not be daunting. Your local college, community, or school district will likely offer introductory courses and provide opportunities for you to attempt various procedures under helpful supervision. In addition they will be able to advise you on which computers and applications will meet your basic needs as a writer: word processing, Internet access, and data management.

With or without a computer, you will have to set up a filing system of some kind. My computer desktop has a folder labeled *Writing*, which holds separate folders for projects I am currently working on, query letters and responses, as well as database files to keep track of what, when, and to whom I have submitted. My *On Hold* folder contains items that have been rejected or temporarily abandoned and are awaiting inspiration.

STEP 7: ORGANIZE YOUR TIME

To maximize your chances of succeeding, it will be important to look at your new pursuit as a bona fide job, with hours of business, a workplace atmosphere, and you on task. I am at my desk by 9:00 in the morning, and I work straight through until about 2 p.m., when I stop for lunch. I try to stand and stretch once every hour, and I take a fifteen- to twenty-minute walk about halfway through the morning. But other than that, it is work time for me. Friends know it, and family members know it. They rarely intrude. If the downstairs phone rings, it goes to muted voice mail.

Unless I have an upcoming deadline, I take afternoons off to catch up with friends, respond to e-mails and phone messages, play tennis, or do household chores. Find your own rhythm, decide what works best for your situation, and then stick to it.

STEP 8: BUILD YOUR OWN RESOURCE LIBRARY

A writer's office space needn't have bookshelves groaning with tomes, but there are three print resources that I could not do without: a good dictionary, a complete thesaurus, and a text of modern English grammar usage. Additional titles that I have used over the years are mentioned throughout this chapter.

STEP 9: LEARN ALL YOU CAN

Using the suggested resources will certainly help you get your ideas down in print, but inspiration and learning rarely occur in a vacuum. Enjoy your solitude, but getting involved in some kind of writing community could be beneficial to your writing and your state of mind.

Colleges and school-district extension programs may offer creative-writing classes, or you might decide to audit a writing class at a university. Membership in community writers' groups or guilds will give you opportunities to attend workshops and seminars on specific topics, and some national writer's organizations may be willing to accept an unpublished writer for membership.

And do not forget the wonderful world of writers' conferences! These are usually two- to three-day events, most held annually, where attendees have an opportunity to participate in sessions and workshops on various topics. Many conferences offer participants one-to-one pitch sessions with agents, selected writers, and editors.

Check out the *Children's Writer's and Illustrator's Market*.[4] In addition to detailed listings of children's publishing markets, this annually updated resource provides excellent information on upcoming conferences. Attendance fees are high for some conferences, and you may have to add travel and accommodation to the overall cost. But the thrill of rubbing shoulders with experienced, knowledgeable, and often famous names in the publishing world is something every writer should experience at least once.

STEP 10: WRITE AND REWRITE

By this point, you will probably have gone back to your draft a number of times and done more writing. Now will be a good time to ensure that you are on the right track.

A wonderful resource for this stage will be *Writing Books for Kids and Teens* by Marion Crook.[5] The author offers excellent suggestions on organizing your writing day and getting balance in your writing life, but the greatest strength of this book is in the area of writing craft. Elements such as point of view, dialogue, pace, and character are presented clearly and thoroughly, with sufficient examples and practice activities to ensure that you have covered all the bases.

STEP 11: PROOFREAD

You are satisfied with the storyline, plot, and pace, and your characters have been developed and presented as effectively as possible. Now is the time to check grammar and punctuation:

1. *Check out one element at a time*—No specific order is recommended, but focusing on one feature at a time (colons, for example) is more likely to yield results.
2. *Work from a printed copy*—I find it easy to miss errors when working on a screen, so I always proofread from a paper copy, with a colored fine-tip marker in my hand.
3. *Double-check spelling with your dictionary*—Since a computer can't tell the semantic difference between *rough* and *ruff* or *two* and *to*, do not rely on your computer's spellcheck feature. It will highlight words that are misspelled but not those that are misused.

4. *Avoid adverb abuse*—If you find a number of words ending with *-ly*, you may be using too many adverbs. Eliminate adverbs by using more descriptive verbs.
5. *Check grammar against a usage* text—To insure that grammatical details are correct, invest in and use a good grammar text. Strunk and White's *Elements of Style* is a classic and my personal favorite.[6]

STEP 12: DO A TEST RUN

All known bugs and weaknesses have been eliminated from your manuscript. Now is the time to test it on a few readers: a couple of children in your target population as well as an adult or two.

Design a set of age-appropriate questions to ask test readers once they have finished the piece. Questions should cover issues such as pacing, images, plot, characters, and vocabulary, the complexity and detail depending on the individual reader's age and reading level.

STEP 13: REVISE

Compiling the comments from your test readers will give you a template for revising and improving your story. Keep in mind that, even though isolated opinions may lead to further investigation, trends are what you are really seeking. No specific numbers constitute what is a trend, but if a quarter or more of your readers are of a similar opinion, it will be worthwhile making revisions that respond to the criticism.

STEP 14: SUBMIT

Your story has been written, edited, and revised, and you finally feel ready to submit it. This will be the time when you will find *Formatting and Submitting your Manuscript* by Jack and Glenda Neff and Don Prues worth its weight in gold.[7] The authors have assembled a trove of information about how to structure submissions, from query letter and synopsis to fundamental issues such as manuscript formatting.

At this stage, returning to *The Children's Writer's and Illustrator's Market* will help you to select the most appropriate markets for your particular genre. Visit the website of each market to confirm that they are open to new authors and to find the name of a specific individual to whom to address your submission.

Most publishers do not want to receive unsolicited manuscripts, so ensure that you follow the specific guidelines for each and send precisely what they want. Submissions generally include:

- a one-page query letter, giving a brief overview of the project, and a few words about your background
- a one-page synopsis of your project, indicating genre and word count
- a separate, detailed bio
- and usually the first few pages of the manuscript.

Adhering to the guidelines will not guarantee that your work will be published, but it will give it a fighting chance to stay out of the slush pile.

STEP 15: THE WAITING GAME

Weeks go by with no response. Then, just as you are about to decide to scrap the whole writing idea, responses start coming in. Typically the first to arrive will be generic, unsigned, form-letter rejections; next will be those that mention your project by name but offer little other than a statement such as "does not meet our current objectives."

Somewhat later, you may receive one or two kindly worded rejections that offer specific (but very brief) critiques of your work. Embrace these, and know that someone liked your work well enough to give it more than a cursory glance. Then one day, when you have all but given up hope, the acceptance letter arrives.

STEP 16: EXPECT THE UNEXPECTED

Readers of children's books are a very special breed. The level of involvement they demand from authors typically exceeds the level demanded by adult readers. You will be expected to make appearances at schools, libraries, and, of course, bookstores. At school visits, children will eagerly ask questions and want to share stories of their own.

At bookstore signings, children will look and listen, but it will be adults who ask the questions. Some of them will even bring manuscripts hoping you might agree to forward them to your publisher. Some will challenge your use of a particular word or point out a perceived weakness in plot. Confident, now that you are a published author, you remain cool, ready for anything.

STEP 17: ENJOY THE REWARDS AND SHARE THE JOY

Your name is in print. Children and parents send you letters. Public libraries feature you on their "author of the month" boards. Schools invite you to give addresses at graduations and Literacy Month kick-offs. You are asked to lead seminars for aspiring writers. And you are loving every minute of it! Now is the time to start on your next project. It is also time to give something back.

Volunteer to give talks on writing at community clubs and libraries or to read to children in hospitals. Donate some of your publisher's complimentary author copies to shelters for abused families, to worthwhile fundraising events, and to hospitals. And do not forget seniors' homes. One of the most heart-warming fan letters I ever received was from a ninety-two-year-old woman. She wrote that after reading *Simon with Two Left Feet* she felt, for the very first time, that she had the strength to finally leave behind the bullying she had received as a child.

Children's writing can inspire, teach, and entertain. It can also heal. So if you are still eager to climb aboard this carousel ride of writing for children, then join me, and be ready for all the ups and downs, the shrieks of delight and the tears of relief, the feeling of sometimes going around in circles, and the wonderful music that never stops.

NOTES

1. Tracey E. Dils, *You Can Write Children's Books*, 2nd ed. (Cincinnati: Writer's Digest Books, 2009).

2. Berthe Amoss and Eric Suben, *The Children's Writer's Reference* (Cincinnati: Writer's Digest Books, 1999).

3. Debbie Dadey and Marcia Thornton Jones, *Story Sparkers: A Creativity Guide for Children's Writers* (Cincinnati: Writers Digest Books, 2000).

4. Chuck Sambuchino, ed., *The Children's Writer's and Illustrator's Market* (Cincinnati: Writers Digest Books, 2013).

5. Marion Crook, *Writing Books for Kids and Teens* (Vancouver, B.C.: Self-Counsel Press, 1998).

6. William Strunk Jr. and E. B. White, *The Elements of Style*, 4th ed. (London: Longmans, 1999).

7. Jack Neff, Glenda Neff, and Don Prues, *Formatting and Submitting Your Manuscript* (Cincinnati: Writers Digest Books, 1999).

Index

About the Editors and Contributors

Supriya Bhatnagar is director of publications at the Association of Writers and Writing Programs (AWP) and editor of the *Writer's Chronicle*. Her short stories have appeared in *Femina* and at *4Indianwoman.com*. Her memoir, *& then there were three . . .*, was published in 2010. Her essays have appeared in *Perigee, Artful Dodge, Drunken Boat, NEO*, and the anthology *Winter Tales II: Women on the Art of Aging* (2012). "Of Kabir and Karma" was nominated for the 2012 Pushcart Prize Award. "Mangoes & Mayhem" appears in the January–February 2014 issue of *Muse India*.

Christine Redman-Waldeyer launched *Adanna*, a print journal for women and about women, in January 2011. Redman-Waldeyer is a poet and assistant professor in the Department of English at Passaic County Community College in New Jersey. She has published three poetry collections, *Frame by Frame, Gravel*, and *Eve Asks* and has appeared in *Caduceus, Lips, Paterson Literary Review, Seventh Quarry, Schuylkill Valley Journal, The Texas Review, Verse Wisconsin*, and others. She earned her doctorate from Drew University and resides at the Jersey Shore.

Carol Smallwood partial credits include *Women on Poetry: Writing, Revising, Publishing and Teaching* (2012) on the list of Best Books for Writers by *Poets & Writers, Women Writing on Family: Tips on Writing, Teaching and Publishing* (2012), *Water, Earth, Air, Fire, and Picket Fences* (2014), and *Divining the Prime Meridian*, a third forthcoming poetry collection. Her library experience includes school, public, academic, special libraries, teaching, administration, and being a consultant. *Bringing the Arts into the Library* (2014) is her sixth book for the American Library Association. Carol has founded humane societies.

CONTRIBUTORS

Sarah W. Bartlett's work has appeared in *Aurorean, Ars Medica, Minerva Rising, Literary Mama, Up the Down Staircase*, and *Shemom*, as well as in the anthologies *Contemporary American Women* (2009*)*, and *Women on Poetry* (2012), *Into the Great Blue: Meditations of Summer* (2011) is a poetry chapbook. *Hear Me, See Me: Incarcerated Women Write* is forthcoming. Following twenty years in health-care planning, Bartlett has operated a creative-writing school for women since 2004. She blogs regularly at SarahScapes (http://sarahwbartlett.com/) and Writing Inside VT (http://writinginsidevt.com/).

Jinny V. Batterson holds a BA in French from Randolph College and an MBA from the University of Richmond. Before retiring she was in teaching and computer software. She has lived most of her life in the United States, with about two years each in Burundi and the People's Republic of China. Jinny has appeared in Richmond's *Style Weekly*, *U.S. China Review*, and *Carolina Woman*. She lives in Cary, North Carolina, and is a member of the NC Writers' Network.

Elizabeth Bodien lives near Hawk Mountain, Pennsylvania, and taught anthropology at Northampton Community College in Bethlehem, Pennsylvania, until 2007. Her poems have since appeared in *red lights*, *The Fourth River*, *Schuylkill Valley Journal*, *Cimarron Review*, *qarrtsiluni*, *U.S.1 Worksheets*, and *Across the Long Bridge: An Anthology of Award Winning Poems*, among other publications in the United States, Canada, Australia, and India. Her collections include the award-winning chapbook *Plumb Lines* (2008), *Rough Terrain: Notes of an Undutiful Daughter* (2010), and *Endpapers* (2011).

Rita Keeley Brown is author, editor, educator, and speaker with careers in music, education, business, and writing. She studied at Northwestern University and UCLA, majoring in music and English. Nonfiction is her specialty: personal essays, poems, and two books published 2008 and 2011—a memoir, *Good Luck, Mrs. Brown*, and an award-winning biography, *A Pawn of Fate*. Her workshop series, Creative Writing: An Unopened Gift and You Have a Story to Tell, are very popular presentations. She is vice president of Programs for the California Writers Club–San Fernando Valley.

Kathleen Clauson, unit coordinator for WIU Physical Sciences Library in Macomb, Illinois, is a successful writer "on the side." She has contributed to *Handling Job Stress: Tips by Librarians* (2013), *Women, Work, and the Web: How the Web Creates Entrepreneurial Opportunities* (forthcoming), and others. Her fiction appears in *Time Intertwined*, *Short-Attention Span Mysteries*, and various literary print and e-journals. Her novella, *Eva Galuska and the Christmas Carp*, a finalist in the 2008 USA Book News National Best Books Awards, was self-published.

Lynne Davis, since retiring from the Center for English as a Second Language, Southern Illinois University–Carbondale, has published articles in *Global Study*, *ESL Magazine*, *Transitions Abroad*, *SAQA Journal*, and the

"Reader's Write" section of *The Sun Magazine*. Her contribution "Just like West Side Story: Teaching English Grammar with Poetry," appeared in *Women on Poetry: Writing, Revising, Publishing and Teaching* (2012), which is included in *Poets & Writers* magazine's list of best books for writers. Lynne currently writes articles for the Yahoo Contributor Network.

Lisa Fraser, services-implementation coordinator for the King County Library System, Washington, has taught courses in marketing and advocacy for libraries at the Information School of the University of Washington. She coedited *Time and Project Management Strategies for Librarians* (Scarecrow, 2013) and contributed to *The Frugal Librarian: Thriving in Tough Economic Times* (2011) and *Preserving Local Writers, Genealogy, Photographs, Newspapers, and Related Materials* (Scarecrow, 2012). She's also been published in a variety of other print and online publications such as book reviews for *Serving House Journal, Adanna Literary Journal*, and *Prick of the Spindle*.

B. Lynn Goodwin is owner of Writer Advice (http://www.writeradvice.com/) and author of *You Want Me to Do WHAT? Journaling for Caregivers*. Her stories and articles have been published in *Voices of Caregivers, Hip Mama, Oakland Tribune, Contra Costa Times, Danville Weekly, Staying Sane When You're Dieting, Small Press Review, Dramatics Magazine, Career, We Care, Thickjam.com, Friction Literary Journal*, and *The Sun*. A former teacher, Goodwin conducts workshops and writes reviews for *Story Circle Network*, and *InspireMeToday*. She's working on a YA novel and brainstorming a memoir.

Stanley L. Klemetson, retired associate dean of the College of Technology and Computing at Utah Valley University, Orem, Utah, obtained his Ph.D. from Utah State University. Klemetson's memberships include the American Society of Civil Engineers, American Society of Engineering Education, League of Utah Writers, and Bayou Writers' Group. He is president elect of the Central Utah Branch of ASCE. His work appeared in *My Love to You Always* (2012) and has published fifty-five journal articles and research reports and several technical books. Klemetson is an avid reader and enjoys the association with other writers.

Barbara Kussow is editor and publisher of *Still Crazy*, a literary magazine that publishes poetry, fiction, and nonfiction by and/or about people over age fifty (http://www.crazylitmag.com/). Her poetry has appeared in *Wild Violet, Kaleidoscope, Dos Passos Review, Hospital Drive, Danse Macabre*, and other publications. Two poems received honorable mentions in *Byline* contests. Three short stories have been published in *The Storyteller* and two in *Wild Violet*. One story placed among the top entries in the 79th

Writer's Digest writing competition. Kussow has also published essays online and in print.

Lori Leger is a self-published author of romance novels. She resigned after eighteen years in road design with the state of Louisiana in 2012 to write full time. Lori is sole owner of Cajunflair Publishing. She has seven novels published in two series, in both electronic-book form and print, all based in her home state of Louisiana. She has also contributed to two anthologies of short stories with several other authors. Several of her books have attained Amazon's best-seller ranking and continue to earn good reviews from readers and review websites.

Alice Lowe is a freelance writer in San Diego. Her personal essays have been published in more than twenty literary journals over the past three years, including *Upstreet, Hippocampus, Switchback, Prime Number,* and *Phoebe*. She was the 2013 national-award winner at *City Works Journal* and winner of a 2011 essay contest at *Writing It Real*. She also writes on the life and work of Virginia Woolf. She published a monograph, "Beyond the Icon: Virginia Woolf in Contemporary Fiction." Lowe blogs at http:// aliceloweblogs.wordpress.com/.

Arlene L. Mandell, retired English professor, was formerly on the staff of *Good Housekeeping* magazine. She has published more than 500 poems, essays, and short stories in newspapers and literary journals, including the *New York Times, Tiny Lights,* and *Wild Violet*. Her work has also appeared in twenty-four anthologies, including *Garden Blessings* (2014) and *Women Writing on Family: Tips on Writing, Teaching and Publishing*. An e-chapbook, *Scenes from My Life on Hemlock Street: A Brooklyn Memoir*, set in the 1940s and '50s, is available free at http://www.echapbook.com/ memoir/mandell/.

Nancy Kalikow Maxwell, MLS, MA, has participated in the development of successful grants totaling more than ten million dollars. Author of *Grant Money through Collaborative Partnerships* (2012), Maxwell owns and operates the grant-development company Kaliwell, Inc. (http:// www.librarygrants.org/). Before retiring from her thirty-year library career, she was library director at Miami Dade College (Miami) and Barry University (Miami Shores, Florida). Her earlier work, *Sacred Stacks: The Higher Purpose of Libraries and Librarianship* (2006), was an ALA bestseller.

Ann McCauley worked as a freelancer for local newspapers and periodicals while working as an RN. She has authored two novels and a revision, *Mother Love* (2003), *Runaway Grandma* (2007), and *Revised Mother Love* (2012). *Mother Love* received a Reviewer's Choice Award in 2005. *Runaway Grandma* was nominated for Book of the Year in Women's Issues in

2008. McCauley obtained her M.A. in Creative Writing in 2014 from Wilkes University. McCauley is currently working on her next novel. She is an avid reader and devoted grandmother. She and her husband love to travel.

Rosemary McKinley's work has appeared in *Examination Anthology, Lucidity, LI Sounds, the poets arts* and *canvasli.com, Newsday, Peconic Bay Shopper,* and *Fate Magazine.* Two short stories have been included online on *Smashwords. Summer Lovin'* won an honorable mention in *Clarity,* an international poetry contest. *The Mouton Coat* was published in the *Treasure Box* edition of *Patchwork Path* (2010), and *Max* was published in *Nurturing Paws.* Her book *101 Glimpses of the North Fork and Islands* was released in 2009, and her YA historical fiction novella, *The Wampum Exchange,* was released in 2012.

Katie McKy has written hundreds of magazine articles for business magazines, women's magazines, travel magazines, and sporting magazines. She is author of *Pumpkin Town* (2008), which has sold more than 800,000 copies in several languages, and has written other picture books and adult nonfiction. As a writer she has taught writing to approximately 300,000 children in states across the Midwest. McKy especially enjoys writing profiles for magazines, as she's gotten to hear some amazing stories and share those stories with folks from coast to coast.

Carole Mertz, organist in Parma, Ohio, attended the Mozarteum, Salzburg, Austria, received her MusB from Oberlin College, Oberlin, Ohio, and was director of development for the Jupiter Symphony in New York City. Her writing appears in *Mature Years, Copperfield Review, The Conium Review, Capper's, The Write Place at the Write Time, Page & Spine,* and anthologies. Mertz won recognition in the Fourth Worldwide Intergenerational Storytelling Contest. Her novel is forthcoming in 2015. She volunteered as a local hospital visitor and is a New York C.S. Lewis Society, and Rockford Writers' Guild member.

Don Mulcahy, born in Clydach, Wales, and Canadian citizen since 1969, lives in Strathroy, Ontario, Canada, where he writes poetry, prose, and book reviews following an academic career in dentistry. His work has appeared in dental journals, newspapers, the *CHS Newsletter* (Wales), the *Prairie Journal, Matrix, Coffee House Poetry* (U.K.), *iota* (U.K.), *Verse Afire, fait accompli, blood ink, Tower Poetry,* the *Antigonish Review, Vallum,* and the anthologies *Butterfly Thunder, Sounding the Seconds, Ascent Aspirations, Voices Israel 2013 Anthology* and has appeared online at http://blueskiespoetry.ca/ and http://www.prairiejournal.org/. He recently completed a book-length political critique.

Angela Narth, after a successful career in education, became a full-time author. Her credits include *A History of Ghosts* (2009), *Great Canadians* (2005), *Fergus, Prince of Frogs* (2003), *The Very Last Ladybug War* (2001), and *Simon with Two Left Feet* (2000). Her stories and articles have appeared in *Room Literary Magazine*, *Corinthian Horse Sport*, and *Manitoba Gardener*. She lectures part-time in educational psychology at the University of Manitoba. Her memberships include the Writers' Union of Canada and the Canadian Authors' Association.

Louise Nayer's most recent book, *Burned: A Memoir*, won the Wisconsin Library Association Award and was listed as one of ten upcoming titles in *O Magazine*. She coauthored *How to Bury A Goldfish: 113 Rituals for Everyday Life*. She has written two books of poetry: *Keeping Watch*, with funding from the NEA, and *The Houses Are Covered in Sound*. She received six California Arts Council grants to teach in senior centers and nursing homes and taught at City College of SF for more than twenty-five years and now teaches memoir workshops through OLLI at UC Berkeley. She's done numerous readings and radio spots, including NPR, and is a member of the SF Writer's Grotto as well as the American Association of Journalists and Authors. Her website is http://www.louisenayer.com/.

John Presley retired in 2013 after a career as a university administrator and professor of English. He writes about British literature, most specifically James Joyce, D. H. Lawrence, and Robert Graves. He has published thirteen books, including a collection of his poetry (with another on the way), and writes and edits in the fields of religion, popular culture, travel, and higher education. His recent publications include "Civic Engagement and Critical Pedagogy" (in *Education as Civic Engagement*, 2012), *The Future of Higher Education*, (2009; paperback, 2011), and *Nazarene Gospel Restored* (2010).

Robert Runté, Ph.D., took early retirement as professor at the University of Lethbridge to pursue a full-time career as editor. He is now senior editor with Five Rivers Publishing and freelances at http://sfeditor.ca/. He was founding director of SF Canada and served on the boards of *On Spec Magazine*, Tesseract Books, and the Writers' Guild of Alberta. In addition to dozens of conference papers, journal articles, and book chapters and a half-dozen entries in the *Encyclopedia of Literature in Canada*, he has won two Aurora Awards for his speculative fiction (SF) criticism.

Stephen Sottong was born in the rust-belt town of Kokomo, Indiana, and spent much of his youth in the public library. He began writing at about age ten and continued sporadically throughout his working life. He worked as a computer programmer, electronics technician, electrical engineer, and academic librarian before retiring. He now lives behind the

Redwood Curtain in Eureka, California, with his wife, four cats, and four hives of bees, while devoting himself to his first love, writing fiction and science fiction. In 2012 he won the international Writers of the Future contest.

Maxine Susman retired in 2011 as professor of English at Caldwell University, Caldwell, New Jersey, and now teaches poetry workshops and adult education. Her doctorate is from Cornell. Susman also taught at Rutgers and Seton Hall Universities and Duksung University in Korea and has been a consultant writer and editor, government worker, and test developer. In five poetry collections she's appeared in *Paterson Literary Review, Colere, Fourth River, Ekphrasis, Poet Lore,* and dozens of other journals and anthologies. She lives in Kingston, New Jersey, and performs with the poetry group, Cool Women.

Christine Swanberg, retired teacher, has published several collections of poetry: *The Alleluia Tree* (2012), *Who Walks among the Trees with Charity* (2005), *The Red Lacquer Room* (2001), *The Tenderness of Memory* (1995), and others. An interview with her appeared in *Poet's Market 2008.* Her poems appear in journals such as *Spoon River, Beloit Poetry Journal, Lilopoh, Conversations across Borders,* and many others, as well as in many women's anthologies. Swanberg is a contributor to *Garden Blessings* (2014). She received the Woman Spirit award from Womanspace and the YWCA award for women in the arts.

CPSIA information can be obtained at www.ICGtesting.com
Printed in the USA
BVOW05s1326290814

364763BV00002B/5/P